PRAISE FOR *INTERNAL COMMU*
IN TIMES OF CRISIS

In the chaos of crisis, it is easy to default messaging focused on external audiences - press conferences, media statements, social media updates etc. What *Internal Communication in Times of Crisis* reminds us of is that some of the most critical conversations must first happen inside the organization. Internal audiences are too often an afterthought, yet they are the lifeblood of clarity, consistency, and trust. This book is a must-read for any communicator or leader who understands that employees are not just recipients of information – they can be trusted voices, steady hands and powerful advocates when they are informed, empowered and valued. If you are looking to level up your crisis communications response from the inside out, start here.
Benjamin Morgan, MA Principal, Centre for Crisis & Risk Communications

The perfect handbook for anyone trying to understand the role of internal communication in a crisis. The frameworks outlined will help anyone in an organization navigate a crisis - communication professional or not. While there is no one-size-fits-all for a crisis, the book captures many of the nuances that need to be considered for leaders when it comes to maintaining relationships with employees. This book is a great blend of academic theory, practical experience and frameworks you can apply straight away.
Jenni Field, leadership credibility and organizational communication expert

The practicality of Alison Arnot's approach – backed by deep personal experience – shines through, covering all the key elements of effective crisis comms: from crisis categorization, internal audience understanding and strategy to content creation, channel selection, leadership communication, internal listening and self-care. *Internal Communication in Times of Crisis* will be invaluable in encouraging practitioners to think more strategically about the internal elements of their crisis comms, while providing practical, meaningful tools for putting that strategy into action.
Rod Cartwright, adviser on risk, crisis, reputation and resilience and Founder of Rod Cartwright Consulting

Alison's practical guide to internal communication in times of crisis creates confidence for communication professionals. In a crisis, internal communication is often an afterthought, but Alison's book is full of actionable advice to implement today. The inspirational stories and hints and tips make this an ideal book to help you plan or oversee crisis communication.
Rachel Miller, Founder, All Things IC, and author of *Internal Communication Strategy*

Alison has put the spotlight firmly on an often-overlooked part of crisis communication. She carefully brings together her own experiences with the views and thoughts of those involved in crisis response and academic research. This is a vital book that delves into the human impact of crisis through the lens of employees.
Amanda Coleman, crisis communication specialist, consultant and author of *Crisis Communication Strategies*

Drawing on current and recent writings, Alison's own real-life experiences and interviews with practitioners, she provides a framework for understanding how crises develop inside organizations and ideas on how to respond when the worst happens. The book explores preparation, explains how the internal communicator's audience insight comes into play and works though the stages of an unfolding event. This beautifully written book is packed full of useful suggestions and ideas which experienced and novice practitioners alike will value.
Liam Fitzpatrick, Change communications author and adviser

Alison offers clear, actionable insights, helping internal communicators navigate the challenges of crisis communication at every stage – from preparation and response to recovery.

What sets this apart is Alison's 7S framework that starts with people's core needs and expands to support the organization as the crisis evolves. It's a structured, people-first approach that helps communicators lead with clarity, empathy, and confidence in times of uncertainty. This book is more than a guide; it empowers internal communicators to be strategic, responsive, and resilient when it matters most.
Nafisa Ali Shafiq, Co-Chair of CIPR Inside, Internal Communications Lead at Yorkshire Housing

A crisis is a crisis, but failing to plan for one is on you. Alison's book is essential for any communication professional ready to take charge and guide their organization through the darkest moments. With internal communication rightly placed at the heart of crisis response, she presents a serious subject in an engaging and accessible way. What struck me most was the focus on people – the needs of the survivors. Crisis preparation has always proven its worth to me, and Alison shows you how.

Monique Zytnik, author of *Internal Communication in the Age of Artificial Intelligence*, communication strategist and IABC EMENA Chair

Internal Communication in Times of Crisis

*How to secure employee trust, support
and advocacy in crisis situations*

Alison Arnot

KoganPage

First published in Great Britain and the United States in 2025

Kogan Page

Kogan Page Ltd, 2nd Floor, 45 Gee Street, London EC1V 3RS, United Kingdom
Kogan Page Inc, 8 W 38th Street, Suite 902, New York, NY 10018, USA
www.koganpage.com

EU Representative (GPSR)

Authorised Rep Compliance Ltd, Ground Floor, 71 Baggot Street Lower, Dublin D02 P593, Ireland
www.arccompliance.com

Kogan Page books are printed on paper from sustainable forests.

ISBNs

Hardback	978 1 3986 2060 5
Paperback	978 1 3986 2059 9
Ebook	978 1 3986 2058 2

British Library Cataloguing-in-Publication Data

A CIP record for this book is available from the British Library.

Library of Congress Control Number

2025939035

Typeset by Integra Software Services, Pondicherry
Print production managed by Jellyfish
Printed and bound by CPI Group (UK) Ltd, Croydon CR0 4YY

To Kieran

CONTENTS

About the author xii
Preface xiii
Acknowledgements xvi
List of contributors xvii

1 Understand crisis 1

What is a crisis? 2
Types of crises 4
Crisis development 7
The impact on the internal community 9
Crisis opportunity 13
References 15

2 Recognize the role of internal crisis communication 17

What is internal crisis communication? 18
Introducing the 7S of internal crisis communication 20
Tips for internal crisis communication success 31
References 33

3 Anticipate and plan for different types of crises 34

Anticipate the crisis 35
Monitor and track issues 41
Tackle problems 42
Dive into different scenarios 42
Prepare your plan 44
Share your plan 48
Practise your plan 48
Identify the crisis 'flashover' 49
Activate the response 51
References 53

4 Understand your internal community 55

Who are your internal community? 56
The need to know them 56

Build knowledge in stable times 58
Dig deeper in the context of the crisis 65
References 70

5   **Define your strategy and agree approach** 71

Assess the situation 72
Set clear objectives 74
Establish the crisis position 74
Confirm your sources of truth 82
Recognize different needs at each crisis stage 84
References 90

6   **Craft your content** 91

Key principles 92
Control the first messages 101
Tell the stories of crisis 103
References 108

7   **Select the right channels** 109

Understand your channels 110
Identify channel purpose 112
Choose a suitable channel combination 123
Put contingencies in place 125
Enable tracking and evaluation 126
References 127

8   **Work with your leaders** 129

The central role of the crisis leader 130
Support your leaders 134
Help yourself 141
References 143

9   **Support your line managers** 144

The critical role of line managers 145
Help your line manager community 153
References 159

10   Listen to your people 160

What is organizational listening? 160
Listen through crisis 162
Respond to feedback 173
References 175

11   Take care of yourself 177

Acknowledge your feelings 178
Look after your mental health 178
Look after your personal wellbeing 180
Look after your professional wellbeing 184
References 192

12   Evaluate efforts and learn for next time 194

The benefits of learning 195
What to measure 196
How to measure 201
Interpret your findings 204
Share learning and evidence action 208
References 210

Index 211

ABOUT THE AUTHOR

Alison Arnot is an award-winning business owner, trainer, consultant and speaker with over 25 years' front-line experience in PR, internal communication and crisis communication. For the past 12 years she has trained communication professionals in these disciplines for the Chartered Institute of Public Relations (CIPR) and has also trained and consulted for global organizations and teams through her business Catalyst Communications. Alison has planned, managed and delivered internal and external crisis communication in diverse crisis and pre-crisis situations, including the 2007 terror attack on Glasgow Airport where she was the first member of the airport's communication team on the scene after the attack.

PREFACE

From my first days working in PR, I've been aware of the potential for crises and the need to deliver a clear and timely communication response. I spent much of my early career in the rail and aviation industries where on-call rotas, planning manuals and tabletop exercises were woven through the job. Crises were something we were taught to prepare for and trained to deal with, yet even so, the idea of something monumental happening to us – and involving me personally – was unthinkable.

Until it wasn't.

Just after 3 pm on Saturday 30 June 2007, during my time as Head of Employee Communication for Glasgow, Edinburgh and Aberdeen airports, a terror attack on Glasgow Airport stunned the nation. Captured in photographs and on video as it happened, stories and startling images of a flaming jeep rammed into the front of the airport terminal were quickly shared, and the demand for more information was immediate. Crisis plans switched into action, and less than a half hour later, I became the first member of the airport communication team to reach the scene, cross an armed police cordon, and enter the crisis room where I'd begin working with crisis management and business continuity colleagues to deliver the airport's internal and external crisis communication response.

Priorities moved at pace – and our focus, needs and objectives shifted as the incident unfolded and things became clearer. We were a few hundred metres from the site of the attack – yet even in this most frightening situation, our rigorous preparation and planning meant that we knew what to do and how to do it. The airport crisis management and business continuity teams were exceptional, and as they worked relentlessly to get the airport back up and safely running within 24 hours of the attack, they also kept the communication team involved and supported so that we could step up and deliver our best too.

Crisis communication was crafted and delivered in stages to support the needs of the airport as we moved through crisis response and crisis recovery back towards business as usual. Together with airport leaders and operational colleagues, our communication team worked hard to establish an open, trusted and helpful narrative from the first moments of impact. And through each crisis phase, we worked round the clock to meet the airport's immediate strategic and operational needs while shaping positive evidence-based stories that our many stakeholders would feel confident to take ownership of, and share.

In doing this, we delivered a multi-award-winning internal and external crisis communication campaign that not only supported Glasgow Airport in its phased reopening and business recovery but also highlighted and celebrated the competence and quality of the airport teams. And as a result, an incident that could have severely damaged reputation instead enhanced internal and external relationships, showcased operational excellence and underlined staff passion and commitment to serve their customers and protect their airport. Staff were praised in the media, by politicians, by business partners and by customers – and the airport's internal and external crisis communication hailed as best practice as the operation strengthened and recovered.

My own personal experience amid all of this and in the weeks that followed was humbling, and at many times, emotional. Through the greatest challenge imaginable, Glasgow Airport's staff showed up, stepped forward as a team, and represented everything that is powerful and extraordinary about their city. I was inspired watching the practised expertise of my crisis management, business continuity and leadership colleagues, and I was moved to see how many employees, contractors and partners from every role, every grade and every part of our airport community volunteered to help in the early and very frightening stages of the attack, and how they continued to help and support each other as the days went on, reality struck, and exhaustion set in.

Most of our crisis-communication planning before the attack had focused on the needs of the media and external stakeholders – and there is no doubt those elements were crucial. But it was also quickly clear that recovery and success would rely on the will, talent and resilience of the airport's diverse internal community, and that meant that internal communication and employee recognition must also play a central strategic role, which it did.

My learning that summer shaped who I am professionally more than anything else that happened to me before, or since. It set me up for a period of exponential growth in my own confidence and competence as a trusted strategic communication adviser and it shaped my interest in crisis communication and in the vital strategic advisory role of internal and external communication professionals at the highest level of organizations.

Perhaps more importantly, it reminded me that when we choose not to splinter, but to support each other, even in the most difficult circumstances, we are always stronger, and that's something to be celebrated and encouraged in life as well as work. The generous guidance and support I received in my time working for Scotland's three largest airports built my desire to help and mentor others as I moved into more senior leadership roles myself, and it continues to shape my professional values as I have had the privilege to build a business as a communication consultant and trainer.

At the time of writing this book, I have over 25 years of fully rounded internal and external communication experience. I have practised it, studied it, talked about it, taught it and absorbed it by osmosis. And every day doing any of these things reinforces my belief in the vital power and importance of effective and considerate internal communication in times of crisis.

In recent years a complex mix of existing and emerging factors have brought the risks we all face into sharper focus and made it clear that the question for most organizations is not now if another crisis will strike, but when. The idea of something monumental happening again to me – or to you – must now be thinkable and expected, and we must be ready.

The organizations that survive and thrive in this increasingly turbulent world are the ones who put meaningful communication with their teams at the heart of organizational strategy, and that means internal communicators must start planning now to support their people, organizations and of course themselves through whatever lies ahead.

Through my own training and consultancy, I see a growing interest, awareness and demand for specialist support in internal crisis communication, and while a level of practical and academic discussion dates back to the 1980s and 1990s there is space to do much more when it comes to providing practical thought leadership for, and more importantly by, internal crisis communication practitioners.

This book looks at crisis fully through the internal communication lens and from the perspective of the internal crisis communication professional – but it has been written for anyone with a passion for enabling their organization through crisis, regardless of sector, company, title or role. It covers the full span of crisis – from risk identification and pre-planning through the acute and chronic crisis stages, to coming out the other side and strengthening the organization.

In simple language, I have set out my own observations on the benefits and needs of internal crisis communication, and I have supplemented this with academic theory and expert commentary where I think it is helpful to give a deeper or more rounded background or perspective.

The book's goal is to offer real world, practical advice, and my hope is that it will help you begin or continue the planning and preparation needed to take confident and well-judged leadership of your organization's internal communication when crisis next strikes.

ACKNOWLEDGEMENTS

I'd like to thank Janet Adeyemi and the training team at the Chartered Institute of Public Relations (CIPR) for helping me to integrate internal communication into their global crisis training provision and for encouraging me to shape my notes on this subject into something deeper. This book would not have been written without Janet's encouragement and I'm grateful for her support. I would also like to thank the CIPR Board and leadership teams for their endorsement.

Thank you to Donna Goddard-Skinner and the team at Kogan Page for backing my idea, to Jeylan Ramis and Bobbi-Lee Wright who provided helpful guidance as I made it a reality and to all the people who shared their stories, experience and expertise as I began to write. I could not have imagined how enjoyable and inspiring each of the different interviews would be, nor could I have imagined how many incredible people would say yes when I asked them to take part. I am very grateful to all of them for sharing their time, thoughts and advice, and I know the book is stronger for being shaped by their different views.

I'd of course also like to thank all the colleagues who have encouraged, mentored and supported my learning in this field over many years, and particularly the members of Team Glasgow who let me into the crisis room, shared their knowledge and sparked my passion for this subject so many years ago.

I want to thank all the different friends and family members who helped me juggle many different responsibilities as I wrote this book, and last but never least, I want to thank my partner Ross and my son Kieran, who were kind and giving as I wrote, and who love and inspire me every day.

LIST OF CONTRIBUTORS

Thank you to the people who kindly shared their ideas and experiences in this book:

Advita Patel, Alison Lochhead, Amanda Coleman, Ben Verinder, Carolyn Bowick, Dan Holden, Derek Provan OBE, Ed Conley, Gillies Crichton, Dr Jacqueline Conway, Dr James Ndone, Jane Leaker, Jarrod Williams, John Bailey, Julian Pike, Kate Betts, Katie Marlow, Dr Kevin Ruck, Leona Deakin, Lucy Easthope, Lulu Arnett-Morrice, Marion Anderson, Mike Stevenson, Piyali Mandal, Rachel Miller, Stewart Kerr, Sue Jane Taylor, Suzanne Goldberg, Dr Timothy Coombs and Victoria Tomlinson.

Thank you to the people who kindly shared their ideas and experience for this book:

1

Understand crisis

Somewhere in the world, at this very moment, a crisis is about to strike.

Sometimes, you'll hear about it straight away. Details will ping on your mobile newsfeed. A friend or family member may send a message, and you might turn to social media or TV as you piece together what went on. Other times, you won't learn about it until later, through a few snatched words on the radio as you drive to dinner. Maybe instead you'll discover that another bad thing has happened as you rush past a newsstand or digital screen on your way to work the next day. Sometimes you'll have more immediate things to think about, and, sometimes, the crisis won't register with you at all.

When crisis strikes, everyone in the wider world feels the impact differently. For some of us, it will be a catastrophic and painful life-changing event, while for others, it will be recognizably bad or sad, but too abstract and far away to be truly affecting. Each crisis is different, but for the people inside the affected organization, it is always personal. Inside the organization, every crisis brings an intense, disruptive and transformative experience that is felt up close in many different ways, which will affect everyone profoundly in the moment and may stay with them for years to come.

Organizational crises trigger different strategic or operational demands and obligations, and they also trigger different emotional, psychological and practical human needs and responsibilities, all of which require internal crisis communication support, and all of which we will discuss in this book. The first step to meeting any of these in a meaningful way is to know your organization, to know your people and to be prepared – and the first step to being prepared is to understand crisis.

To begin, you need to know what organizational crises are, how they differ from business as usual, and what forms they can take. You need to know why and how they could hit your organization; you need to know how they could evolve and with what impacts; you need to know how people will naturally respond; and you need to know what all of this means for the planning and activation of your internal crisis communication strategies.

This chapter sets you up with the knowledge and understanding necessary to make a credible and well-judged contribution to internal crisis communication in the most challenging times your organization will face. First, it defines the exceptional nature of organizational crises and explains how crises differ from regular challenges and bumps in the road. Next, it describes a range of crisis types, causes and triggers, and it explains how crises develop in stages which each present different needs. From there, it discusses how your people might feel in times of crisis, what they might do, and how you can use this insight to unlock the power of internal communication and confront the challenges ahead.

What is a crisis?

People who juggle competing problems in busy and complex organizations often complain they're in constant crisis as they lurch from one drama to the next – but while that's possible, it's also unlikely. That's because in contrast to risks, issues, changes, challenges, difficulties and disruptions which ebb and flow in everyday organizational activity, crises are bigger than normal bumps in the road. They don't characterize business as usual, and they can't be juggled alongside normal daily tasks.

Formal definitions of crises and their impacts vary, yet most experts agree with Karl Weick's (1988) assertion that organizational crises are characterized by a 'low probability/high consequence event that threaten the most fundamental goals of an organization'. Most also agree that crises are events or processes that have the potential to cause significant human, environmental, financial, operational or reputational harm; that have the potential to affect or endanger the entire organization's growth, profitability or existence; and that require a specialist approach to management and communication.

Crisis communication consultant and trainer Ben Verinder is Founder and Managing Director of Chalkstream, a public relations company based in England. He has led the communication response to diverse crises and potential crises in the education system including fires, floods, chemical spills, on-campus assaults and murder so he knows well how crisis feels. He says:

> Dealing with a crisis is often very different to dealing with everyday activity.
> There is potentially much more at risk, and so it calls for a different

communication approach. For the people inside your organization, a crisis can feel personal, raw and dangerous. It's typically experienced in a completely different way inside the organization than it is outside of it, and managing it well requires clear and careful understanding of what has happened, what is likely to happen next, and what the possible impacts on all of your different internal and external stakeholders will be.

We will see later in this chapter that all crises are unique – they have different causes, they have different effects and they require different solutions. To the wider population, who are bombarded with stories of horror and outrage on a daily basis, they vary in scale, and they vary in significance. Some, such as the 9/11 terror attacks, or the Covid-19 global pandemic and lockdown, stop us in our tracks, reshape our collective consciousness and leave a lasting imprint on history. Others barely register and pass in the swipe of a device.

But, for the people working inside the affected organization, the crisis is always personal. Inside the organization, the crisis is an intense, disruptive and emotional life event which will affect everyone profoundly in the moment and may stay with them for years to come. And for that reason, the crisis deserves a carefully tailored and properly considered internal crisis communication response.

When it hits, your organization's crisis will be the number one topic of conversation inside and often outside of work. It will interrupt normal activity, command everyone's attention, and demand that everyone stops everything to focus on the operational, tactical and strategic activity necessary to prevent, limit or repair further harm.

When that happens, you too will need to put aside everyday activity to help people across the organization to access and share the carefully crafted and emotionally and logically meaningful internal crisis communication that will:

- keep everyone safe and supported
- help them make sense of the evolving situation
- help them stabilize, restart and remotivate through the challenges they face
- help them identify and minimize future risk
- help them achieve the overall crisis goals
- help the organization strengthen and pull through

Types of crises

When you imagine an exceptional and harmful incident in your own organization, you might picture a scenario that was also unexpected – a natural disaster or shock event that rose without warning and struck to devastating effect. In the preface to this book, I shared my own experience of a terror attack at my place of work. Later, we'll hear from people who have experienced or dealt with hacks, hurricanes, floods, pandemics, crashes and explosions. These real stories eliminate all doubts that shock crises must be anticipated, and prepared for – but they are not the only type of crisis you could face.

In fact, as well as the malevolent attacks and natural, biological or operational crises described above, experts such as Lerbinger (2012) and Coombs (2015) suggest that organizations endure many other different types of crises, including those caused by confrontation, mismanagement, misconduct and misbehaviour that could and should have been predicted and prevented.

These self-inflicted crises are more common than shock happenings, and they're often caused by resolvable issues, such as a regular technical breakdown that's worked around rather than fixed, the concealment of important information under a landslide of data, or whisperings of strange behaviour that everyone's heard about, but no one has confronted. They creep up and grow over time because people fail to acknowledge or deal with them while there's a chance to put things right, and they are a problem that Kate Betts knows well. Kate is a former BBC journalist and director of Capital B Media, a company that specializes in crisis communication consultancy and training. Based in Yorkshire, England, she has advised on many of the highest profile and most sensitive national crises in the UK, and her unique mix of experiences gives her a wide understanding of different crisis types. She says:

> One of the biggest problems I see in organizations who have gone on to experience a crisis is a lack of listening and a lack of wanting to hear about risk and issues when there was still an opportunity to make a change. Leaders, managers and communication professionals need to be listening to whatever is happening in and around the organization, good and bad, and we need to be on the lookout for red flags and warning signs.

> Over and above that, we need to understand the issues raised, and we need to tackle and deal with them. Leaders and managers need to realize that avoiding problems doesn't make them go away, it just pushes them below the surface

where they remain potent and unresolved. Sometimes it takes weeks, sometimes months, sometimes even years – but in my experience if they have not been tackled, problems always return, and they usually return in a bigger and more dangerous way.

Seymour and Moore (2000) paint a vivid picture when they describe the two different manifestations of crisis as *Cobras* and *Pythons* – the Cobra being the sudden or surprising crisis, and the Python being the slow creeping crisis that steals up and strangles the organization issue by issue.

Some organizations and industries are more volatile and complex than others, but every company is vulnerable to different risks, and every company must set up the flexible plans and processes to help employees function and perform well in difficult times. To do this best, robust systems must be used across the whole organization to scan for, detect, highlight and understand warning signs, and everyone involved in crisis scanning must be aware that new risks are emerging all the time so it's important to hear different perspectives and be alert to different scenarios.

Jane Leaker has worked in the internal communication and engagement function at Transport for London (TfL) for 20 years. In that time, her teams have experienced everything from terrorism to cyber-attacks to other complex incidents on the network. She tells me that her organization is crisis aware, well-prepared and well-rehearsed to deal with major incidents and human harm, but she points out that as the world changes, our thinking about crisis needs to change too.

> At TfL, we have a very structured approach to crisis management and communication. We know what a major incident is, and we know how to deal with it. Through real world experience and through scenario planning, our approach is tried, it's tested, and it's something we do very well. When we face a major incident, in whatever form, we are ready.

> At the same time, it's important to be aware that the world is constantly changing. The crises companies must prepare for today are not the same ones they prepared for 20 years ago, and they won't be the ones they'll prepare for in 20 years' time, so we need to remain alert to new and unseen situations. And as we re-evaluate risk, we must be very considerate that a crisis may nowadays encompass more than the obvious major incident we have in the plan. It may not even happen directly inside the organization, and we need to think more about how we become just as effective as we plan for that.

> Many companies did not traditionally build issues like war, social unrest or rioting outside the organization into their crisis communication plans, yet they

have a huge impact on your people and their ability to feel safe and function at work. That means we still need to think about if and how we step in and use our people and communication channels to engage and support.

Across the world, these big polarizing social and political issues have an impact and so we need to think about how we deal with them, and we need to build them into our planning to show people that leadership have considered their needs and have thought about them.

We will dive deeper into different crisis types in Chapter 3. However for now, it's important to know that to fully understand your organization's vulnerabilities, you must look and listen for slow-and fast-moving risks or issues outside and inside your own organization, and you must recognize a wide range of perspectives to build a full and informed understanding of the negative or harmful effects different crises may have.

Crisis causes and triggers

Crises are caused by a mix of deep underlying factors and triggered or 'set off' by a more immediate issue or event. Those that are caused or triggered outside of the organization are as varied as the world we live in. They can be harder to predict than those that grow inside the organization, and they are harder to prevent. Scanning for them involves anticipating multiple local or global factors that might negatively impact your organization, sector or community.

External causes and triggers may relate to environmental change, social unrest, political shifts, legal change, economic turbulence, technological change, cultural change and more. Their impacts are as diverse as their triggers, and include earthquakes, tsunami, floods, fires, illness, disease, confrontation, terrorism, product tampering, cyber-attacks and supply chain challenges. Some external events, such as health pandemics or war, can be considered a crisis in one company, and a crisis cause or trigger in another, depending on the impact they have on the organization and on its people.

Internally caused or triggered crises are more personal to the organization than external ones, and while statistics change each year, they are more common than many people realize. They can arise anywhere in the organizational hierarchy, and they are usually symptomatic of deeper sores or self-harm such as ineffective management, toxic cultures, skewed values, abuses of power, unethical conduct, deception, bad behaviour, negligence, poor processes, a lack of training, a lack of resources and an inability to listen. Huge organizations such as Wells Fargo (Berry, 2016), France Télécom (Waters, 2014) and the UK Post Office (McCapra, 2024) have all seen once strong reputations left in tatters because of deeply painful crises of their own making.

Experts such as Pearson and Mitroff (1993) and Coombs (2007) advise that crises caused or triggered by the organization are often more reputationally damaging than those that originated externally, because they relate to issues that could and should have been seen and averted before they caused harm.

It takes courage to help everyone face and deal with all the potential causes and triggers your organization may face, but prevention is better than cure. Every company must put systems, processes and safety nets in place to ensure that employees, contractors and consultants can talk frankly and regularly about red flags outside and inside the company walls, if it is to develop a broad and meaningful understanding of what could go wrong, stop the crisis before it strikes or deal with it if it does.

Internal communicators can support this process by helping employees see the implications of unsolved challenges, by communicating openly about issues as well as opportunities, and by putting safe and trusted channels in place for everyone to help anticipate, identify, report and understand risks and issues. We'll talk more about this in Chapters 3 and 10.

Crisis development

Regardless of type, and regardless of cause or trigger, once they begin to accelerate, crises take on a lifespan that can be seen to extend far before and beyond the point of immediate impact. Crises all travel at different speeds, they can seed multiple interconnected issues, and they never evolve exactly as you might expect – but they do follow patterns, and understanding these patterns is critical if you are to think forward and be ready for whatever comes next.

Crisis stages

In the simplest of terms, every crisis has a beginning, a middle and an end which come in three stages:

- A **pre-crisis stage**, when warning signs are detected and the organization takes steps to eliminate them, minimize them or plan for impact.

- A **crisis stage**, when the crisis hits and concentrated efforts are made to manage, contain and minimize harm.

- And a **post-crisis stage**, when the organization either dies, survives or strengthens and moves into recovery, learning and a new normal.

Many experts suggest you can further dissect any of these stages, often showing them as models that can be used to better understand and manage the crisis. Fink's four-stage model (1986), for example, is the one I will refer to throughout this book. It's simple, but it's useful for internal communication because, as well as the pre- and post-crisis stages shown above, it observes that the main crisis stage has a first and second part which are experienced very differently, so in fact every crisis has four rather than three stages:

- A **pre-crisis stage**, when warning signs are detected and the organization takes steps to eliminate them, minimize them or plan for impact.

- An **acute crisis stage**, which occurs when the crisis hits with a bang, everything is at its most urgent, confusing and intense and the focus is on activating a response to contain the situation and prevent escalating damage and harm.

- A **chronic crisis stage**, when the crisis lingers, ripples and aftershocks are felt, and the focus turns to long-term management and recovery.

- And a **post-crisis stage**, when the organization either dies or strengthens and moves into recovery, learning and the new normal.

Lots of planning and training is focused on the acute stage of crisis, because this is often where external interest is most intense, but if you have experienced them before, you'll know that there can be a profound difference in internal need as the crisis moves from a big bang to little ripples, and so you must also consider how internal crisis communication must adapt as the crisis moves from the acute to the chronic stage, and how internal crisis communication activity must evolve to meet predicted and emerging human, operational and reputational needs. This is a key focus of our discussion in Chapters 2 and 5.

Importantly, thinking forward will also prompt you to look at the crisis and the organization's future in its entirety. This in turn will inspire you to lift your head, look at the bigger picture and better consider the ripple effects and long-term impact of your advice and decisions as you react in the moment of greatest pressure.

The risk of a 'double crisis'

It's also important to understand that bad management or ill-judged internal or external communication related to the initial problem can either bounce the organization into a deeper and more dangerous situation or catapult it into another crisis altogether.

Research by Pearson and Mitroff (1993) found that it's normal for organizations to experience more than one crisis simultaneously, and that a mismanaged single crisis can set off a *chain reaction* of other crises and difficulties, while Johansen and Frandsen (2007) coined the term *double crisis* to describe a situation made worse by poor communication, a lack of communication or wrongful communication.

Good communication is never a fix for bad behaviour, and it should not be considered so, but poorly timed or poorly judged communication always makes a painful situation worse. This means internal crisis communication is vital in the overall crisis management, business continuity and business recovery processes, and internal crisis communication professionals must think forward and strive to get their facts straight, communicate quickly, evidence compassion and listen carefully at every crisis stage.

Failure to fully recognize internal crisis impacts or to acknowledge and accommodate employee experience and attitude is a key crisis-communication failing, and the reason for countless difficulties that follow. This means that more than anything, as it seeks to support, engage and enable the internal community in the crisis response, an organization must also seek to understand their unique needs and expectations at every step of the way, as Seymour and Moore (2000) explain: 'In a crisis you must, more than in any other business situation, put yourself in the shoes of your audience, see the problem from their perspective, and shift your communication to accommodate the disturbing emotions they now feel.'

The impact on the internal community

Crises affect everyone differently. If you have experienced them before, you'll know that some employees feel the harm of the crisis more than others, some feel the blame and some play a more obvious role in fighting the challenge or finding its solution. You may also have felt or observed how the impact causes a surge of adrenaline that triggers everyone's natural 'fight, flight or freeze' response, leading some staff to become more active, energized or aggressive; cause others to hide, deny or distance themselves from the problem; and cause others to stop or stall work – not knowing what to do or say.

Everyone is different, and individual reactions can't be accurately predicted, but whatever the circumstances, their physical and emotional proximity to the crisis and to the organization itself means that the internal community will feel an initial sense of disruption, disorientation, shock and uncertainty which can have negative effects, and which internal crisis communication must address if the company is to:

- keep everyone physically and psychologically safe
- help everyone cope and function in the evolving situation
- help everyone advocate and support the organization through the challenges ahead

Regardless of whether they become victims, potential victims, survivors, onlookers, defenders or champions, every employee will become a high-power, high-interest stakeholder who is affected by or can affect the crisis, and who requires deeper and more direct communication than many of those on the outside looking in. Their demand for information and understanding will be limitless, and they will observe, analyse and interpret every experience and every piece of information available (or unavailable) to them as they quickly form an attitude or opinion about what is happening, why and with what effects. All of this will shape and seed:

- how they think and feel about the crisis
- how they think and feel about the organization
- how they think and feel about themselves
- what they say and do next

This is important, because practical understanding and a growing body of academic evidence, for example from Frandsen and Johansen (2011), Heide and Simonsson (2019) and Mazzei and Ravazzani (2022), shows that as active receivers, senders, sense makers and sense givers of crisis information, and as potential enactors of crisis management, business continuity, business recovery and reputational recovery activities, an organization's employees are powerful advocates or detractors and persuasive actors in shaping what comes next.

Internal crisis communication academics and practitioners agree that employees are different to other crisis stakeholders. Time and time again, we see up close and in detail how our internal stakeholders feel different crisis impacts and how they stimulate different crisis effects – in part because of their relationship to the crisis itself, and in part because of their different roles, relationships and personal identification with or within the organization.

Occupational psychologist Leona Deakin tells me:

> Our life and work are intertwined. One of the first questions we ask people when we meet them is 'What job do you do?' and that's because so much of our personal identity is wrapped up in our jobs and organizations. Social identity theory tells us that our jobs and workplaces are a huge part of how we see ourselves – they give us purpose, belonging and self-worth. So, when crisis strikes, it doesn't just affect how the employees feel about the organization, it also affects how they feel about themselves, and it affects what they say and do next.

> Different organizational setbacks or traumas have different impacts depending on how they are caused and managed, and employees can decide to fight against the organization or fight for it. A poorly handled crisis can trigger feelings of anger, shame or embarrassment which will cause employee purpose, desire to belong and self-worth to drop, while a well-handled crisis can reinforce a strong connection with the company and boost employee pride, self-worth and belonging.

Even when employees aren't considered direct crisis victims, they will still face emotional, psychological and practical challenges that require tailored internal communication strategies. That's because depending on how and why they are caused, and depending on what people witness as they occur, crises can either shatter a general sense of justice and control inside the organization, leading to feelings of betrayal, insecurity and sadness that erode trust, commitment and effort; or they can evidence fairness and bravery that unite people, build pride and galvanize effort and advocacy. Leona Deakin continues:

> If the company has done wrong, behaved badly or is seen to be the villain in the crisis, your employees will distance themselves, and they will be thinking of moving on, particularly if they have seen or heard of behaviour that goes against their values of right and wrong. They'll worry that the crisis is going to taint them, and they'll worry that others might think they did something wrong. They may feel a sense of sadness, anger or betrayal; they may feel a loss of trust; and they may also feel embarrassment, shame and guilt if they had some complicit knowledge and didn't speak out.

But, if the company hasn't done anything wrong, if it is considered the victim of a crisis, then the employees may feel that they have been a victim too. They may feel pain, indignation, unfairness and sadness, but they'll be able to live with that. They will continue to function in the organization, and they may go out in the world and advocate for it. They may say 'This is really unjust, and we need to fight it because it's not fair.'

And then of course if something bad happens but the company deals with it well and fends off harm, the employees will feel pride that people are grateful. Their sense of belonging and sense of identity will be strong, they'll feel good about the organization, and they'll feel good about themselves. They'll be proud to tell people what happened, and they'll go the extra mile to advocate and offer support.

There is no single internal crisis communication approach that works in every situation, but most academics and practitioners agree there are principles and tools you must consider and apply for best success. Authorities such as Coombs (2007) suggest the most relevant, helpful and appropriate communication response will be empathetic, forward-looking, and based on a firm understanding of what happened, why it happened and how people feel about that. This means different crisis positions, strategies and approaches are required to engage, empower and enable employees in different circumstances; we will talk about this in more detail in Chapter 5.

As you develop your internal crisis communication strategies, you must accept that people won't go the extra mile for a company they believe is unrepentant for having caused harm so it's necessary to back words with action, evidence fairness in the treatment of victims and in the management of the crisis, and rebuild relationships by considering all the needs of everyone involved.

It's also important to accept that your employees' attitudes to the crisis and their desire to support or otherwise will be shaped not just in the moment, but they will also be based on their previous experience in the organization (Ndone, 2023).

Social psychology and the principle of reciprocity tells us that we are all more likely to support people and organizations that we know well, that we think have a good reputation or that have helped and supported us the past, and so it follows that employees and contractors who already like and respect the organization and who feel consistently feel heard, valued and supported are more likely to remain loyal, engaged and active during a crisis than those who do not.

Dr James Ndone is Assistant Professor in Crisis Communication at Costal Carolina University, South Carolina, USA, and he is a specialist in emotional crisis communication. He tells me about his research into the impact of negative employee-organizational relationships on crisis outcomes:

> My research found a negative employee-organization relationship damages internal reputation by creating a perception that the organization doesn't care about its employees. This lack of trust and lack of respect leads to employees being less willing to support the organization, especially during crises. Unsupportive behaviour might include reduced productivity, spreading negative sentiments or even actively working against the organization's interests.
>
> To overcome the damage the organization must rebuild trust. This can be done by improving communication, showing empathy and actively addressing the concerns that led to the negative relationship in the first place. Implementing fair and transparent rebuilding strategies can help to mend relationships and encourage more supportive behaviour during crises – but of course for best success, organizations should prioritize maintaining positive everyday relationships with their employees as a proactive strategy. Doing so not only helps in day-to-day operations but also serves as a buffer during crises, making it easier to navigate difficult times with the support of the workforce.

There are layers of nuance in every situation, and later chapters will touch upon all the organizational and audience insight you need to deliver a carefully tailored and well-judged internal crisis communication response, but for now it's important to understand that trust, effort and commitment are reciprocal, and that relationships may become weaker or stronger based on how each party is seen to respond in challenging times.

Crisis opportunity

All crises are intense, disruptive and transformative experiences that have the potential to cause significant disruption and harm. They will challenge and disorientate people right across the organization's community, and they will push everyone out of their comfort zone – but they don't have to lead to ongoing chaos, and they don't have to be lethal.

Eventually, the crisis will be over – and while some companies never recover, experts such as Mitroff (2005) have advised widely on how, with sensitive, empathetic and effective management, communication and relationship building, others will emerge operationally, financially and reputationally stronger and more resilient.

Most often, the companies that strengthen and thrive are the ones that:

- prepare effectively and plan ahead
- understand the crisis and meet a full range of operational needs
- understand how people feel about it and meet a full range of human needs
- strategically consider the long-term impact of everything they say and do
- consider their purpose and values, and make decisions that stand up to scrutiny
- communicate regularly in a logically and emotionally meaningful way
- and adopt a learning mentality, constantly listening and adapting as required

The rest of this book discusses the key strategic and tactical internal crisis communication understanding necessary to help your organization do just that.

KEY TAKEAWAYS

- Crises are low-probability, high-impact events or processes that have the potential to cause significant human, environmental, financial, operational and reputational harm and that require a specialist approach to management and communication.
- They come in many different forms and can emerge from inside or outside of the organization, arising suddenly or creeping forward over a long period of time.
- Many crises bring warning signs that should be anticipated and dealt with to prevent or minimize harm, and these can be more reputationally damaging and harder to forgive than those that were beyond a company's control.
- Crises are not static events. They twist, turn and evolve in stages that require different approaches to internal crisis communication at different times.
- A poorly managed and poorly communicated crisis can set off a chain reaction of further crises and difficulties.

- Employees are high-power, high-interest crisis stakeholders who often feel crises more intensely than external stakeholders because they are closer to the impact and have a deeper personal tie to the organization.

- Regardless of whether they become victims, potential victims, survivors, onlookers, defenders or champions, all employees will observe, analyse and interpret the information available to them as they quickly make sense of what is happening and why, and as they decide what they will say and do about it.

- The employee perspective on the crisis is driven not just by the type, cause and impact of the situation as it is observed by others, but also by their distinct personal and professional observations and experiences at each crisis stage, and by their past, current and expected future relationship to the organization.

- There is no single internal crisis communication approach that works in every situation, but there are principles and tools you must consider and apply for best success, and the most relevant, helpful and appropriate communication response will be human-focused, forward-looking and based on a firm understanding of what happened, why it happened and how people feel.

- Finally, as well as challenge, crises bring opportunity. With strong management, internal communication and relationship building, the company can emerge operationally, financially and reputationally stronger and more resilient.

References

Berry, K (2016) How Wells Fargo mishandled reputational crisis, *Bank Investment Consultant*, New York, 23 September, www.proquest.com/docview/1912118469?sourcetype=Trade%20Journals (archived at https://perma.cc/27S5-JM2V)

Coombs, W T (2007) Protecting organization reputations during a crisis: The development and application of situational crisis communication theory, *Corporate Reputation Review*, 1 (3), 163–176, www.researchgate.net/publication/247478499_Protecting_Organization_Reputations_During_a_Crisis_The_Development_and_Application_of_Situational_Crisis_Communication_Theory (archived at https://perma.cc/S7CH-KK9E)

Coombs, W T (2015) *Ongoing Crisis Communication: Planning, managing, and responding*, SAGE, Los Angeles

Frandsen, F and Johansen, W (2011) The study of internal crisis communication: Towards an integrative framework, *Corporate Communications*, 16 (4), 347–61, www.emerald.com/insight/content/doi/10.1108/13563281111186977/full/html (archived at https://perma.cc/D3UH-7T8K)

Fink, S (1986) *Crisis Management: Planning for the inevitable*, American Management Association, New York

Heide, M and Simonsson, C (2019) *Internal Crisis Communication: Crisis awareness, leadership and coworkership*, Routledge, Abingdon

Johansen, W and Frandsen, F (2007) Krisekommunikation: Når virksomhedens image og omdømme er truet, Samfundslitteratur, Frederiksberg. As cited in Frandsen, F and Johansen, W (2017) *Organizational Crisis Communication*, Sage, London

Lerbinger, O (2012) *The Crisis Manager: Facing disasters, conflicts and failures*, Routledge, New York

Mazzei, A and Ravazzani, S (2022) Chapter 19: The strategic role of internal crisis communication, *Research Handbook on Strategic Communication*, Edward Elgar Publishing, Cheltenham

McCapra, A (2024) Opinion: Public relations lessons from the Post Office scandal: Recent revelations from the Horizon IT Inquiry illustrate what happens when you get it wrong, *Management Today*, 27 June, www.managementtoday.co.uk/opinion-public-relations-lessons-post-office-scandal/reputation-matters/article/1878676 (archived at https://perma.cc/WF54-Q4YP)

Mitroff, I (2005) *Why Some Companies Emerge Stronger and Better from a Crisis: 7 essential lessons for surviving disaster*, HarperCollins Leadership, Nashville, TN

Ndone, J (2023) Internal crisis communication: The effects of negative employee-organization relationships on internal reputation and employees' unsupportive behaviour, *Public Relations Review*, 49 (4) 102357, ISSN 0363-8111, https://doi.org/10.1016/j.pubrev.2023.102357 (archived at perma.cc/URG7-4PSK)

Pearson, C and Mitroff, I (1993) From crisis prone to crisis prepared: A framework for crisis management, *The Executive*, 7 (1), 48–59, www.jstor.org/stable/4165107 (archived at https://perma.cc/5YZM-WVVR)

Seymour, M and Moore, S (2000) *Effective Crisis Management: Worldwide principles and practice*, Cassell, London

Waters, S (2014) A capitalism that kills: Workplace suicides at France Télécom, *French Politics*, 32, 10.3167/fpcs.2014.320307, www.researchgate.net/publication/268038922_A_Capitalism_That_Kills_Workplace_Suicides_at_France_Telecom/link/5612312c08ae6b29b49e4d6c/download?_tp=eyJjb250ZXh0Ijp7ImZpcnN0U GFnZSI6InB1YmxpY2F0aW9uIiwicGFnZSI6InB1YmxpY2F0aW9uIn19 (archived at https://perma.cc/43VY-6JVU)

Weick, K E (1988) Enacted sensemaking in crisis situations, *Journal of Management Studies*, 25, 305–17, https://doi.org/10.1111/j.1467-6486.1988.tb00039.x (archived at https://perma.cc/E4UW-JZYZ)

2

Recognize the role of internal crisis communication

The internal community are high-power, high-interest crisis stakeholders, and when a crisis strikes, whatever happens next will be shaped on one hand by their talent, commitment, resilience and advocacy; and on the other by the strength, influence and impact of the leadership, relationships, culture and communication they enjoy.

Success or failure often sits on their shoulders, yet time after time, as company leaders plan to deal with their next disruptive or potentially devastating event, they look outside first, leaving communication with the people they'll rely on to confront the challenge as an afterthought or a box to be ticked. All too often, they include internal communication as an action, an output or an endnote. They seldom consider specific or flexible objectives, approaches or impacts, and they rarely think about the full range of employee needs, let alone how these needs might differ in different parts of the company or change as the crisis evolves.

The result is that in far too many organizations, meaningful internal crisis communication is either non-existent or it's pieced together using crumbs of content that were originally gathered and shaped for the outside world. People hear about their own company's difficulties through mainstream or social media, or from friends, neighbours and customers. This not only frustrates and disempowers them, but it also signals to them that they sit low in the crisis hierarchy, and that in turn weakens the relationship, lessens the desire to act or advocate, and leaves an unnecessary vulnerability in the organization's ability to respond and recover as well as it could.

Internal crisis communication is different from everyday internal communication. It meets markedly different emotional, psychological and practical needs in markedly different circumstances, and if it is to deliver its potential, it must be strategically planned, judged and implemented. To do it effectively, you need a clear understanding of what it is, where its true power lies and how to harness that power to meet different needs and drive meaningful results.

This chapter begins with an explanation of what internal crisis communication is, why it's important and what it aims to do. From there, it introduces the 7S of internal crisis communication, a hierarchy of human and organizational internal crisis communication needs created to help you take a more forward-looking approach to your thinking. The chapter then ends with some key tips to get you best set for success as you begin or continue your internal crisis communication planning.

What is internal crisis communication?

Internal crisis communication is the planned, sustained and tailored effort to keep everyone inside the organization informed, engaged and involved through every crisis stage, from pre-crisis prevention back to post-crisis recovery and a new normal. It involves multiple formal and informal communication methods, channels and messages, and multiple formal and informal communication senders and receivers. Done well, internal crisis communication doesn't just keep the internal community informed, it also keeps them feeling safe, supported, empowered and enabled all the way through the most challenging time their company will ever face. Ultimately, it aims to:

- protect all stakeholders and minimize crisis harm
- help people make sense of what is happening
- activate internal support, action and advocacy for overcoming the crisis and strengthening the organization as it recovers and enters a new normal

It is closely aligned with external crisis communication, crisis management, business continuity and business recovery, and it may require collaboration with strategic and operationally focused colleagues across the organization and with HR, organizational development and training.

As well as employees, the internal community may be made up of contractors, subcontractors, freelancers, partners, volunteers, employee unions, representative committees and board members – so while the term 'employees' is often used as a summary term through this book, the needs of all these groups should be considered and built into your internal crisis communication plans and activity as necessary.

We established in Chapter 1 that different crises prompt different reactions so they require different flexible and adaptable internal crisis communication strategies and approaches. These must be carefully considered to create a meaningful crisis position and conversation that is delivered by leaders, role models, influencers and ambassadors inside the organization as well as through a selection of carefully chosen communication channels – and they must be designed to support, motivate and sustain the whole of the internal community through the challenges that a crisis brings.

We will focus on this in detail in Chapter 5, but for now let's focus on some elemental internal crisis communication needs.

Crisis communication authorities such as Coombs (2015) are clear that the goal of all crisis communication is to reduce the damage a crisis causes to both the stakeholders and the organization, putting the stakeholders first, and so it follows that internal crisis communication must first aim to protect and support all stakeholders, and it must then aim to enable employees so they can advocate for the organization and participate effectively in the crisis response.

To do this, academics such as Frandsen and Johansen (2011), Heide and Simonsson (2019) and Mazzei and Ravazzani (2022) propose that internal crisis communication requires a direct and personal approach. Sometimes, this must mirror the external crisis communication response and sometimes it must be more specifically tailored to employee and organizational needs at different crisis stages. This may include:

- instructive content to protect people from harm
- informative content to build understanding, minimize uncertainty and help people adjust to the crisis environment
- identification content to build or rebuild trust, belonging and engagement in the organization
- Action-oriented content to enable different crisis goals, and activate advocacy
- bespoke content to meet specific emotional, psychological, or behavioural reactions and practical needs

Every situation is different, but key needs and priorities emerge time after time. Based on this observation, I would like to introduce a new framework that clearly sets out each of the different human and organizational internal crisis communication needs you must consider as you take a forward-looking approach to internal crisis communication.

The new framework, which I have called the 7S of internal crisis communication, prioritizes essential human needs and moves incrementally to meet fundamental interconnected organizational needs as the crisis evolves and continues through each stage of its life cycle. I believe the ability to meet each new set of needs is enabled by what came before, so I would encourage you to think about them in the suggested order as you shape your strategies and activities:

- surviving needs
- supporting needs
- sensemaking needs
- stabilizing needs
- stimulating needs
- sustaining needs
- strengthening needs

Introducing the 7S of internal crisis communication

How and what you communicate will ultimately be determined by the cause, scale and impact of the crisis, and by its effect on the individuals inside and outside your organization; however, the 7S of internal crisis communication can help guide and clarify your thinking about different human and organizational needs as the crisis evolves, and we will refer to these needs throughout this book.

It is important to recognize that each of the seven needs are often closely linked and compressed very tightly together, so much so that in some situations it can feel as if they run in parallel, while in others it's clear to everyone that nothing can move forward until a critical step has been addressed and satisfied. Regardless, the point is that you put people first and begin with a clear primary objective to protect humans from harm. From there, you can think of the 7S of internal crisis communication as an interconnected hierarchy where the satisfaction or realization of each subsequent set of needs is enabled by what came before.

- Surviving needs: to keep people safe from harm
- Supporting needs: to deliver practical, emotional and psychological support
- Sensemaking needs: to build crisis understanding, explain the crisis position, re-establish trust and enable crisis advocacy
- Stabilizing needs: to restore a sense of organizational confidence, competence and belonging, and to take the first steps to recovery
- Stimulating needs: to enable the full strategic and tactical crisis response and get people energized and engaged as they achieve crisis management, business continuity and business recovery goals
- Sustaining needs: to build resilience, maintain a sense of progress and help teams continue towards recovery as crisis lingers in the slow chronic stretch
- Strengthening needs: to help the organization recover and come back stronger

Surviving needs

Surviving needs must be met first to keep people safe from harm.

When there is a danger of human harm, all needs related to physical safety and the reduction of human harm must be considered first and fast. That's not only because taking care of people is the only ethical thing to do, but it's also because any organization that fails to prioritize human need, safety and welfare is heading towards failure. People simply will not forgive, forget or comply, and that's a problem when you are relying on them to help.

This means that as a crisis hits, or as it changes shape and returns, the primary objective of internal crisis communication must be to disclose what is happening and offer the instruction necessary to keep people safe, to shield them from further harm, and to enable them to do the same for all the company's other internal and external stakeholders. Surviving communication is about quickly protecting and preserving life, then critical assets and the environment. Nothing else matters until these needs have been met, and this means that surviving needs remain the priority for as long as there is danger or risk of harm.

Because it is delivered in the acute stage of the crisis, when disruption, confusion and danger are all around, surviving information must be hyper-focused. It must be short, sharp, simple and directive to ensure critical information is understood and acted upon and to avoid unnecessary overload and overwhelm.

Each situation is different, but it can relate to anything from the disclosure of the problem and an instruction to evacuate a site, to shelter in place or to shut down a piece of machinery. On occasion, it can be to take no action and await further instruction. Where the risk is not of human harm, surviving information can also include instruction to avoid other forms of harm, for example not to click on an email link during a cyber-attack.

Surviving communication should ideally be sent from the top/centre of the organizational hierarchy to everyone else using one or more of the verified informing channels discussed in Chapter 7. It must be consistently tested for accuracy, then echoed and repeated without interference for as long as there is danger or risk of harm.

Supporting needs

Supporting communication must directly follow surviving communication and it should focus on the other emotional, psychological and practical help necessary to re-establish personal and professional wellbeing to begin healing and to help people to function within the complex and volatile situation they now face.

Because crises differ, supporting needs differ too, and they may change as the crisis evolves. Like surviving communication, supporting communication must be timely, simple and reassuring but it should also enable a greater level of conversation and consultation. A poorly judged supporting message can spark a sense of anger, betrayal and outrage, so it must show empathy and compassion for everyone affected by the situation, and it must be tailored to focus on the needs of the individual or group(s) it is directed towards.

Suzanne Goldberg has led internal communication at Channel 4 television, the Royal National Lifeboat Institution (RNLI), BBC News and Burberry in the UK. She has specialist experience supporting welfare and trauma response in human crises and she says it's vital that we understand the different crisis support that's required in different situations:

> Not every crisis is traumatic for employees, but you need to recognize that
> trauma comes in many forms and people feel it in different ways – so effective

supporting communication is vital. Support is needed very early in the crisis process and it may continue for a long time, as the need won't stop just because everyone's had a message or two or because they have been given a link to your Employee Assistance Programme.

Different people will require different types and levels of support as they experience the crisis and as they feel different effects, so supporting communication needs to plan for initial crisis impact and also for later trigger events and aftershocks. Take, for example, a technical malfunction that causes the death of a colleague. That's a devastating thing, and people will require support to process it. But the incident is just the beginning because as an investigation takes place, more information may come to light that is upsetting, so there may be more potential trauma. And then there may be additional triggers sometime later, such as special dates or events. All of those are touchpoints where people might still need supporting communication, and a leader who will stand up and say 'We know this is hard, but we've got it. We've got you. We've got your backs.'

While some people may feel trauma very directly, others will be exposed to it in less direct ways, but they may still be affected so we need to take a tailored approach. Our role as internal crisis communicators is to make sure that everyone knows what support is available to them; to help leaders to show up with empathy and authenticity to reinforce the central communication; to make sure managers have the tools, systems and processes they need to provide or signpost the support for their teams; to let people speak; and to listen, understand and respond to what they need, for as long as they need it.

Supporting communication can be delivered through a mix of personally tailored and company-wide messages. In some crises, the need will relate to shelter or financial support, so content must relate to working locations and conditions, job security, salaries and benefits. In other crises, the need will relate to physical or mental health and wellbeing, so the focus is on guidance, advice or training. In others still, the need will relate to complex feelings of shock, trauma, guilt or grief which must be acknowledged and understood as colleagues are guided towards specialist help.

Regardless of the situation, supporting communication must acknowledge and answer specific employee questions and demands. This means that while published materials are important, communication may be better delivered directly person to person, or in a group setting at a carefully considered place and time, through a credible and trusted leader or third party. Whatever the situation, people must also be allowed to speak, to be heard, and to have their questions quickly and compassionately answered.

Sensemaking needs

Tightly associated with surviving and supporting needs is the vital task of framing the crisis, helping people make sense of what is happening and – as far as is realistic – getting them onside. The need to make sense of unfolding events will be greater in some crises than others, but it will always exist in some form and even less directly affected employees may catastrophize or disassociate without it. This means that support for the sensemaking process must start early, satisfy demand, and continue through each crisis stage if the organization is to build understanding, re-establish trust and enable advocacy in the most difficult situations imaginable.

Academics such as Ancona (2011) explain that sensemaking involves interpreting and creating meaning out of uncertain or ambiguous circumstances. Often likened to exploring or mapping out a situation to better understand it, it is necessary to help people adjust and function in unfamiliar, shocking and harmful situations, and it's something that everyone will do with or without corporate support. That makes it a vital element of internal crisis communication, because if any members of the internal community don't get the information they want and need from the organization, they will simply seek and find it elsewhere, leading to weakened employee-organization relationships and greater risks of misinformation, disinformation and alternate agendas spreading and shaping the overall crisis narrative.

If they have a negative experience and interpretation of the crisis, how it was caused, and how it's being dealt with, your people will make sense of it accordingly and be less likely to support the recovery effort. But if they see, hear and, importantly, experience everyone in the organization behaving competently and humanely in even the most devastating of circumstances, they will have a more positive sense of what is happening and so will become more likely to step forward and assist. That means that facilitating positive crisis sensemaking through words and, importantly, through action and behaviour, is vital to shape employee attitudes to the crisis, and it's vital to determine what they decide to say and do next. Academic internal communication researcher and author Dr Kevin Ruck explains:

> When a crisis happens, one of the first things employees feel is uncertainty.
> They will be thinking 'I'm not sure what's happening. I've not been here before.

I don't know how to deal with this. I don't know what the organization will do or how it affects me and my future.' Uncertainty is the enemy of basic performance and engagement as you can't perform effectively, and you can't be engaged with the organization if you are uncertain about what's happening in that moment. If internal crisis communication does not address that uncertainty, there will be an immediate hit on performance and engagement, and so a critical early and continuous role of internal crisis communication is to help people make sense of what has happened, why and what is coming next.

People who are trying to make sense of a situation may replay and re-examine it repeatedly in their mind as they seek to re-establish a feeling of comfort and clarity. They might ask questions like, *What's happening? How could this happen? How do I feel about it? How does this reflect on me?* or *What should I do now?* They will focus on little else until their questions are answered, and they'll speak with others and observe and interpret everything that is going on around them as they seek, review and analyse as much information from inside and outside the organization as they can.

No organization can fully control the sensemaking process, nor should it attempt to, but all organizations can and must share information and involve people in different types of crisis understanding and activity if they wish to minimize uncertainty and to avoid chaos, confusion and catastrophizing. That means that regardless of whether the news is considered good or bad, sensemaking communication involves publishing information regularly, facilitating formal and informal conversation, and positioning the company as the number one source of trusted truth. If you don't do that, the organization is less likely to secure the support it needs to recover.

Central, leader-led messages should be used to disclose or confirm, map out and frame the crisis; and to explain the crisis position while offering a sense of purpose using the different strategies we will discuss in Chapter 5, while line manager conversations should be used to help people feel comfortable with the information and interpret what it means to them.

Like supporting communication, sensemaking communication puts the individual before the organization and begins by confirming the answers to basic questions such as *When do I work? Where do I work? What do I do?* before moving on to *Why should I care? Why should I stay? Why should I help?* and *What more can I do?* Content must seek to discuss the situation and the scope of the challenge in a way that people can relate to personally, and stories and evidence should be shared to show fairness in the treatment of victims and the management of the process, as well as a capability to move forward positively in the situation.

Sensemaking communication should be delivered through a mix of different channels and it benefits from published and spoken expressions of care, competence and reassurance as well as high levels of facilitated conversation, negotiation and debate. Face-to-face conversations are necessary, and team reflection or problem-solving exercises can be helpful as they let people share views with their peers. Beyond that, leaders and managers must get out and about to help colleagues make sense of the crisis by responding to the conversations they hear, by acknowledging emotion, by acknowledging difficulties, by replaying common values and aspiration as they explain and receive feedback on crisis positions, priorities and outcomes, and as they role model expected behaviours.

Occupational psychologist Leona Deakin says:

> When a crisis hits, people can feel like their world has been turned upside down. That sense of 'if I do the right things, everything will be okay' gets shattered, and they're left feeling like they have no control over what's happening. It's a tough realization, and it can lead to lingering feelings of fear, guilt or overwhelm.
>
> So, as soon as you are able, what helps is giving people certainty through clear information about what is happening and additionally involving them and giving them something they can control. This is where communication comes in because involving employees in understanding challenge and finding and implementing solutions can make a huge difference. It gives people a sense of purpose and reminds them they're part of a team working towards something better.
>
> That need starts early but it continues through each crisis stage so internal crisis communication must keep up the sense of purpose by sharing a well-developed and clearly articulated mission, vision and set of values to direct behaviours, align everyone in the recovery process, support decision-making and give people something meaningful to work towards.

Stabilizing needs

Once each of the aforementioned critical human needs have been satisfied, or are on the way to becoming satisfied, attention can turn to organizational need. This means the next priority is to stabilize – to confirm the crisis position, to restore a sense of organizational confidence, competence and belonging, and to take the first steps to recovery.

Jane Leaker has worked in the internal communication and engagement function at Transport for London for 20 years. In that time, her teams have experienced everything from terrorism to cyber-attacks to other complex incidents on the network and she knows first-hand the necessity to meet emotional and psychological needs, stabilize a situation and then help get things moving again. She tells me:

> Once we have established safety, it's all about making people feel safe and empowered to make their own decisions, and to guide them on how they need to adapt their work processes. If you think about a cyber-attack, or terrorism or something like Covid for example, you'll recognize that the organization must adapt its work processes to keep the wheels moving. Internal communication has a vital role stabilizing and restarting the organization by giving people the information that enables them to pivot how they work and to carry on doing the job that's required.

> A lack of guidance can lead to all sorts of operational inefficiencies, and it can also have a negative impact on wellbeing. It can increase anxiety and stress which affects mental health and overall job satisfaction. And of course, it can damage customer relations and reputation as a result, so it's important that we get it right.

Stabilizing content seeks to confirm the crisis position, while returning to a positive routine, building confidence, and evidencing a commitment to safety, fairness, wellbeing and company values as people get ready to go back to work and keep the organization functioning. It is the necessary link between human needs and organization needs, so it's very important at this point that people know what's happening and where they fit in. This means that stabilizing communication can be quite operationally focused and locally led, and while a central message remains important, some elements may be quite tailored to the needs of different regions, functions or teams within the organization. At this stage, even the smallest wins make a big difference, so you may wish to recognize progress and (if appropriate) celebrate early success.

Leaders and line managers take on a critical role in delivering personal and meaningful stabilizing communication, while central one- and two-way informing channels should be used to discuss the bigger picture, even if it's to confirm nothing has changed. If it had been necessary to switch away from the company's normal internal communication channels in the acute stages of crisis, this is the time to look at whether they can be reintroduced, but either way, the organization must keep updating employees as new information becomes available, and leaders should continue to listen and gather views about what people think needs to happen next.

Stimulating needs

If stabilizing is about getting set for the future, then stimulating is all about pressing 'go' and getting people engaged and excited about what comes next. Stimulation is vital to enable a tactical response and so it runs parallel with crisis management, business continuity and business recovery needs, but it's also very much about connecting people physically, intellectually and emotionally to the crisis response, energizing them and building a desire to go the extra mile and help each other succeed.

This is the point at which internal crisis communication really begins to broaden out and include higher levels of message co-creation and control, and so you must use a wide mix of content and channels to confirm that all employees understand and believe in the crisis position; appreciate and support the wider strategy; connect the dots between task and vision; and accept the stretch targets ahead.

At this time, it's critically important to start and continue putting individuals, roles and teams at the centre of every positive crisis story so that across the organization, people feel valued and acknowledged in their contribution to the crisis response. We will discuss in Chapter 6 how best to involve lots of different voices as you share interesting and useful advice, information, and tell stories as you accept what happened and work to rebuild a sense of identity, and to re-establish confidence and resilience within each of your teams.

When it's done well, stimulating communication brings an acceleration point where the organization reiterates its positive values, instils a new sense of purpose and sets a clear future vision. It gives everyone a clear role to play, gains commitment to the challenge and re-empowers people to support the organization through the crisis back to business as usual or into a new version of normal. This means it must be very active and involving, and communication must use a mixture of involving and engaging ways to celebrate the individuals in the organization as part of the bigger team.

A tip is to ask people what they think as you set out a vision or call to action, to promote and share good ideas widely, and to think about how you might use immersive content and a mix of audio and video to evidence progress in a memorable way.

Sustaining needs

And just as you think that the organization is well on its way to recovery, get ready for a bump. Because just as sociologist and organizational expert Professor Rosabeth Moss Kanter (2009) argues that organizational change is hardest in the *miserable middle*, many organizations find that maintaining engagement and motivation is hardest in the slow chronic stretch where the crisis grinds on with fewer regular and easily identified milestones. People are tired. They are fed up, and with adrenaline no longer pumping at 100 miles an hour, there's a risk that if sustaining needs are not met, things will slip.

To the outside world, it may look like the crisis is over. They've made their judgement on how well or badly the organization has handled the situation, and they will alter their behaviour accordingly. Their interest drops, and it moves elsewhere. External crisis communication stops, and all too often, internal crisis communication stops too. That's a mistake, because the internal community are still working hard behind the scenes to help the organization continue to operate and continue to recover. They are still making sense of what happened, they are not yet back in their comfort zone, they are at risk of burnout and – in some types of crises – they are still grieving.

If you've experienced it yourself, you'll know that it's normal at this point for employees to feel mixed and changing emotions, and it's normal for their motivation to rise and fall, particularly if they are seeing little crisis progress or if they are feeling uninvolved and out of control.

Some people need to be held psychologically and emotionally and cared for very closely as they recover. Others simply need a boost and a level of recognition of the challenging work they continue to do, so sustaining communication should be employee-led. If trauma or human harm has been felt, it must involve lots of opportunity for discussion and conversation and it must support continued healing.

Where the harm was environmental, operational, financial or reputational, it's about keeping people active and onside. In these instances, it can be delivered through continued working groups, brainstorming events and problem-solving activities and it must be backed up with shareable stories, images, data and information, and little rewards to keep informal conversations going in a positive way.

At the same time, getting it right involves recognizing and accepting the natural dip, so it is also about continuing to be there emotionally – acknowledging that feelings will naturally go up and down, recognizing effort and showing compassion as everyone continues to give their all. Human contact, staff recognition and a meaningful focus on mental health and wellbeing is vital, so you must encourage your leadership teams to get out to hear success stories, thank everyone, role model positive behaviours and keep morale high.

Strengthening needs

Finally, as we discussed in Chapter 1, some companies don't just recover from crises, they come back stronger and more resilient. If the organization is open to it, even the most challenging crises can bring opportunity for growth, innovation and enhanced relationships, and so careful and considerate strengthening communication is critical to present, reinforce and celebrate this outcome as employees continue to go the extra mile and help the organization to succeed

Crisis leadership experts James and Wooten (2022) suggest that to best recover, the organization must embrace a learning culture, with processes and protocols in place to surface and share information, to resolve blockages, and to capture and integrate lessons learnt. This, they say, requires leaders to rebuild relationships forged on trust and openness, and it relies on a diversity of skills, knowledge and perspectives to see the picture as fully as possible. They argue it also requires leaders across the organization to work consciously on their own critical thinking and self-awareness, guarding against bias, deferring to the expertise of others, building the trust to delegate, letting go of things that no longer work, and enabling collaborative creativity to reframe problems as opportunities wherever possible.

From there, strengthening communication is all about using a wide mix of the involving and engaging channels described in Chapter 7 to evidence learning and change while sharing crisis success and building reputation back from the inside out. It's about rebuilding pride and re-establishing the employee's positive relationship with the organization as they overcome the challenge and move to better times.

Strengthening communication is hugely powerful, and it is the necessary final step to recovery, but it must be well-timed and well-judged. Celebrate or 'shut down' the crisis before people are ready, and particularly before the surviving, supporting and sensemaking needs have been met, and you will hurt people, you will make them angry and, ultimately, you will fail.

To keep it palatable, it must be well-judged, and it must be fully victim and survivor aware, and it must be inclusive of everyone as it celebrates crisis defenders and champions. If it is appropriate, this is the time to include small events, recognition ceremonies and tokens of thanks that place employees firmly in the hero role as you encourage teams across the organization to recognize milestones, reflect on their achievements and embrace opportunity for the future.

Tips for internal crisis communication success

Internal crisis communication is complex, it's nuanced, and it's often misunderstood. It is a proactive and forward-looking discipline which must be strategically and considerately delivered using all the information available to guide your thinking in the most difficult of times.

The quicker people know there is risk, danger or threat of any type, the quicker they can respond to minimize harm, so a considered, timely and directive response is required to keep people safe; while long-term employee-centred involving content and activity is needed to help the organization rebuild and recover over the longer term.

As we will find out in Chapters 3 and 5, your strategy requires detailed insights that you can't make up or guess in advance, but that doesn't mean you need to wait. There are lots of things you can do to prepare, and success relies on beginning early, planning ahead and starting now.

Beginning early means:

- developing a full understanding of the types of crises your organization might face and how it might deal with them
- forming a full understanding of your organization, your people and the types of support they may need
- recognizing and preparing to meet the different human and organizational needs you may have to cater to
- establishing a robust, human-focused and fully functioning internal crisis communication infrastructure and approach within your organization
- fostering an organizational culture that is grounded in open and effective listening, transparent reporting and respectful relationships

Planning ahead means:

- building strong relationships with all the colleagues and groups at all levels across the organization that are focused on different elements of risk, issues, and crisis management and communication
- working with colleagues across the organization to establish and agree a robust but adaptable internal crisis communication plan, and discussing potential strategy and approach using the tools and techniques suggested in the rest of this book

---

KEY TAKEAWAYS

- Internal crisis communication is the planned and sustained effort to keep all members of your internal community involved throughout every stage of an organizational crisis from crisis prevention through crisis management all the way back to business recovery and a new normal.

- It is different from everyday internal communication. It meets markedly different emotional, psychological and practical needs in markedly different situations, and so it should be specifically planned and considered, and tailored to each unique situation.

- Its main aims are to protect all stakeholders and minimize crisis harm, and to activate internal support, action and advocacy for overcoming the crisis and strengthening the organization.

- Every situation is different, and while different strategies, content and channels are required in different contexts, key needs and priorities can be seen to emerge time after time.

- This chapter introduced a new framework, the 7S of internal crisis communication, that puts critical human needs at the centre of all internal crisis communication activity and moves incrementally to meet critical organizational needs as the crisis continues through each stage of its life cycle. In doing so, it guides the user through an interconnected hierarchy of internal crisis communication needs where the realization of each new set of needs is enabled by what came before.

- The needs identified in the 7S of internal crisis communication are surviving, supporting, sensemaking, stabilizing, stimulating, sustaining and

---

strengthening. For best effect, internal crisis communication must consider all these needs, alongside the other strategic and tactical tools and techniques we will discuss in the rest of this book.

- Success relies on preparing early, planning and recognizing how to adapt in different situations.

References

Ancona, D (2011) Sensemaking: Framing, and acting in the unknown, *The Handbook for Teaching Leadership*, Sage, Los Angeles, www.sagepub.com/sites/default/files/upm-binaries/42924_1.pdf (archived at https://perma.cc/EQJ2-SKKA)

Coombs, W T (2015) *Ongoing Crisis Communication: Planning, managing and responding*, Sage, US

Frandsen, F and Johansen, W (2011) The study of internal crisis communication: Towards an integrative framework, *Corporate Communications, An International Journal*, 16 (4) 347–61, www.emerald.com/insight/content/doi/10.1108/13563281111186977/full/html (archived at https://perma.cc/D3UH-7T8K)

Heide, M and Simonsson, C (2019) *Internal Crisis Communication: Crisis aware-ness, leadership and coworkership*, Routledge, Abingdon

James, E H and Wooten, L P (2022) Prepared leadership as your fourth bottom line. *Stanford Social Innovation Review*, 11 October, https://ssir.org/books/excerpts/entry/prepared_leadership_as_your_fourth_bottom_line# (archived at https://perma.cc/8VGQ-4P84)

Mazzei, A and Ravazzani, S (2022) Chapter 19: The strategic role of internal crisis communication, *Research Handbook on Strategic Communication*, Edward Elgar, Cheltenham

Moss Kanter, R (2009) Change is hardest in the middle, *Harvard Business Review*. 12 August, https://hbr.org/2009/08/change-is-hardest-in-the-middl (archived at https://perma.cc/5X3X-4YFD)

3

Anticipate and plan for different types of crises

In Chapter 1, we established that all crises are unique. We saw that there's no quick fix to guarantee your company will survive a crisis and come back stronger, but we also came to see that with the right attitude, effective preparation and a well-informed approach, success is more than possible.

Of course, the best outcome is always that the organization anticipates escalating issues and takes action to stop harm before it happens, but it's also necessary to plan for other eventualities, so the organization is ready to look after its people, respond well to whatever has occurred and to meet each of the 7S of internal crisis communication first identified in Chapter 2.

The secret to success is taking fast, effective control, and the secret to taking control is to prepare in advance. Best practice involves working with crisis management, business continuity, external communication and operational colleagues to identify, understand and tackle potential vulnerabilities and dangers in stable times and to prepare and test the plans that will guide you in less predictable situations. Nothing else will work better to ensure that everyone is physically, mentally and emotionally ready to stop potential crises before they escalate or to tackle them effectively when they hit, and nothing else will ensure you are best placed to act quickly, confidently and with the full support of your company leaders when you need to do so.

This chapter advises how you can work with others in the organization to detect and deal with known issues before they escalate, and to scan for emerging trends that are not yet on the radar. It sheds light on the different types of crises you should consider as you seek to identify any gaps in your thinking. Next, it explains how you might prepare for different best- and worst-case situations before they strike, it offers tips for shaping and practising your crisis communication plan, and it explains how to identify a crisis and activate the response.

Anticipate the crisis

We recognized in Chapter 1 that every organization is vulnerable to internally and externally triggered crises, and the best-prepared companies constantly and systematically scan for warning signs related to both. No one can predict exactly how things will play out, but we can all analyse past and present activity in and around our organizations to anticipate what might cause future harm.

Crisis anticipation involves working with specialists from across the company to understand complex risks, embed detection systems, and scan for issues and trends. Excellence lies in getting as many people involved as possible, being open and non-defensive as together you question 'what if?'

Understand your risk

Every organization, every industry and every geographical area is vulnerable to its own unique risks, so if there's a risk register in your organization, you must use it as the starting point for your internal crisis communication planning. Doing this won't just ensure you are preparing for the right things, it will also show senior leaders and crisis management colleagues that you have your finger on the pulse of the organization, that you are there to add value and you are working with them, rather than against them.

The risk register is a live document which is updated and reviewed to track patterns and identify areas of rising and falling concern inside the organization, industry, geographical area and, where relevant, in the wider world. It's typically owned by someone who has full oversight of crisis, business recovery or business continuity activity in the company, and it is used to monitor, manage and mitigate all forms of organizational risk.

Many registers are split into crisis categories and include:

- risk description
- risk likelihood
- potential impact or harm
- allocated owner

No register is identical, but they may incorporate risks such as extreme weather, cyber-attack or technological malfunction. Generic risk and impact descriptions are less powerful than defined and detailed ones, so the best registers include background and analysis on what is known about the internal and external history of the risk, and what is not known but must be monitored or assessed.

As you consider internal communication needs related to each risk, look at the organization and its decisions through other eyes. Closely examine and reflect on its performance, practices, products, services, activities, behaviours and culture from different internal and external points of view. Assess how well everyone follows the rules, regulations and values that are in place to guide them, listen to what is not said as well as to what is said, and try to understand what could trigger harm from other perspectives.

Recognize changing internal and external attitudes towards your company and its activities and be considerate that what amounts to a crisis for your people may be different to what you've traditionally identified in your plan. Try to see different points of view as you seek to understand the impact of political, economic, social, environmental and legal complexity, turbulence and disorder in the organization, in its networks and in the wider world.

Think the unthinkable

Common sense dictates you must be ready to deal with the most obvious and immediate risks first, but the examples in this book make it clear that there are other issues to consider. This means that when you are fully clear on your company's direct set of risks, you should also use the insight you have gathered to imagine and plan for less likely events or processes that would stop the organization from delivering its core activity, or that would have other harmful human, environmental, financial, operational or reputational consequences.

There are lots of helpful lists you can use to identify a full range of possibilities, and one of the best known was developed and refined by Dr Otto Lerbinger. In his book *The Crisis Manager: Facing disasters, conflicts and failures* (2012), Dr Lerbinger identified nine crisis types which every company needs to anticipate and prepare for. He called these: *natural crises, biological crises, technological crises, confrontation crises, crises of malevolence, crises of mismanagement, crises of skewed management values, crises of deception* and *crises of management misconduct*.

As you go through each possibility, consider whether similar risks are already included on the risk register or not. If they are, imagine how they might change or manifest in different ways. If they are not, look at trends occurring inside and outside the organization to identify any gaps. You don't need to plan for absolutely every type of crisis, but you do need to consider different possibilities and decide if they are a risk for your organization.

NATURAL CRISES

Natural crises, or disasters, include earthquakes, tsunami, wildfires and floods. They can cause devastation over wide areas, and they can have profound, long lasting and multifaceted human, economic, social and environmental impacts. They can also trigger a chain of further crises if they are handled badly, communicated badly or if they are overwhelming in scale.

In 2011, a major earthquake hit the seafloor northeast of Tokyo and triggered a 15-metre-high tsunami which wiped out miles of infrastructure across Northeastern Japan and disabled the power supply and cooling of three Fukushima Daiichi reactors, causing a nuclear accident that led to the permanent evacuation of more than 100,000 people.

Even though many had lost homes and families in the tsunami, hundreds of Tokyo Electric Power Company (TEPCO) employees and contractors were housed in temporary accommodation and faced personal risk as they worked alongside firefighting and military personnel to restore heat removal from the reactors and cope with overheated spent fuel ponds (World Nuclear Association, 2024). Many years later, TEPCO are still implementing a complex decommissioning project that will take 30 to 40 years to complete while also working to revitalize the living environment and industries of Fukushima (TEPCO, no date).

If natural crises are a risk for your organization, you should seek specialist and expert local knowledge as you plan and think not just about how you will communicate the obvious survival and support messages before and as the crisis hits, but also how you will continue to meet sensemaking, stabilizing, stimulating, sustaining and strengthening needs afterwards.

BIOLOGICAL CRISES

Biological crises cause widespread harm when outbreaks of natural or man-made disease spread rapidly between humans or animals leading to contamination, public health emergencies or widespread disease, disability or death.

They can be overwhelming, not just for health, but also for society and the economy, and they impact us all. When they are badly handled, they can lead to multiple other difficulties, as the Covid-19 pandemic showed. Most experts agree that increased globalization, urbanization, climate change, antimicrobial resistance and biosecurity threats mean that future biological crises, including pandemics, are likely, so it's important that all organizations are fully prepared to support their employees through a range of different scenarios.

TECHNOLOGICAL CRISES

Technological crises are classified as such when technology fails or malfunctions leading to human, environmental, financial, operational or reputational harm, and they include software failures, mechanical breakdowns and industrial accidents.

Global aerospace company Boeing experienced a technological crisis when two separate Boeing 737 MAX airplanes crashed in 2018 and 2019 due to a malfunction in the software that was designed to help prevent the aircraft from stalling. The fatal accidents killed 346 passengers and crew (Boeing, 2019; BBC, 2020)

Two crashed planes are devastating for any organization, and dealing with such a happening is hard to comprehend, especially when the organization is considered at fault. But the reality is that technological crises kill hundreds of thousands of people every year and they affect millions. The damage and the pain are the same, whether a son, daughter, partner, parent or beloved friend dies alone, or in an incident that involves many others, so an organization that relies on complex and interlinked technologies must consider and seek to mitigate and plan for different types of technological risk.

CONFRONTATION CRISES

Crises of confrontation arise when people criticize, boycott or attack an organization, product or service because of real or perceived wrongdoings, and they can begin internally as well as externally.

A long-term example is the boycott of Nestlé products following concerns about the way it marketed breast milk substitutes in developing countries. The boycott from the Infant Formula Action Coalition began in the US in the 1970s and ended when the company refined its policy in 1984, although some boycott activity continues to this day (Nestlé, no date).

Every company is vulnerable to criticism, and this can bring a particularly strong need for supporting and sensemaking communication. People at all levels of the organization can naturally become defensive and emotional so it's critically important that organizational leaders are able to accurately differentiate between peaceful protest and violent confrontation or abuse then respond accordingly. Failing to respond proportionately in either situation can prompt further harm, widespread condemnation and a potential double crisis focused on how badly the organization responded to the situation it faced.

To best prepare, a tip is to gather people from all generations, all backgrounds and all regions of your organization to agree how they define a crisis of confrontation, what a proportionate response would feel like, and what information, support and flexibility they would need from the company in different situations. A tip to guide the conversation may be to discuss the purpose and intent of the people involved, the methods used to draw attention to their cause, the consequences of their action and the impact on your people.

CRISES OF MALEVOLENCE

Acts of malevolence include terrorism, cyber-attacks, workplace violence, contamination, tampering, hacking and the deliberate spread of disinformation. Examples through this book show they can cause significant operational, financial and human harm and they're something that all organizations must be ready to deal with.

No organization is exempt from risk, and it is as necessary to be prepared for physical acts of violence as it is for cyber-attacks and the spread of disinformation. As you prepare, you must work with security specialists in the organization to discuss what measures are in place to protect people, physical assets, electronic assets, information and processes, as well as what communication needs your staff would have in relation to each of the 7S of internal crisis communication in different scenarios, with a focus on surviving and supporting needs. If there are any gaps, you must address them as a priority.

CRISES OF MISMANAGEMENT

Crises of mismanagement occur because of management negligence, incompetence, illogical decision-making or issues denial. They can happen in any organization, of any size, and while they are often screened by silos or submerged in bureaucratic confusion, they can be foretold by many bubbling warning signs.

An example is the British Post Office scandal, also known as the Horizon scandal, which came to public attention after decades of mismanagement which saw hundreds of sub-postmasters wrongly accused of theft, fraud and false accounting when using faulty accounting software between 1999 and 2015. Despite knowing about system errors, the Post Office pursued prosecutions, leading to wrongful convictions and imprisonments (Post Office, 2024).

Many former sub-postmasters and sub-postmistresses say the scandal ruined their lives. Some used their own money to cover non-existent shortfalls because their contracts said they were responsible for unexplained losses. Others faced bankruptcy or lost their livelihoods. Marriages broke down, and some families believe the stress led to serious health conditions, addiction and even premature death (BBC, 2024a).

CRISIS CAUSED BY SKEWED MANAGEMENT VALUES

Skewed management values cause harm when companies knowingly sacrifice health, safety or basic human values in favour of personal, financial or corporate gain, sometimes with terrible consequence.

In 2013, more than 1,100 garment factory workers died and many more were injured when the poorly constructed and overloaded eight-storey Rana Plaza building near Dhaka, Bangladesh collapsed sparking local protest and global outrage. Reports state large cracks appeared in the building the day before the collapse, yet factory staff were told to re-enter the building and return to work (BBC, 2013).

The victims and survivors of Rana Plaza were making clothes for multiple big brands and global retailers, highlighting every organization's duty of care for contractors and subcontractors as well as for their own people, and for the need for organizations to identify and consider skewed management values not just inside their own walls, but in supplier and partner organizations too.

CRISIS CAUSED BY DECEPTION

Crisis caused by deception can involve fraud, false reporting, false promises or hiding important information. They can have devastating and long-lasting consequences, particularly when human harm is felt.

The horrifying fire which killed 72 people at Grenfell Tower in London in 2017 was an avoidable tragedy that revealed multiple serious failings including systematic dishonesty and the concealment of known safety concerns highlighting the critical importance of rigorous audit, confidential reporting and whistleblowing opportunities in high-risk sectors and organizations (Apps, 2022; BBC, 2024b; Walker, 2024)

CRISES OF MISCONDUCT

Finally, misconduct can occur anywhere in any organization, and managers and employees who behave unethically, violate trust or abuse their power can cause lasting human harm.

In 2018, the charity Oxfam GB faced a major organizational crisis after it was uncovered that some of its employees sexually exploited survivors of the 2010 Haiti earthquake, and the company had failed to properly investigate (Oxfam, 2019) while retail giants Harrods (BBC, 2024c) and Abercrombie & Fitch (BBC, 2024d) have both had public allegations of systematic abuse, harassment and rape at the highest levels of their organizations.

It takes bravery to surface and tackle internal misconduct, or indeed any other crisis related to management deception or failure, especially when the perpetrator(s) are acutely aware of the power dynamics in a situation, and you feel that you are perhaps one or two steps removed, but it is impossible to turn back the clock after harm is felt, so it's necessary. As well as offering opportunities to whistle-blow and prevent future harm, internal communication is vital to support victims and survivors and to help them make sense of what has happened.

Monitor and track issues

Recognizing the full range of potential issues is a vital first step to creating an early warning system, but it's equally important to monitor and track how situations evolve, as global crisis communication consultant John Bailey explains. John is Managing Consultant at Global Communications Consulting, a company specializing in crisis communication that is based in Singapore and Switzerland working with clients in more than 50 countries. Over the past 25 years, he has advised on some of the largest and highest profile global crises in the aviation industry as well as in the hospitality, manufacturing, sports and FMCG sectors, and he is a firm believer in an early and proactive approach. He says:

> Identifying and tracking internal and external issues serves as a great early warning system. Sometimes the analysis is subjective but if you regularly monitor and track the damaging impact of your issues, you'll see that some will drop off over time, while others will start climbing.

> A simple tip is to use a basic scoring system and an X/Y axis. On one axis, rate how likely the issue is to happen, and on the other, how much damage it could

cause. The issues that end up in the right-hand corner are the ones you should focus on now, and the ones that are moving towards that corner, no matter how slowly, are the ones to think about. Sometimes an issue that has been around for years can suddenly flashover into a crisis, and tracking helps you anticipate and get ready for that shift.

Tackle problems

Beyond identifying, tracking and communicating through crises, John Bailey also tells me that communicators can help business leaders to understand and tackle potential problems before they cause harm:

> As we identify and track issues, we also have a role in bringing crisis concerns to the table. We need to help management understand what could happen and how they could be perceived if they follow through on the decision they're about to make.

> We need to be able to say, hold on a second, before we do that, have you thought how it could play out? Have you thought how that will be interpreted? Have you thought how people will respond?

It becomes clear that our value as internal communicators is not just planning to tackle the crisis, it's also about changing the course of damaging events to make sure the crisis never happens. As well as guiding decisions, internal communication can coach employees on risk, set clear expectations around values and behaviour, clarify and role model obligations to transparency and accountability, and embed a positive culture of listening and reporting. We will discuss the role of listening further in Chapter 10.

Dive into different scenarios

As you monitor, track and tackle organizational risks, you should also consider how the business would deal with each situation if it was to escalate in unexpected ways.

Scenario planning lets you visualize different best- and worst-case situations in a safe environment. It won't give you a detailed prediction of what will happen, but it will stimulate the conversation about different situations and their impacts.

The process can involve anything from simple discussion to tabletop exercises, to full role play simulations that imagine how a crisis might be triggered and evolve with different turning points, ripples, aftershocks, and that test how different crisis positions, messages, spokespeople and channels might be received in different situations. This helps you identify and remove snags, barriers and communication breakdowns in stable times, it can prompt discussion around the impact of different decisions, and it gives you helpful insight to develop both your plan and strategy.

Victoria Tomlinson ran an award-winning communication business based in England for 30 years before becoming Founder and Chief Executive of Next-Up, and she has advised in multiple crisis and pre-crisis situations. Her top tip is to involve everyone who interacts with your many different stakeholders or who delivers or represents your brand experience:

> You need to involve people with different perspectives and specialisms from across the whole organization, from all generations, from all roles and from all points in the hierarchy. You need to move out of the boardroom and make sure that you involve people from the frontline. That means bringing in people who interact with your customers, and people who work in the supply chain and people who work in the operation so that you see the issue from different points of view.
>
> You need to consider different situations, and you need to ask the challenging questions ahead of time. At all times, consider 'How does this feel for the different humans involved?' Go through the big, difficult issues, the really tough ones, and discuss how they might arise, how they might play out. Discuss what information, support and flexibility your people might need in different scenarios and consider how you might use different approaches to deal with them.

Building in difficult questions and worst-case scenarios makes your planning as robust as possible and it's essential to get you ready for the most harmful crisis situations. It can also help build confidence and a sense of psychological safety in the organization by letting people know that nothing is 'off limits' and there is nothing they need to hide.

Consider all needs

As you consider your scenarios from diverse perspectives, recognize that some employees may have specific needs that you must consider, and we'll talk about this more in Chapter 4.

Find out about different employee needs relating to medical treatment, hygiene, diet and places for prayer if these are required, and beyond that, make sure that you consider and test language, channels and other activities that will be inclusive and accessible to everyone.

Consultant, author and business owner Rachel Miller is a global authority on internal communication. She tells me that an emerging area of internal communication practice is communicating well with neurodivergent employees, and she says it's appropriate to purposefully build their needs in the internal crisis communication planning process:

> I recommend involving your neurodiverse colleagues when you are planning and practising crisis situations. If you have network groups, invite them to be part of the discussions and open the invitation wider to capture parents and carers and those who have not disclosed their neurodivergence at work.
>
> I know from my own family's experience, when you're dysregulated, it is hard to follow instructions or processes. As the neurodivergent parent of two neurodivergent children, I know how distressing fire alarms and increased noise can be. This inhibits their ability to follow safety instructions, and requires a different approach, which must be considered and planned ahead of time.

Prepare your plan

With a strong understanding of the issues you face, and the needs your employees may have, your next step is to write an internal crisis communication plan to help the organization act quickly to protect the internal community from harm and from there engage, empower and enable them in the crisis response.

At this point, it's important to be very clear about the difference between this document (the internal crisis communication plan) and the one that comes later (the internal crisis communication strategy).

The plan is all about getting up and quickly running. With a focus on surviving, supporting, sensemaking and stabilizing needs, it sets out the pre-agreed, pre-approved and fully signed-off set of guidelines, protocols and steps required to quickly and confidently flip from business as usual to crisis mode, and it offers adaptable guidance or suggestions about the communication tactics that you should and shouldn't consider in range of harmful and fast-moving crisis situations.

But it is not your strategy. Your strategy is a longer-term, forward-looking approach to framing your crisis, achieving your objectives and meeting each of the 7S of internal crisis communication through each crisis stage, and it requires detailed crisis insights so you can't guess it in advance. We'll talk more about strategy, approach and crisis positioning in Chapter 5.

Gillies Crichton is director at Resilire Assure. Based in Glasgow, Scotland he has spent over three decades at the sharp end of crisis preparedness, response and recovery for the aviation industry, and in that time, he's dealt with gas leaks, fires, vehicle collisions, aircraft crashes and terrorism. His advice is simple:

> Plan for anything, not everything. There may be six or seven hundred things that could go wrong, but if you try to create six or seven hundred different plans, you'll tie yourself in knots. Six or seven adaptable scenarios is more effective. In an airport, for example, the impact of a runway closure can be immense. It doesn't really matter whether snow causes the runway to be closed, or a storm causes the runway to be closed. What matters is that weather has caused the runway to be closed. So, make sure you have an adaptable plan in place to effectively communicate the fact that the runway is closed and adapt from there.

As you pull it together, make sure that you include key foundational elements, as well as elements related to crisis activation, crisis management, internal crisis communication and internal stakeholder information.

Foundational elements

Your document must be easy to identify and easy to scan when time is at a premium. It therefore requires:

- a clearly titled cover with revision dates, owner details and senior sign off
- a content page with page numbers
- a signed policy or mission statement specifying key internal communication commitments, high-level objectives, obligations, principles, duties of care

Elements related to crisis activation and management

You will be acting with wider crisis management, crisis communication, business continuity and business recovery teams, and you must be part of those teams from the start, so your document should also outline all key issues related to crisis activation and management:

- The process for 'calling' a crisis and activating the plan
- Named crisis leader and deputies
- Crisis steering/management roles and responsibilities including gold/silver/bronze or strategic/tactical/operational contacts if appropriate in your company or sector
- Business continuity/recovery roles and responsibilities
- Internal and external crisis communication roles and responsibilities
- The process for mobilizing the team, including an out-of-hours call tree that shows who will be contacted, by whom and in what order
- A directory of other key contacts
- Guidance on co-ordinating with other parties (i.e. police or partners)
- Virtual and in-person crisis control centre location and access requirements
- Key crisis meetings and/or reports
- Necessary checklists, e.g. for Personal Protective Equipment (PPE)
- Necessary logging forms, e.g. to capture communication outputs or feedback
- Physical and virtual passwords and codes
- Pre-agreed internal crisis communication budgets and finance codes

Elements related to internal crisis communication

Next, your plan should outline everything that's going to get you ready to deliver a fast, strong and effective communication response as your crisis hits:

People

- Internal communication roles and responsibilities
- Named internal crisis communication leader and deputies
- Named internal spokespeople and deputies for different subjects and scenarios
- Named language translators if required

Process

- A list of identified risk/crisis scenarios and suggested approach

- Guidance to help quickly define your full strategy and approach
- A clear, simple and speedy sign off process for internal messages
- Critical tasks for the first hour, day and week

Content

- A list of key needs/questions based on the 7S of internal crisis communication
- Skeleton holding statements for different scenarios and channels
- Skeleton information/update statements for different scenarios and channels
- Skeleton positioning statements for different scenarios and channels
- Skeleton statements and information related to essential employee needs
- Skeleton statements and information related to company values and behaviour
- Information about employee assistance programmes and helplines
- Adaptable key messages about the organization, its mission and its activities
- Adaptable descriptions of key products and services
- Adaptable descriptions of key issues and events
- Maps of key buildings and surrounding areas
- Images of key people, buildings and products
- Facts and figures
- Common FAQ

Channels

- Key sources of truth, and backup channels to use
- Key sources of listening, and backup channels to use
- Pre-allocated internal telephone helpline numbers or email addresses

Internal stakeholder information

- An internal stakeholder register and map which includes all employees, contractors, sub-contractors, freelancers, partners and volunteers
- Any specific internal stakeholder needs or insights to consider

When your plan is complete, you should save it electronically and keep a printed version of each updated revision, so it is instantly accessible in different formats. And when speed is of the essence, an additional tip is to store key contacts, building codes and passwords in your personal device or on a wallet-sized card you keep with you.

Share your plan

There's a reason that fire evacuation plans are visible on the back of hotel room doors. They will most likely not be needed, but if they are, they could be the difference between life and death. Your internal crisis communication plan is the same, so don't be fooled into thinking it's something that should be hidden away, because it's not. If it is to be effective, it must be shared with everyone you'll rely on to help deliver it, and it must be embedded in the company's wider crisis management and external communication plan, so people know that it must be adhered to when crisis strikes.

Practise your plan

From there you must regularly discuss, review and practise the plan with your internal and external communication colleagues, with your crisis management team and with all the departments, locations and stakeholder groups identified within it.

- Test all colleagues are clear about how and where to get updates.
- Test the tools, channels and processes work as you expect them to.
- Test the language and tone in holding statements feels human and helpful.
- Test how different messages will be received in different scenarios.
- Test all colleagues know how to report a problem.
- Discuss ways to form a crisis position and meet the 7S of internal crisis communication in different situations.
- Identify and capture new or unanswered questions or gaps.
- Debrief and make required improvements.

Crisis expert Gillies Crichton tells me that regular testing, practise and exposure to anticipated and new situations builds capability across the whole team, strengthens relationships, and helps develop a kind of 'muscle memory' which means everyone is confident, resilient and ready to act when the unexpected happens. He says:

> Share the plan and empower everyone to do what's required. Take it step by step and practise, practise, practise. If you are practised, if you are rehearsed, and if your plans are in place, then you are ready.

Identify the crisis 'flashover'

If your train crashes, your ship sinks or your factory explodes, then it's obvious the organization is in crisis, and it must activate its plans. But when a slower moving situation is less clear cut, leaders must decide when to make the switch from crisis anticipation to crisis response.

Global crisis communication consultant John Bailey advised earlier in this chapter of the need to track and monitor issues to be ready for the 'flashover' from issue to crisis, and he tells me timing is critical so it's important to make the call correctly:

> Every organization is different, but it's important to agree a set of simple criteria or a decision tree that you'll use to recognize and evaluate the flashover from issue to crisis.
>
> Some of the things you might consider are:
>
> o Has the issue caused a significantly high volume of internal or external negative sentiment towards the organization?
>
> o Are key internal or external stakeholders demanding a response?
>
> o Are you aware of additional facts not yet in the public domain which would spark criticism or controversy?
>
> All you need is a set of three or four questions like these and all you do is move from one to the next answering 'yes' or 'no'. If the answer to one or more questions, is 'yes', it's time to call colleagues together and activate the response. If the answer to all of them is 'no', you put it back and keep monitoring it until it changes again.

John tells me that when you call a crisis, the first thing the CEO or their deputy must do is activate the call tree that brings the crisis steering team, crisis management team and crisis communication team together, and the next thing they must do is clearly identify and assess the known and unknown issues being faced and the resources available to deal with them.

You need to have all the right people in place, and you need to have that clear partnership between the crisis steering group, the crisis management group and the crisis communication group from the get-go.

What the business is essentially doing at this point is activating the strategic management of the organization in response to the crisis. Typically, the comms team doesn't make all the strategic calls, but we do need to be able to communicate them, so we have an important advisory role in helping business leaders see the internal and external reputational impact and ripple effects of different decisions and positions.

No one at this point should be working in a silo, and the internal and external communication team must have a seat at the table to understand what's happening, observe decisions being made, share insight, and to offer advice in real time if we are to deliver the best possible communication strategy and approach.

When crisis hits, an organization's ability to accurately assess and define the problem is critical to the success of everything that follows. That's clearly because understanding a crisis is the first step to fixing it, but it's also because it's the only way to clearly explain the situation, assess communication need, and judge how different strategies, messages, channels and spokespeople will be received.

Not all facts will be immediately known, so it's OK not to understand everything straight away – but it's not OK to cut corners, make things up or omit important points because of that. You must get on top of everything as soon as you can and work with leadership, crisis management and business continuity colleagues to understand:

- What happened?
- Why did it happen/who was responsible?
- Whether it could have been foreseen and/or prevented?
- What forms of harm has it caused?
- How widely has the harm been felt?
- What have the ripple effects been?
- How do people feel about it?
- What is the organization going to do about it?
- What might happen next?

Clarify and verify everything before you share it forward, and never be afraid to question, challenge and interrogate the points that you don't understand or can't explain. Crisis expert Gillies Crichton says this means not just asking the questions you *want* to know the answer to, but asking the ones you *need* to know the answer to as well:

> When crisis hits, it's natural for people to prioritize personal interest and agenda. That means they start by asking questions that satisfy their personal needs or responsibilities, rather than by gathering the information that is essential and important to everyone at that point in time. And while the questions they ask may be interesting, they may not be immediately relevant in that moment, so spending too much time discussing the wrong information could distract from understanding and addressing the urgent needs at hand.

To get to the source of the problem, you must talk to the experts, and you must talk to the different people affected. Look at both the big picture and the critical detail, and make sure you fully understand why the information you are collecting is necessary, how it should be shared, and what it means for the operation and for the humans involved.

As you gather and verify the facts, recognize that every question brings forward different answers, and don't assume that everything you hear is correct. Misinformation and disinformation circulate at all levels inside and outside an organization because people naturally have different priorities, outlooks or experiences – so don't judge, dismiss or accept information too soon. Gather evidence from different sources, explore alternatives, double-check critical information, and make sure verified facts are date-stamped and logged in a central repository. That helps make sure all information shared by anyone in the company is consistent and fact-checked too.

Activate the response

As you do all of this, you'll also need to activate the early stages of the internal crisis communication response in parallel with the external crisis communication, crisis management and business continuity response, so work closely with leadership, crisis management, business continuity and external crisis communication colleagues as you use your plan to decide what first steps you take and how.

Within the first hour of a crisis (and preferably within the first minutes), you must agree and release an internal statement to disclose or confirm that the organization is aware of the crisis and to set a tone of compassion and control. Balance surviving, supporting and sensemaking needs with key strategic and operational requirements as you:

- understand what happened, why it happened and what might happen next
- develop, draft and deliver the first message
- activate your crisis communication intranet or web page
- establish a set of frequently asked questions (FAQ)
- seek other forms of employee insight and feedback
- agree a rhythm of hourly, daily and 'breaking' updates
- agree your crisis position, and use insight to fully develop your longer-term internal crisis communication strategy and approach

We'll talk more about the full crisis response in the chapters that follow.

KEY TAKEAWAYS

- The secret to communicating well through a crisis is to be prepared. To succeed, you must put robust systems in place to help anticipate, identify and understand all the risks and issues the organization may face.
- Start in stable times and work with colleagues to understand the risks in the organization and how they might evolve.
- Think the unthinkable, monitor, track and tackle issues to prevent problems before they occur.
- Dive into different scenarios and work with people from across the organization to test what does and doesn't work.
- Use the insight you've gained to prepare for your crisis with a pre-agreed and pre-practised internal crisis communication plan.
- When the crisis 'flashes over' move quickly to activate your response. Work with colleagues to gather insight and involve everyone in the process of crisis understanding so you are ready to deliver the best possible long-term internal crisis communication strategy and approach.

References

Apps, P (2022) *Show Me the Bodies: How we let Grenfell happen*, Oneworld Publications, London

BBC (2013) Bangladesh factory collapse probe uncovers abuses, www.bbc.co.uk/news/world-asia-22635409 (archived at https://perma.cc/T6XN-R4BB)

BBC (2020) Boeing's 'culture of concealment' to blame for 737 crashes, 16 September, www.bbc.co.uk/news/business-54174223 (archived at https://perma.cc/8U9E-GGZJ)

BBC (2024a) Post Office Horizon scandal: Why hundreds were wrongly prosecuted, 30 July, www.bbc.co.uk/news/business-56718036 (archived at https://perma.cc/33R6-YJFB)

BBC (2024b) Grenfell Report: Key findings from the enquiry, 4 September, www.bbc.co.uk/news/articles/c049yvrd5qxo (archived at https://perma.cc/ZPW2-HUJH)

BBC (2024c) Mohamed Al Fayed accused of multiple rapes by staff, 19 September, www.bbc.co.uk/news/articles/cz6x635wpjxo (archived at https://perma.cc/7ULX-X8LF)

BBC (2024d) 'I tried to say no repeatedly': More men accuse ex-Abercrombie boss over sex events, 14 September, www.bbc.co.uk/news/articles/cj9l9dlgpmno (archived at https://perma.cc/GBL7-E7DA)

Boeing (2019) Statement from Boeing CEO Dennis Muilenburg: We own safety 737 MAX software production and process update, 5 April, https://boeing.mediaroom.com/2019-04-05-Statement-from-Boeing-CEO-Dennis-Muilenburg-We-Own-Safety-737-MAX-Software-Production-and-Process-Update? (archived at https://perma.cc/PRB4-PZEY)

Lerbinger, O (2012) *The Crisis Manager: Facing disasters, conflicts and failures*, Routledge, New York

Nestlé (no date) Ask Nestlé: Nestlé boycott, www.nestle.com/ask-nestle/our-company/answers/nestle-boycott (archived at https://perma.cc/F3A5-6W6U)

Oxfam (2019) Oxfam GB 'deeply sorry' for sexual exploitation in Haiti and flawed investigation, 11 June, www.oxfam.org.uk/media/press-releases/oxfam-gb-deeply-sorry-for-sexual-exploitation-in-haiti-and-flawed-investigation/ (archived at https://perma.cc/8NGY-XJWA)

Post Office (2024) Horizon Scandal context, 24 April, https://corporate.postoffice.co.uk/horizon-scandal-pages/context (archived at https://perma.cc/K34Q-SEDZ)

TEPCO (no date) Fukushima decommissioning and revitalization are our top priority, www.tepco.co.jp/en/hd/responsibility/index-e.html (archived at https://perma.cc/QK6M-YCNR)

Walker A (2024) How Grenfell exposed our moral bankruptcy, *Construction Management Magazine*, https://constructionmanagement.co.uk/grenfell-tower-tragedy-exposed-our-moral-bankruptcy/ (archived at https://perma.cc/DQ94-5X8G)

World Nuclear Association (2024) Fukushima Daiichi accident, https://world-nuclear.org/information-library/safety-and-security/safety-of-plants/fukushima-daiichi-accident (archived at https://perma.cc/559X-TR96)

4

Understand your internal community

When a crisis strikes, the internal community experiences the impact and after-effects intensely and in many different ways. Some people feel the harm more than others, some feel the blame, and some will play a more obvious role in fighting the challenge or finding its solution. Some may become victims and potential victims, some may become survivors, some may become witnesses or onlookers, and others may become crisis defenders and champions.

But whatever their circumstances, everyone will feel a deep sense of disruption, everyone will feel a deep sense of uncertainty, everyone will want to know what is happening, and everyone will have thoughts, feelings and ideas they want or need to share. As they assess what's going on, people across the organization will observe, analyse and interpret information from many different sources and they will reflect on past experience to form opinions and ideas about what is happening, why and with what effects. This information will shape:

- how they think and feel about the crisis
- how they think and feel about the organization
- how they think and feel about themselves
- what they say and do next

Clunky channels, short-sighted statements and impractical ideas that fail to consider real-world emotions, motivations and preferences simply won't stick and in some situations could hurt people, make them angry and push them to seek information and alliances elsewhere. If you want it to be both helpful and effective, your internal crisis communication must be grounded in the realities of the organization and in an understanding of who your people are, how they feel, and what they want and need.

To meet their needs, you'll need a deep understanding of the organization's structure, culture and history, a deep understanding of the internal community, their shared characteristics, values and experiences, and a deep understanding of where, how and why these characteristics, values and experiences differ. You need to know:

- who your people are
- what they do
- what they care about
- how they experience the organization in normal times
- how they experience the organization as the crisis unfolds

This chapter explains why an effective approach relies on being able to connect with all the people in your organization and being able to dig deeper into their different characters, capabilities, experiences, aspirations and motivations as well as the challenges, frustrations and barriers they face. It explains what you need to know about your own people in stable times and what you must find out to supplement this understanding as the crisis becomes clear.

Who are your internal community?

In the simplest terms, your internal community is made up of everyone who is involved in making your organization work in both good times and bad times. It encompasses everyone who is seen, either by themselves or by others, to be part of the organization, and as well as employees, it can include long-term and zero-hour contractors, subcontractors, freelancers, partners, volunteers, employee unions, employee and contractor representative committees and board members.

It is made up of a diverse assortment of groups and subgroups with different roles and responsibilities, and importantly it is made up of a diverse assortment of unique individuals with formal and informal connections, contracts, stakes, alliances and responsibilities to each other, a life outside of work, and a variety of wants, needs and expectations.

The need to know them

Your people come from different countries, cultures, religions, backgrounds, families and social groups and they all have different hopes, fears, interests, personalities and priorities inside and outside of the organization. They may be strategists, creatives, technicians, administrators or caregivers; they may be parents, partners, sons, daughters, friends or neighbours; they may be customers, service users, shareholders or members of other communities; and when crisis strikes, they may be victims, potential victims, survivors, witnesses, onlookers, crisis defenders or champions.

All of their characteristics, all of their experiences, all of their assumptions and all of their allegiances will bump and blend to shape not just what your people will need, but also what they will think, feel, say and do in complex and challenging times, and that means that all kinds of similarities and differences must be considered and catered to rather than ignored. If they give to the organization, your employees will expect to receive back from it, and they will expect to be heard and seen by it. They will expect to be protected and cared for, they will expect to be heard, and they will expect that their crisis efforts are recognized, appreciated and enabled through open and timely content and conversations that have been shaped with compassion and understanding, and crafted to meet their specific needs.

Properly knowing them is vital if you want to protect and support them in the face of crisis harm, and also if you want to understand the problem from their perspective, acknowledge their contribution, secure their trust and confidence, and if you want to activate their support, action and advocacy.

When it's done badly, the impact of poor communication and relationship building can be devastating, and it causes a pain that can last for years. Seymour and Moore (2000), Mitroff (2005), Coombs (2015), Coleman (2023) and many more have consistently argued that the humans affected by any crisis must be understood and held at the centre of the response, yet an organization's inattention to the needs of its own people is a failing we see time and time again, and is something that must be addressed.

Every company and every culture are different. What matters to the people in your organization will be different to what matters to the people in mine, so it's important that wherever you work, you connect with colleagues on a human level.

Build relationships, recognize organizational reality from different perspectives, see the unique strengths and vulnerabilities in different teams, and ask 'why' as well as 'what' as you seek to better understand your colleague's experience, expectations, emotions, aspirations and behaviour. You can't properly support or persuade people if you don't know what they think, so properly understanding the people you are communicating with is not only necessary, but also, in the words of Dewhurst and Fitzpatrick (2022) 'one of the most important investments you will make as a communicator.'

Build knowledge in stable times

In Chapters 1 and 5, we discuss how the most credible and effective internal crisis communication response and position must be based on a deep knowledge of the crisis, the company and the community – and while the cause and nature of the crisis itself will drive a lot of what people think, feel and do, it's important to know that some employee thoughts and behaviours will have been seeded before.

Some crisis perspectives and behaviours will be influenced by your employee's background, past experiences, personal values and daily expectations as well as by their job role, tasks, responsibilities, relationships, working patterns and workspaces – and you can build knowledge of all of this in stable times.

To begin, you need to know who your people are, what they do, what they care about and how they experience the organization in good times and bad. You can gather this insight through:

- Existing information – such as organizational charts, organizational demographics, organizational profiles, management information, feedback and analytics
- New research – such as polls, surveys, questionnaires, focus groups, interviews and content analysis
- Observation – such as getting 'out and about', building relationships, talking and listening to people

Who they are

The first step to building effective relationships and communicating well is to take an interest in who your people are.

Different people in your organization will always have basic needs, interests and priorities that are determined by who they are, how they identify personally and how they identify in the company, and they will not be able to participate effectively at work if these basic needs, interests and priorities are not satisfied. This means that it's helpful to work with HR teams and other colleagues to build a realistic picture of the human beings who make up your organization. Consider contractors, subcontractors, free-lance staff and volunteers as well as employees while you come to understand the whole community:

- Language
- Age
- Gender
- Ethnic background
- Religion
- Accessibility and participation requirements
- Personal needs and responsibilities
- And other additional needs or characteristics

These demographics and characteristics can help you better identify key needs related to each of the 7S of internal crisis communication first identified in Chapter 2 – and it helps you better converse with different groups, subgroups and individuals on their terms in both good times and bad.

Seeking a proper appreciation of different colleagues can also help you be more considerate and inclusive in understanding their tolerance and capacity to accept different types of information at different times, for example during local or religious holidays or during extremely busy periods at work. It can shape decisions related to strategy, content, channels and spokespeople, and it can help meet other critical needs that empower or enable people to function effectively in a range of different situations.

More than that, getting out and about to meet people and know them better can help you build the trusted networks, relationships, insights and goodwill that you'll have to call on in complex and volatile times, and so it's a fundamental part of the internal crisis communicator's job.

Alison Lochhead has had a 30-year PR and communication career spanning environmental protection, the railway industry and the university sector in Scotland. She explains that if you want to build strong and reliable relationships in your organization, you must get out and about well before the crisis begins, and you must keep doing so when it strikes:

> People need to know you personally. They need to know you're an honest broker, and that you 'get it'. They need to know that they can speak to you frankly and that they can trust what you say in return. Building trusted

relationships takes time, and it takes effort. You can't do this only by email or on a video call, you need to get out there and be curious about every bit of your organization. You must get to know it back to front and inside out. Visit different locations and interact with everyone – senior leaders, managers, receptionists, operations, facilities, IT – listen and ask questions.

If you have established good relationships across the organization before crisis hits, people will know they can approach you early. They will be honest with you, and they'll know they can trust your advice to help tackle a situation before it makes impact or to deal with it when the worst happens. And if you have that, you're already a step ahead.

What they do

It's absolutely possible to inspire, motivate and engage people in the most challenging times and against all odds – but it's equally possible that barriers to access, unachievable asks or poorly judged attempts to 'rally the troops' will instead frustrate people, sending them into secret subgroups and silos, or turning them off altogether, meaning that crisis goals are not met, or that they are achieved in spite of, rather than thanks to, the organization's official internal crisis communication.

There's a real tendency for people in organizations simply to dismiss or work around information that doesn't meet their need, and Miller (2024) explains that whenever there's a gap that's not met by official communication, employees find their own ways to get the right information at the right time to help them do their jobs. This is never more obvious than when messages are prepared and delivered at the wrong time, in the wrong way, or by an unfamiliar individual with a clear lack of knowledge or meaningful interest in the realities most employees face.

For best success, internal crisis communication messages must get through to the right people at the right time, they must land well and meet their purpose. The difference between getting it right and getting it wrong is the ability to recognize what does and doesn't realistically work, as well as to understand practical and emotional need. This means that as well as being based on an understanding of who people are, crisis conversations and requests must be grounded in an understanding of what they do:

- The job they do
- The facilities and location they work from

- The culture and environment they operate in
- The skills and responsibilities they have
- The resources and support available to them
- Their daily frustration, challenges, opportunities and aspirations
- The impact of time zones, working patterns, workload and shift systems

Getting messages through to the right people involves making sure the message and channel is considered, delivered, received, processed, considered and acted upon without unnecessary interruption or delay. And landing well and meeting their purpose means achieving established communication objectives in a way that is acceptable, believable and meaningful to all the company's different internal stakeholders, or better tailoring it for identified individuals and groups until it is.

Advita Patel is an internal communication consultant, author and business owner who is based in Manchester, England. She helps organizational leaders understand how they can create more inclusive cultures so all colleagues can belong and thrive in their work. She explains:

> As well as understanding demographics, understanding who people are
> according to criteria such as their role and location is also useful as it helps
> you plan to reach them and communicate in a more meaningful way. There
> is no point in complaining that a nurse has not read your digital newsletter if
> you know they spend their whole shift on their feet and have not even had two
> minutes to grab a coffee that day. So use the information you have about their
> job role, working patterns and their daily experiences to provide them with
> something more useful and accessible instead.

Beyond this, it's worth remembering Frandsen and Johansen's (2011) observation that employees have formal and informal roles as both senders and receivers of crisis communication. If you want to help them meet their formal responsibilities and if you want them to advocate informally as well, it's helpful to know what their networks and touchpoints are.

Internal communication consultant and trainer Dan Holden reflected on his own experience in dealing with crises in the UK aviation and manufacturing industries as he told me that the best way to check your assumptions about what communication in your organization is really like is to get out and experience it yourself:

> When you're close to the centre of the organization, you feel more informed
> and equipped because you've seen something on the intranet, received an email

or had a line manager come out of a briefing to share updates. But what about the harder to reach employees? What about those on shift and who have less touchpoints within the company? You can't make assumptions about how and when they receive company updates, you've got to ask, you've got to get out and about in the operation, on the different shift patterns, and you've got to experience it for yourself.

You might assume that staff arrive, clock in, pick up their schedule, chat to the boss and move on, so you figure you can catch them with an email or a team meeting at the beginning of their shift. But that's not actually the case. In a distribution centre for example, not everyone has a company email. Some managers might not even see a couple of their drivers every day. The drivers arrive before them, head out on the road, have a quick lunch and then clock out without crossing paths. It's important to think about the reality of the timeline you're working with. Just publishing a message won't solve it, because some colleagues might not even receive message one and two before you're sending message three.

Not all employees, let alone contractors, subcontractors, freelance staff and volunteers, can or will access formal company communication channels in the way managers assume they do. Instead, their views of the organization are shaped in a secondary infrastructure, passed on informally and through unexpected routes, in canteens, corridors and car parks as well as in corporate suites. As you seek to understand how communication is received by everyone in the organization, you also need to consider how it is informally processed, how people enter or initiate a conversation about it, and why some people find certain messages or channels acceptable and motivating while others do not.

Walk around every part of the organization and recognize the barriers that people face when trying to communicate well. General access to people, channels, networks and touchpoints are well-recognized examples; but outdated processes, excessive bureaucracy, inadequate resources, internal tensions, broken distribution lists, broken technology, broken relationships, ineffective leadership and psychologically unsafe cultures all make communication harder.

When you understand these constraints, you can work towards fixing them, and you can work towards creating cultures, systems and processes that genuinely support a full range of internal needs and establish a more positive employee-organizational relationship in good times and bad. At the same time, you must be careful that workarounds are not simply quick fixes with unintended consequences – let's go back to Dan Holden's driver, or indeed anyone else who spends hours out on the road. A common suggestion is to communicate via their personal device so they can pick up and reply to urgent messages while they are driving – but is that really the best solution when you are trying to prevent crises and protect people from harm?

As you get out and about and to learn more about daily life and daily communication in your company, you should seek to understand different perspectives too. In the rail industry, for example, the same organization feels very different in head office than it does in a remote single person signal box. Both experiences of the organization, of its purpose, values and activities, are real, both bring their own joys and frustrations, and neither is more 'correct' than the other – so they must both be considered and accounted for. Internal communication consultant, author and business owner Advita Patel says:

> If we are doing all that we can to help the people in our organizations belong and thrive in both good times and bad, then we must understand we're not talking to a homogenous group.
>
> We must make sure we are doing everything we can to recognize different needs, meet different needs and help everyone succeed. This means we need to be aware of our own bias or assumptions or preferences and we need to go out of our way to understand the gaps in our own knowledge. We need to get out and about in the organization, be curious, and pay attention to who our colleagues are and what they need from us.
>
> Even if you are not part of a particular location or department or community, you must still build the trust and relationships that will enable you to know it better. So whether your people work in offices, shops or factories, you should get out and about so you can stand or sit beside them, shadow them, and talk to them to properly to understand what working in the organization feels like and means to them.

What they care about

Finally, if you want crisis communication to resonate, you need to show that leaders in the organization care about the same things that the rest of the internal community do, and that everyone is working towards the same goals, in the same way and with the same values.

We know from many years of research that employees are more motivated when they find value and meaning in their work, we know they are more engaged when they see a sense of organizational integrity, and we also know that understanding what gives people a sense of personal and professional purpose is key to developing meaningful employee-organizational relationships and engaging internal communication.

Our purpose and values can ignite our passions and our sense of fair and unfair, good and bad, right and wrong, and, as we discussed in Chapter 1, our personal identity can also trigger different thoughts, feelings and behaviour in different crisis situations, perhaps fuelling our desire to fight for the organization – or against it.

This means that an understanding of how happy people are, how valued they feel and what they care about superficially, and at the deepest levels is important to help them make sense of the crisis and to encourage their trust, advocacy and support. What motivates and demotivates them? What binds them together? What drives them to support each other and work as a team? … And what causes them to fracture? All of these questions are important as you stabilize the organization, stimulate and sustain the response, and attempt to strengthen into the future.

Lulu Arnett-Morrice joined the communication team at Epsom and St Helier University Hospitals NHS Trust in England at the height of the Covid-19 pandemic in July 2020. Based in an office in the heart of the hospital, Lulu and the communication team saw first-hand the impact the pandemic was having on healthcare staff. She tells me that it was important to continue linking personal stories to common values and common purpose as they worked to sustain the crisis response:

> Working in the hospital during the pandemic was intense. The pandemic was hard for everyone, but it was particularly hard for the people working in the frontline of healthcare. Everyone was stretched, exhausted and morale was impacted as the pandemic continued and pressure mounted on the NHS. As a communications team, we felt it was necessary to show staff that they were valued as individuals, and we wanted to remind everyone of the important common purpose that we share across the hospital trust.

> Humans of Healthcare was inspired by Humans of New York, a catalogue of photographs and stories that shows the lives of people living and working in New York City. We knew people in the hospital would have interesting stories and we wanted to tell these to help our employees reconnect with their personal purpose, shining a light on the diverse and dedicated staff at the trust.

> We talked to people across different departments, job roles and levels and from different ages, backgrounds and length of service in the organization. Sometimes we asked people to volunteer themselves and sometimes we asked people to

nominate their colleagues. Either way, we began with 10 standard questions, and we used these as talking points to speak with people about their memories, about the things that made them proud and about the things that they were finding difficult. All of our meetings were conducted as one-to-one interviews and recorded, so we could tell the stories in each individual's real voice and we had a photographer capture pictures of them in their working environment.

The Humans of Healthcare campaign was designed to engage and lift people back up by celebrating the fact that we are all unique individuals bound by a common and important purpose. We wanted people to reflect on their career journey and remember their 'why' to help them get through such a difficult time.

We know colleagues were inspired because of the new conversations and relationships the campaign helped build, because of the numbers of likes and comments on each story, and because of the number of people who got involved. My personal favourite stories were those of Junior Doctor Vedang Tyagi, who had arrived in England with an ambition to work for the NHS 11 months previously, and of Sister Patricia Mendonsa, Care of the Elderly Ward Manager, who was preparing to retire after 33 years working for the Trust and who was extremely proud to have been invited to attend a special reception at Buckingham Palace to celebrate the nursing profession. Every story we told was unique, interesting and most of all inspiring. I loved developing this campaign and it became one of my favourite parts about my job.

The campaign showed the human side of what we do, and the pictures and stories reminded everyone that working for the NHS is more than just a job. More importantly, they connected people, and they gave us meaning and value in such a difficult time.

Lulu reflects:

Understanding people and their diversity is key to landing effective communication, but it's also valuable when you are trying to build greater engagement. We need to recognize and make sure all people feel included regardless of role, level, experience or any other factor. It's so important in both crisis and in everyday communications, and it's really at the crux of everything we do.

Dig deeper in the context of the crisis

The knowledge you build about your internal community helps you communicate well with them in stable times, and it helps you plan and prepare for what they might need if crisis strikes. It helps you understand what approaches, content, channels and spokespeople might work best to achieve your crisis aims. But it's not a full picture, and pre-crisis data can't be used as your only source of intelligence.

That's because all crisis communication must be shaped in the light of the new and changing situation – the severity of the crisis, the harm it has caused or may still cause, the experiences people have of it, and the attitudes of internal and external stakeholders towards different issues, individuals and groups within the organization.

When crisis strikes, some of your employees may become victims and potential victims, some may become survivors, witnesses or onlookers, and others may become crisis defenders and champions. They will all have surviving, supporting, sensemaking, stabilizing, stimulating, sustaining and strengthening needs, but their closeness to the crisis, to other crisis stakeholders and the harm that they feel will have a profound impact on how each of their needs manifest as well as what internal crisis communication they require. Coleman (2023) explains: 'Managing a crisis requires empathy and it is vital to remember all the ways the situation has, or can have, an impact on people. This includes understanding the psychological, emotional and physical impact of what has happened.'

This means that as people across the organization begin to navigate the crisis together, you must dig deeper to continuously check and understand how different groups, subgroups and individuals feel about what's happened and why. You must observe what they are doing, and you must be aware of their crisis traumas, vulnerabilities, pain points, opportunities and responsibilities, as well as what they are able to further tolerate.

If you are unsure how people are feeling, you need to ask. More than that you need to put yourself into their shoes, and seek to see the problem from their perspective. You can't assume anything, and you must recognize that ignoring or trying to downplay anger, fear, frustration, confusion or disappointment will always make a bad situation worse, as will failing to acknowledge people who are clearly going above and beyond what is reasonably expected.

Get out and about to be with people in the company and supplement what you see, hear and sense with short sharp measurements to dig deep into what people are saying, what they are doing, how they are feeling and why. If you can do this, your internal crisis communication will be more effective as it seeks to facilitate meaningful and constructive conversations that will help:

- support different groups effectively
- meet their sensemaking needs

- diffuse anger and avoid overwhelm
- understand how they are likely to respond to different crisis positions
- understand what they're likely to say and do next
- tailor messages appropriately
- take well-judged action to build the understanding, trust, advocacy and support needed to stabilize the organization and begin the tactical response

Remember that while there are critical moments, particularly at the beginning of the crisis when the same crisis message or content must be prioritized and delivered to everyone at the same time and in the same way, there will be other moments when different people will have very different communication needs, and they will require more focused or personal communication support. This means keeping everyone up to date with a consistent message and position, as we will discuss in Chapter 6, but it also means understanding and offering specific focus and care to the employees who have been harmed or who are directly at risk of harm, as well as to those who are directly facing the crisis and its fallout in other ways.

We have already established that surviving needs come first, and nothing else matters until everyone is safe. If there's a fire in one of your factories, it goes without saying your focus turns to the people trapped in the building and those trying to rescue them before it turns to the others who use the building but are safe somewhere else. But these are not your only stakeholders. You also need to think about the colleagues observing the situation from a factory on the other side of town and wondering if they, too, are in danger at work, and you need to think how all these needs will change as the crisis evolves. You can't forget anyone, because everyone will be making sense of the situation, and everyone will require support to help the organization recover.

The simplest way to assess who needs the most urgent help and then who you must also consider next is to identify which groups, subgroups or individuals within the internal community have been most directly affected – perhaps as victim, potential victim, survivor, witness, defender or champion, perhaps because of their role in supporting crisis victims or survivors, or perhaps for another reason entirely – and then work through the impact on everyone else who is affected until you come to those who are impacted simply because they are part of the organization, because they are making sense of what has happened, because they are required to keep things going, and so should be kept informed. Doing this helps you prioritize and target meaningful conversations and content for the people who have most need and you can tailor content, channels and personal touchpoints accordingly.

Amanda Coleman is a crisis communication consultant, trainer and author. She has over 20 years' experience in emergency services communication, and she has led the crisis communication response to high-profile situations, including the terrorist bombing of an Ariana Grande concert at Manchester Arena, England in 2017. She tells me:

> Crises affect everyone differently and you need to consider everyone, but you also need to be aware of your priorities so that you can communicate effectively and put the right support in place. I like to think of it as a pebble that is dropped in a pond and spreads ripples out from the point it was dropped. First, make sure you know who's directly affected, who is in the centre of the crisis at the point of impact, for whatever reason, and from there graduate outwards towards other interested staff, suppliers, contractors and so on.

> That lets you put the most affected people at the heart of your thinking, and it helps you to prioritize what you're doing, while being inclusive and considerate of everyone else and tailoring different messages to meet different needs. It's very easy to be one step removed from the reality of situations, to go through the checklist, send the emails, tick the boxes and believe that our task is complete. But it's not about that. You've got to know the crisis and its impacts on everyone to make sure you are meeting every different need. When the crisis hits you've got to be looking at things, listening to things, understanding practicalities, and gathering, understanding and responding to all the different emotions.

> You've got to use your internal networks to understand what staff are seeing and hearing, what they are doing, how they are feeling, what they need and why, and then recognize and reference the human reality through your internal comms.

As you seek to understand how the crisis is experienced by different colleagues, recognize that getting out and about in crisis must be done in a considerate way. This means thinking about the needs of the people and parts of the organization in advance so that your questions and comments are well-judged and meaningful, and your visit comes at an appropriate time. It means having all the equipment you need ready and available, and it means making sure your visit is a help rather than a hindrance. Make sure you bring your own hard hats, safety glasses, ear defenders, safety shoes or boots, hi-vis jackets, PPE, hairnets, masks, passes, keys, certifications or whatever else you need. Listen more than you talk, and make sure you are not making demands that cause extra and unnecessary work for busy colleagues.

Once you have satisfied the urgent and immediate surviving and supporting crisis needs, you must also use the insight you have gained to inform sensemaking, stabilizing and recovery communication. That means as well as understanding immediate priority, you should also seek to find out more about colleague attitudes, interest and influence within the context of the crisis as you assess how different people might perceive different crisis strategies and positions and what they might say or do in response. This insight can identify whether support or resistance is likely from different individuals or groups and so helps you tailor the positioning and framing strategies needed to bring different employees on board with the crisis response, and it also helps you decide who to prioritize for detailed and ongoing two-way engagement, who to inform, who to satisfy in other ways and who to monitor. We will discuss positioning and framing strategies in more detail in Chapter 5.

KEY TAKEAWAYS

- Understanding a wide range of internal perspectives and adapting or tailoring messages to meet specific priorities, interests, wants, needs and motivations is vital for an effective and well-judged approach to internal crisis communication.

- Each of your people are different, so if you want to communicate well, and if you want to secure trust, advocacy and support through the crisis, you need to understand them as multidimensional beings.

- Truly understanding who your audience is and what they need involves understanding who they are, what they do, what they care about, and how they send, receive and respond to information in stable times as well as through the lens of the crisis.

- To do this best, you must get out and about in the organization to see and hear first-hand what people are experiencing, how they are feeling and what they are doing.

- The knowledge you have about your employees helps you communicate well in stable times, and it helps you plan and prepare for what they might need if crisis strikes but it's not a full picture, and pre-crisis data can't be used as your only source of intelligence.

- Internal crisis communication must be considered in the light of the new and changing situation – the severity of the crisis, the harm it has caused or may still cause, and the attitudes of internal and external stakeholders towards different issues, individuals and groups within the organization.

- Use the insights you have gained to best decide who to communicate with, how often, in what order, and with what content, channels, style and tone as well as to determine your overall internal crisis communication position, strategy and approach.

References

Coleman, A (2023) *Crisis Communication Strategies: Prepare, respond and recover effectively in unpredictable and urgent situations*, Kogan Page, London

Coombs, W T (2015) *Ongoing Crisis Communication: Planning, managing, and responding*, Sage, Los Angeles

Dewhurst, S and Fitzpatrick, L (2022) *Successful Employee Communications: A practitioner's guide to tools, models and best practice for internal communication*, Kogan Page, London

Frandsen, F and Johansen, W (2011) The study of internal crisis communication: Towards and integrative framework, *Corporate Communications, An International Journal*, 16 (4) 347–61, www.emerald.com/insight/content/doi/10.1108/13563281111186977/full/html (archived at https://perma.cc/D3UH-7T8K)

Miller, R (2024) *Internal Communication Strategy: Design, develop and transform your organizational communication*, Kogan Page, London

Mitroff, I (2005) *Why Some Companies Emerge Stronger and Better from a Crisis: 7 essential lessons for surviving disaster*, HarperCollins Leadership, Nashville, TN

Seymour, M and Moore, S (2000) *Effective Crisis Management: Worldwide principles and practice*, Cassell, London

5

Define your strategy and agree approach

At the beginning, your crisis will feel like an impossible scribble – a plate of spaghetti or a scramble of jigsaw pieces tipped out of the box. As they face it, your people will have all kinds of changing emotional, psychological and practical needs. Everything will feel uncertain and overwhelming, but the crisis can be ordered, it can be made sense of, and internal crisis communication can have a profound and powerful effect.

Your most critical role is to facilitate communication that will help people survive the crisis, that will help them feel supported and that will help them make sense of what's going on. It is to reassure them that everything will be OK, and to help them see that the puzzle can be sorted, the spaghetti untangled and the scribble made sense of.

When you have achieved that, your focus will shift to secure employee trust, advocacy and support to enable operational and reputational recovery. Your role then will be to facilitate communication and engagement that will help stabilize the organization through the long tail of the crisis and stimulate, sustain and strengthen the organization as it transitions into a new normal.

None of this can be achieved by chance, and a well-considered and forward-looking internal crisis communication strategy which encompasses both word and action is needed to help crisis efforts, and to engage, empower and enable every employee. This chapter begins with a reminder of the insights that will set you up for best success. Next it explains how you must set clear internal crisis communication objectives, and it discusses the different positions you can take in different situations and what these involve. It then touches on the importance of spokespeople and advocacy to your strategy, and it explains how internal communication must evolve through each crisis stage.

Assess the situation

Too many internal crisis communication strategies are thrown together in the moment without consideration of the many unique needs involved, and as result, they don't work as well as they should. Employees are bombarded with rushed 'inspirational' initiatives that fail to recognize the complexity of the situation, or worse, with ill-judged or unrealistic demands that cause division and anger to spike rather than settle.

Balance and proportionality are necessary to acknowledge the gravity of the situation without causing further panic and harm, while carefully and ethically judged crisis frames are required to offer a sense of meaning or purpose and present the crisis in a way that will encourage the internal community to support and advocate for whatever comes next. This means an effective crisis response relies on understanding the issue at hand as well as the personalities and feelings involved. To get it right, you must consider the needs of the crisis, the needs of the company and the needs of the internal community from many different logical and emotional points of view.

The crisis

Most experts agree that different types of crises require different types of response. So, in the first instance, as we discussed in Chapters 1 and 3, you need to know what has happened. Work with operational colleagues and the crisis management team to understand what is known, what is not known, what others are saying and what all that means for your communication strategy:

- What happened?
- Why did it happen/who was responsible?
- Could it have been foreseen and/or prevented?
- What forms of harm has it caused?
- How widely has the harm been felt?
- What have the ripple effects been?
- How do people feel about it?
- What is the organization going to do about it?
- What might happen next?

Think of the crisis as a whole process rather than a static event. Consider what took place before, what might come next and what needs to happen now for the best possible result. And as you assess it, be aware that your crisis does not exist in a bubble – and neither do your teams. There will be other things happening politically, economically, socially, technologically, legally, environmentally and culturally inside and outside the organization, and there will be many different takes on what happened and why. To really understand what's going on, you must recognize different perspectives and question how different scenarios could play out today, tomorrow, next week and longer term.

The company

As you assess the crisis, you also need to understand the context it occurred and will evolve in, so a deep organizational understanding is critical to explain why – when faced with seemingly similar situations – some companies energize their people and emerge stronger where others fail to connect.

We discussed in Chapters 1 and 4 that everything that enables or detracts from a successful crisis response was seeded before. Your workforce's past and current experiences of company leadership, culture, reputation, relationships, interactions, history and physical and psychological safety will simmer and churn to shape how they feel in the moment. Will they step forward to make things better? Will they freeze in disbelief? Will they sever ties and look for the closest exit? Or will they rise in protest that enough is enough and push publicly for justice or change?

Scratch beyond superficial or one-off highs and lows to understand how it feels to be part of the company, and how past moments of joy and despair might trigger employee desire to act for or against the organization in the present.

The community

Finally, you must also recognize the needs of the people involved. As we just discussed in Chapter 4, your employees are human beings with hopes, fears, frustrations and feelings. Beyond the fact that some may experience the crisis more directly than others as victims, potential victims, survivors, observers, defenders or champions, seemingly similar people will react differently and sometimes unpredictably in complex, ambiguous or volatile situations, so you need to understand all elements of the problem – and its opportunities – from their point of view.

Set clear objectives

With a rounded understanding of the situation, you must next establish and agree what internal communication can deliver in the short, medium and long term.

Crisis objectives vary, but those related to physical safety and psychological wellbeing always come first, as we established in Chapter 2. Reflect on each of the 7S of internal crisis communication as you agree your objectives and follow the order of the framework to focus first on human survival, support and sensemaking needs before you go on to consider objectives to help the organization stabilize, stimulate, sustain and strengthen. Go beyond vague aims such as 'keep people up to date' and use the insight you have gathered to determine:

- Which calls to action are needed in light of the situation?
- What do you need people to think, feel or do at each crisis stage?
- Which objectives best align to the needs of everyone involved?
- What impact do you need to have?

Ground everything in insight, and have confidence that stretch targets can be achieved, but only if they are considerate of everyone who'll be relied upon to deliver them. SMART objectives set you up for success because they are:

- specific
- measurable
- achievable (with the resource available)
- realistic (in the wider internal and external crisis context)
- timebound

Establish the crisis position

The company's success relies on people being willing and able to step up and go the extra mile, even when this comes at a personal cost. But we've already established that employee commitment can decrease after crisis due to a loss of trust, a loss of respect and diminished job security. Trust, effort and commitment are reciprocal, and people won't make sacrifices if they are uninformed, unsupported or unconvinced, so internal crisis communication objectives must be framed and enabled by a well-judged and compassionate internal crisis position that:

- discloses or acknowledges the crisis
- helps people make sense of what's going on
- shows how the organization is taking accountability
- offers a sense of meaning or purpose
- encourages, motivates and empowers everyone to support

The internal crisis position is key to meeting sensemaking, stabilizing and stimulating needs, and it's critical for bringing people on side and influencing what they decide to do next. It sets the tone for everything that follows, and it drives how people perceive and experience the challenge ahead. It informs the language, content, activities and actions used to explain the crisis in a way that aligns with crisis goals while resonating with employees, and although internally tailored, it must be consistent with core external messages.

Lucy Easthope is a global disaster responder and author who has advised on everything from the 2004 boxing day tsunami and the 7/7 bombings, to the Grenfell fire in London and the war in Ukraine. She says:

> You can't speak with two faces. If you're saying to the rest of the world, we've really messed up here, let us investigate ourselves, you can't then run an internal comms campaign that says we're the best. You have to behave candidly, and you have to remember that the internal message can go external and vice versa.

There are infinite positions you might take, and Dr Timothy Coombs (2015) suggests the most common fall within four main *postures – denial, diminishment, rebuilding and bolstering*. Any of these can be constructive in one situation but damaging in another, so a position that feels justifiable to the CEO in a crisis of mismanagement, but condescending, arrogant, bizarre or hurtful to anyone else must not be used.

If you are unsure what position to take, Dr Coombs' Situational Crisis Communication Theory or SCCT (2007) will help you assess what strategies might work, when and why. SCCT advises that the appropriate communication response will be determined by the level of responsibility people believe the organization must take for the problem then adjusted to account for company history and reputation. In other words, an organization that is judged either by its internal or external stakeholders to have caused the problem must be much more conciliatory than one that's considered the unfortunate victim of circumstance – especially when it has a history of broken trust and bad behaviour.

It's an approach that particularly resonates for internal crisis communication, where the relationships are so close, and the stakes so high, but getting it right involves challenging all your assumptions about how employees really feel and understanding the nuances in each situation, as crisis communication consultant, trainer and author Amanda Coleman explains:

> Don't apply an approach just because you've seen it work before. Each situation is unique, and little differences have a big impact. Gather all the information you can to consider the differences rather than the similarities in the situation before you decide what's best for your own organization.

There's rarely one perfect answer, so you must weigh up different positions, different approaches, and the outcomes and reactions they will produce. A crisis that causes injury feels very different to one that causes inconvenience for example, but there are other needs to consider too. A key tip is to put human beings who have felt harm at the heart of your thinking, then test if your position is fully acceptable to everyone else before you commit.

Denial

A denial position aims to reject crisis blame or responsibility. It may involve attacking the accuser through internal, social or mainstream media, through advertising or through more formal proceedings. It is a damaging strategy when used dishonestly or in error, because it can add profile and polarity to the issue, and it can also cause added unnecessary physical or psychological harm to crisis victims, potential victims and survivors.

Even so, there are circumstances where clear, consistent denial and correction has a critical place – for example when an organization is subjected to a deliberate campaign of fake news or disinformation about its people, products, services or activities, particularly if the false narrative stops or slows it from delivering important work.

An organization that denies a crisis must have all the facts available to evidence its case and be very confident that staff agree that the company should fight an allegation and will back the position. Communication must:

- explain why there is no crisis or why the company isn't involved
- correct mis- or disinformation
- point all internal stakeholders to clear and simple sources of truth
- establish simple fact-checking or myth-busting channels

- ensure leaders and managers know the facts and can answer questions
- share evidence-based case studies and stories featuring trusted experts
- reach everyone through a mix of audio, video, leaflets and posters
- enable space for discussion, conversation and debate
- give people simple content to share

Diminishment

Diminishment sets out to close a crisis and move on. It might minimize responsibility or deny harm using carefully chosen words to paint the difficulty as an isolated event, a mishap or a blip. It can be effective where the organization has a positive history and crisis harm is not widely felt, and it can be necessary where the harm caused by the crisis 'punishment' would be greater than the harm caused by the issue itself.

However, like denial, diminishment will backfire if wrongly applied. No company can dictate how people should feel, and so dismissing or failing to understand legitimate trauma, anger or concerns won't make them go away. Instead, it will fracture relationships and could lead to confrontation, strikes, boycotts or calls for justice. This means that an organization that seeks to diminish a crisis must fully understand all the interest and emotions around the issue before proceeding. Communication must:

- acknowledge the issue, explain why it happened and how it has been solved
- give evidence to show how the crisis 'punishment' is disproportionate
- point all employees to clear and simple sources of truth
- explain the issue in a wider context
- ensure leaders and line managers can echo the position and answer questions
- share positive and future-focused news and case studies
- enable space for discussion, conversation and debate
- avoid drawn-out arguments or drama

Rebuilding

Rebuilding involves taking accountability, and it's the necessary option when the organization has caused harm or is seen to be failing in the crisis response. It can take various forms, and the approach to rebuilding will differ depending on the cause and scale of the company's problems.

That's because your employees will respond differently to a crisis caused by accident or incompetence than they will to a moral violation, and they'll have different demands and expectations for what must happen next. But they'll also have different needs in a crisis caused by systemic problems in the hierarchy versus one caused by a few individual co-workers, they'll have different feelings about an ongoing problem than an isolated difficulty, and they'll have different emotional and psychological needs depending on the level of trauma that has been seen or felt.

Rebuilding often involves apologizing or expressing care and concern, taking full responsibility for what has occurred, asking for help and forgiveness, minimizing disruption and explaining and demonstrating learning and change over the longer term. As well as addressing the here and now, it also presents a clear vision of the future – What will tomorrow look like and how will it be better? What milestones can people expect on the way, and what is going to happen when?

REBUILDING AFTER A CRISIS OF INCOMPETENCE

Mistakes happen. When they do, you disclose this and roll out the infrastructure and training needed to avoid a similar future mishap. To rebuild following an issue of internal in competence communication must:

- disclose or acknowledge the crisis and explain (without blame) what went wrong
- point to sources of truth, advice and support
- explain the training, investments, resources and opportunities being put in place
- explain what action is required from employees
- involve everyone in finding and implementing solutions
- use clear messages to maintain dignity as you embed learning and change
- ensure leaders and line managers can answer questions
- invite employee champions to role model and reinforce values and behaviours
- pause activity that is inappropriate or inauthentic in the crisis
- share case studies and stories of feedback, progress and best practice

- enable space for discussion, conversation and debate
- reinforce with digital screens, posters and stickers in operational areas

REBUILDING AFTER A MORAL VIOLATION

An issue created by deliberate wrongdoing is tougher to deal with than one caused by mistake because it breaks trust and can spark feelings of betrayal, anger, grief or shame which cause employees to disengage, disassociate and question their connection to the company. To rebuild commitment, the organization must provide emotional and psychological support where it's needed, and it must restore trust through meaningful change and transparent communication. The company must:

- disclose or acknowledge the crisis and explain what went wrong
- clearly state that what happened was unacceptable
- clearly state what structures, policies, systems will change
- evidence fairness towards victims and in the management of the crisis
- point to sources of truth, advice and support
- point to reporting systems, feedback platforms and whistle-blowing hotlines
- demonstrate total leadership visibility and accountability
- ensure leaders and line managers can answer questions
- pause activity that is not appropriate or authentic in the crisis
- involve everyone in finding and implementing solutions
- enable space for discussion, conversation and debate
- share case studies and stories of feedback, progress and best practice

REBUILDING AFTER A SMOULDERING CRISIS VERSUS A SUDDEN CRISIS

Communication should also consider whether or not the crisis had been foreseen.

In a smouldering python style crisis, the workforce will be frustrated and angry that red flags were ignored, and they will need a lot more explanation and engagement as to how things will be different in future. That means, that as well as the steps above, the compan must additionally:

- accept the warning signs were there
- accept that feedback was not acted on

- offer opportunities for staff involvement in change
- evidence listening, openly acknowledge, share and respond to feedback

Meanwhile, a sudden Cobra-style crisis brings shock, and it breaks feelings of control which can be very distressing. Providing psychological and emotional support in such a situation is vital, as is giving people the opportunity to discuss what occurred and agree what they can do to stop it happening again.

REBUILDING AFTER TRAUMA

All rebuilding positions require a clear focus on the victims, potential victims, survivors and witnesses of harm, a deep expression of care or regret, and an understanding that 'sorry' is often the only word that will help people heal and move forward.

Every single piece of communication, every single activity, and every single event must be sensitively and compassionately considered from the point of view of the worst affected person outwards, and you should use messaging strategies such as the CARE Formula and the 5 Cs that we'll discuss in Chapter 6 as you encourage leaders to take accountability and explain how the company is taking clear and meaningful steps to fix the issue, to help healing, and to support everyone affected. Global disaster responder and author Lucy Easthope tells me:

> We must think about how we really, genuinely support people after times of trauma. Are we doing enough? In a corporation where harm has been seen for example, if you feel part of the problem, that's a whole different level of toxic.
>
> Employee assistance programmes are not always enough. They are not always supplying psychologists or psychiatrists; they're not dealing with complex trauma. So normal employee assistance might not pick up things that sit and fester, because it is designed for individual people to see the number on the back of the toilet door and ring it. It's not designed for 80 staff to call on the same day, and say I think I'm developing a severe issue around this.
>
> Often the crisis provokes an acute loss of trust in the organization and more generally. Often people will take that home with them. It's not fully a communication issue, but the communication needs to be very considerate of what people have been through.

She continues:

> And if the crisis has involved fatalities, before you can even think about proper recovery, you've got a really difficult phase to get through. There's a rhythm in

in organizations going through mass tragedy and, as well as in communication, there needs to be parity in who attends funerals and in what you do for people and how you recognize what has happened.

You can't start with the Chief Executive and then drop down the management chain as the funerals carry on. You've lost parity. You've lost your sense that there are 15 people here, not one or two. Every funeral is equally important.

At the same time, you offer the choice to families. Quite often they don't want you there, and that can feel like a rebuttal. But corporations cannot insert themselves into the early stages when survivors are very traumatized. Those judgement calls are really important, and I think we also see it with suicides where the company is implicated, and may be told to keep away.

Experiences of grief and trauma are deeply personal and communicating with damaged people is difficult because everyone grieves differently, and everyone has their own crisis truth. Old wounds can reopen, and past resentments can reappear. Communication must be compassionate towards people who are hurting, and it must be personal, tailored and sympathetic to the emotional and psychological distress that has been felt. Minimize discomfort and strive to heal the past before moving into the future.

Good non-judgemental leadership is essential, and it must be centred on what the victims, survivors and witnesses want and need. It's also very important to evidence fairness and parity as you accommodate diverse needs and as you help people to grieve, remember and heal. We will talk more about this in Chapter 7.

All rebuilding strategies require considered, long-term engagement to highlight visible actions and proof of progress over time. They also require communication that is specific about what went wrong so it can be specific about how to fix it. 'We stepped away from our values in pursuit of profit', 'We broke the rules', or 'We acknowledge a toxic and damaging culture' may feel like difficult things to write or say but you cannot move forward until they are faced.

Bolstering

Finally, if and only when it's appropriate and acceptable to everyone, and most importantly to the victims of crisis inside and outside the organization, bolstering strategies can be used to supplement the other three positions, and enhance a sense of unity and purpose as the organization begins to stabilize, stimulate, sustain and strengthen.

Internal bolstering strategies are celebrations of people. They are empowering and enabling strategies that remind people about the good work of the organization and use thanks or praise to bring everyone back together stronger. You must:

- acknowledge the issue/crisis and explain how it has been/is being solved
- point all employees to clear and simple sources of truth
- enable space for discussion, conversation and debate
- involve everyone as you seek opportunity and solution
- share stories of progress, 'heroic' behaviours, best practice and innovation
- celebrate hard work and effort
- recognize milestones and moments of success
- say thank you, reward and recognize effort both publicly and personally
- offer opportunities for mentoring and further training

As you recognize effort, don't just thank the usual suspects. Consider anyone and everyone across all levels, roles and locations, including contactors, volunteers and partners, because widening the circle of appreciation makes it more meaningful to all.

A thoughtful, handwritten note from a company leader or line manager has a huge and lasting impact, while a surprise meal, a random act of kindness, a development opportunity, an award or a small gift can all be appropriate in different situations and can all get messages across in a memorable way. Build in opportunities and allocate funds to reward and take care of your staff as you bolster and strengthen.

Confirm your sources of truth

In every type of crisis, regardless of the company position, your workforce will need simple, accessible and transparent information when and how they need it most. If they don't get that from the organization, they will look elsewhere, and that could lead to the spread of misinformation, mistrust and mistakes.

This means that long before the crisis occurs, everyone must know where they'll find the most up-to-date company information and you must confirm this again (or give an alternative if they become unavailable) when crisis hits – then you must commit to updating these formal channels together with trusted informal channels as a priority. Join the conversation wherever it's happening, talk in human terms and give people something to share.

Select and support your spokespeople and role models

Crisis spokespeople can significantly influence what employees think, feel and do when they receive the message, and they can also formally and informally role model expected crisis behaviour, so they are also a strategic consideration. Just like your channels, your spokespeople must be recognized and credible sources of truth, and they must be fully visible and supported in their role. Select and train a group of internal experts who:

- fully understand what's happening
- are interested in what's going on and able to listen and gather feedback
- are committed to the organization, its purpose and values
- are liked, trusted and respected within the organization
- are actively involved, visible and hands-on in their own specialist area
- can speak about the situation with confidence, care and humility

And help them by giving them:

- clear and up-to-date notes
- fully up-to-date facts and figures
- a platform that will help them to be visible and responsive

Enable wider advocacy

Beyond that, remember that your employees are connected to other people, and they collaborate and interact with different individuals, groups and systems inside and outside the organization. To many people, their closeness to the crisis makes them a source of truth and, whether you like it or not, they will talk about the situation to colleagues, families, friends, customers, service users, suppliers, distributors and more. Some will also share on social media, and others will talk to bloggers or journalists. When they do this, their voices are powerful as global disaster responder and author Lucy Easthope explains:

> The company is porous. If it's very embedded in the local area, say, in the big nuclear industries, for example, your men and women are so much part of the community that when you get it wrong, you've not just lost them, you've lost a whole cohort of people beyond your walls.
>
> If your employees are going home and saying they've heard nothing from the company, or saying the managers are cutting corners or saying somebody has died and nobody's told anyone where the funeral is, then it's not separate. It leaks into the external conversation and shapes a wider understanding of what's really going on with that organization.
>
> If you lose your staff, you lose everyone. For too long crisis communication specialists have sold external comms and media relations as the reputational knife edge, but internal communication is equally critical because poor internal communication makes it harder for an organization to recover.

Gagging your people is not the best approach. Information always leaks out, so it's better to recognize this and help your people to take on a positive ambassadorial role.

Frandsen and Johansen (2011) note employees can be mobilized in crisis communication, not just as receivers but also senders of information whose voices can 'meet and compete, collaborate, or negotiate with other corporate and non-corporate voices', so you can guide by giving them valuable facts, stories and experiences to share. As you do this, help them to help themselves. Be prescriptive about any red lines and legal obligations when it comes to sharing work-related information while allowing them their authentic voice.

Recognize different needs at each crisis stage

In Chapter 1, we established that all crises have a lifespan that extends before and beyond the point of immediate impact, and they move in stages which you must recognize if you are to step out of the moment and get ready for whatever comes next.

This means that once you have established your position and sources of truth, you must be aware of how communication needs to evolve with the crisis. Tailoring your internal communication to crisis stage is a critical strategic activity which begins with listening, establishing trusted relationships and building psychological safety before the crisis strikes; and concludes (or rebegins) with learning as the crisis ends. In Chapter 1, I introduced Fink's four-stage model (1986) to show that as well as a beginning, a middle and an end, the crisis has two separate parts which are experienced very differently:

- An **acute crisis stage**, which occurs when the crisis hits with a bang, everything is at its most urgent, confusing and intense and the focus is on activating a response to contain the situation and prevent escalating damage and harm
- A **chronic crisis stage**, when the crisis lingers, ripples and aftershocks are felt, and the focus turns to long-term management and recovery

Planning for both stages will not only enable you to sustain the company through the long tail of crisis, but it will also help you to fully reflect on the longer-term impact of what is said and done in the moment of greatest pressure.

Informing, engaging and involving everyone is important throughout, but there are times when the grip must be tight, and communication instructive, directive and explicit, and times when the grip must be looser, and communication more consultative, encompassing and employee-led.

Acute stage

As we have established though the 7S of internal crisis communication, information in the acute stage should focus on surviving information that seeks to prevent and minimize harm, first to humans and then to assets if necessary and it should be quickly followed by supporting and sensemaking information to help people adapt psychologically and function effectively in the crisis.

In the first instance, this means removing all obstacles to understanding, focusing on critical information, and using established sources of truth to send out clear and useful surviving instruction. Restrict all messages to the issue at hand and use direct fact and instruction to tell employees what has happened and how to protect themselves and others from harm. Nothing else matters until everyone is safe.

Direct instruction seems counter-intuitive to anyone used to engaging colleagues in an involving and consultative way, but it's vital to help people and assets survive. Misinformation and disinformation can be devastating, so messages must be timely and explicit, and you must collect feedback in short, sharp measures where you can.

Guidance published by the US Department of Health and Human Services Centres for Disease Control and Prevention Crisis and Emergency Risk Communication (CERC) in 2019 states that by understanding how people take in information during a crisis state, we can better plan to communicate with them when it strikes.

The paper suggests that when crisis strikes, human beings:

- simplify messages
- hold on to current beliefs
- look for additional information and opinions
- believe the first message

In response, it states that communicators must:

- use simple messages
- ensure messages come from a credible source
- use consistent messages
- release information as soon as possible

The first message will be the one that's most widely remembered and it's important that it is sent to the internal community before it's sent externally. When companies self-disclose, or when employees hear about the crisis from the company first, it helps establish the control and credibility needed to secure trust, advocacy and support, and it fills a void than can otherwise increase stress and fracture internal reputation and relationships.

Dr Timothy Coombs is a university professor and a globally celebrated researcher, consultant, trainer and author in crisis communication whose writing and research is referenced throughout this book. He tells me:

> Early in my own career when I first became interested in crises, I remember hearing about a Union Carbide employee who was driving to work when he heard about the terrible industrial accident that his company was involved in at Bhopal. He had to pull onto the side of the road because he was so shocked to learn what happened in his company and to hear it on the car radio before he heard from anyone else. The situation affected him so deeply that he disidentified from the company to the point where he could not even say the company name when asked where he worked.
>
> Internal crisis communication can help overcome that kind of situation because while a major crisis will always bring shock, the information and framing

that helps people understand and respond to what's going on is always better to come from within the company than from an outside source. When an organization tells people about a crisis before they hear it from other sources, it's called 'stealing thunder'. It brings benefits to both internal and external crisis communication as it shows the company is in control and taking action, so it leads to less reputational damage both internally and externally.

A quick initial response is important as it helps get the organization's side of the story out quickly, but it's also necessary internally because your employees need instructing information to protect themselves physically and they need adjusting information to cope psychologically, especially in a crisis that involves stress and trauma.

The external audience are interested, but with a few exceptions, they don't live the crisis like the employees do, and so whenever possible, the internal audience should get the message first. We're not talking huge timelines, it could be a few minutes, but the message should go to employees, then to the media. That way, even if the employees hear about the crisis through the media, then look at their email or phone, they'll see a message from the company is already there for them. They'll get the information they need as fast as possible, and they'll be reassured that the best source of instruction or explanation will be from the company itself.

Even if they are not the most affected stakeholder, employees still need to quickly know what happened and what is being done about it. They are still interested and reassured by the fact that their company is treating their stakeholders well, and that's what it's about. A good crisis response is about empathy, and your employees want empathy for themselves, and they want empathy for others. They want to see that their company cares for their other stakeholders and is acting appropriately.

As the imminent danger passes, communication focus in the acute stage must turn to support and sensemaking needs to help your people feel psychologically safe and secure within the crisis situation.

Make sure you:

- share any new information with colleagues first and fast
- protect and update your key spokespeople and sources of truth
- communicate when you say you will
- keep tight control on central content to combat misinformation
- facilitate conversations to help people process what's happening, suggest solutions and adjust for what comes next

If there are obligations not to talk about specific crisis elements, acknowledge the desire for information, explain why you can't say more and offer a timeline for updates. Use a myth buster or FAQ to quash misinformation, keep the conversation going and continue to prepare behind the scenes so that you are ready to share more as soon as you are allowed to do so.

Chronic stage

The crisis doesn't end when the sirens stop, but it does change and that means the approach to communication must change too. The chronic stage can feel messy, uncertain and unending as shockwaves and ripples continue to be felt, so communication must maintain the strategic position and sources of truth but evolve to focus on content and activity that will help stabilize, stimulate, sustain and strengthen the organization.

Consult and engage in person as you offer evidence to restore trust, reinforce values and rebuild unity; and feature people from every part of the organization as you explain new policies, systems and structures, and pinpoint milestones and momentum.

Consider using a creative campaign to embed a vision, learning point, call to action, challenge or common purpose, and reinforce this with stories that move the conversation from what's important to the company to what's important to employees and the people they serve. Make sure you:

- ensure communication is open and transparent
- evidence safety and allow vulnerability
- evidence fairness, equity and inclusivity
- say thank you and show that people are valued in all roles and locations
- present a shared future or common goal
- give people a stake in the outcome
- involve people in the decisions that affect them most
- invite ideas and suggestions from all parts of the company
- allow all voices to be heard equally and enable 'sideways' and 'up and down' conversations to take place

Finally, help people come back together and reunite. Many of the people I spoke to as I wrote this book explained how a shared vision and a shared identity with colleagues made them feel more motivated to help one another and to support and advocate for the organization as their crisis lingered. Often, they said this came organically, and some warned it shouldn't be forced in case it becomes less authentic. But you can enhance unity through stories, language and symbolic acts. After the terror attack at Glasgow Airport, for example, we celebrated the whole of Team Glasgow in recognition schemes, articles, videos and events, and we gave each employee a small metal badge to recognize their efforts. This tiny gesture was inexpensive yet meaningful, and the badges were worn or displayed across the organization for many years. I still have mine and I know others do too.

KEY TAKEAWAYS

- Crisis success cannot be achieved by chance, and a well-planned, well-considered and forward-looking internal crisis communication strategy is needed to help rather than hinder and confuse crisis efforts, and to engage, empower and enable every employee.

- Your internal crisis communication strategy should be firmly grounded in insight and adapted to meet the needs of the crisis, the company and the community.

- SMART objectives are necessary to establish and agree what internal communication can deliver in the short, medium and long term.

- Your crisis position is critical to getting people on side. It sets the tone for everything that follows, and it drives how people perceive and experience the challenge ahead.

- Different approaches are required in different situations, and strategies such as denial, diminishment, rebuilding and bolstering can all be constructive in one situation but damaging in another, so they must be carefully considered and agreed upon.

- There is a difference in strategic, operational and human need between the acute and chronic crisis stages and so you must tailor your approach to internal crisis communication accordingly.

- In every situation, you must confirm your sources of truth, support your spokespeople and enable wider employee advocacy.

References

CDC (2019) CERC Psychology of a crisis, https://emergency.cdc.gov/cerc/ppt/CERC_Psychology_of_a_Crisis.pdf (archived at https://perma.cc/6B63-KDEF)

Coombs, W T (2007) Protecting organization reputations during a crisis: The development and application of situational crisis communication theory, *Corporate Reputation Review*, 10 (3), 163–76, www.researchgate.net/publication/247478499_Protecting_Organization_Reputations_During_a_Crisis_The_Development_and_Application_of_Situational_Crisis_Communication_Theory (archived at https://perma.cc/5DPE-RKJ8)

Coombs, W T (2015) *Ongoing Crisis Communication: Planning, managing, and responding*, Sage, Los Angeles

Frandsen, F and Johansen, W (2011) The study of internal crisis communication: Towards an integrative framework, *Corporate Communications*, 16 (4), 347–61, www.emerald.com/insight/content/doi/10.1108/13563281111186977/full/html (archived at https://perma.cc/D3UH-7T8K)

6

Craft your content

When crisis strikes, your people will seek information from many different sources inside and outside the organization. They'll have access to eyewitness accounts and diverse analysis. And as well as facts, they will possibly hear or see inaccurate information, extreme views and conspiracy theories too. Most of them will get involved in the conversations around them, and they'll trade information face-to-face and online with others who are as invested and interested in the situation as they are.

They'll demand context, details, updates and predictions, and they will use this to work out what the crisis means for them, what it means for the people and things they care about and what they will do and say next. You can't expect to be their only source of information, but you should aim to be their most trusted, and you should aim to deliver the live and on-demand content that meets their needs, shapes their understanding, holds their interest and helps the company to recover and come back stronger.

To do this, you must cut through the noise and share interesting and useful advice, information and stories like a real person would. You must listen and respond if you want to keep and hold attention, and you must constantly check people are getting everything they need to satisfy each of the 7S of internal crisis communication identified in Chapter 2.

Your first message is the one that's remembered. It's the one everyone will read, watch or listen to, it's the one everyone will talk about, and it's the one they'll use as a reference point for whatever comes next, so it's important to get it right. But then what? The crisis is not a static event, so your content and messaging can't be static either. It must flow from the first moment when the focus is on surviving, supporting and sensemaking needs all the way through to the stabilizing, stimulating, sustaining and strengthening content that will help the organization come back stronger.

Crisis demands that you must first deliver short, clear messages that meet critical surviving and supporting needs, and when these have been met, you must build on this with inspiring and engaging content that draws on pride and passion, and makes employees feel valued, respected, motivated and willing to go the extra mile.

This chapter offers simple advice to help you create content with purpose and impact. It begins by outlining key principles for helpful and engaging internal crisis communication and goes on to explain how to develop that critical first message and how to move forward using strategy, structure and soul to tell the stories that will engage, empower and enable your people through the crisis as it evolves.

Key principles

Your internal crisis communication may be the most important information your employees receive in their whole career. You owe it to them to make sure that your content is trustworthy, understandable, actionable and sincere, and you owe it to them to make sure it's meeting their very specific needs in a time of extreme stress and possibly trauma.

To do this, communication must:

- be open
- be accurate
- be clear
- be effective
- be human
- be memorable

Be open

Some business leaders think it's necessary to shield people from bad news, either because they underestimate the team's ability to process it or they fear blame. Yet people can't participate effectively in the crisis response if they don't know what's going on, and you can't build trust in an information vacuum. If people need to know something, you need to tell them, otherwise they will seek information elsewhere.

Global crisis communication consultant and trainer Piyali Mandal is the Founder and CEO of The Media Coach and a specialist in reputational, operational and cybersecurity crisis based in Mumbai, India. She tells me:

> When your employees are not getting information from you, they will instead get it from TV, newspapers and social media. This is damaging because it reduces morale, heightens stress and anxiety, and erodes trust within the organization.
>
> When they are kept in the dark, people have no way to differentiate fake news and real information. So, rumours will spread, sides will be taken and instead of advocacy, you'll start to see murmuring, bickering and fear mongering. All this directly affects your productivity, your reputation and your ability to recover – and all of this can be addressed with transparency. Not only during crisis, but always. Bake transparency through the business and you will be better placed to succeed.

Piyali Mandal's advice highlights a need to include all essential information as a critical part of your content strategy. You can't cut something out because it's too complicated, or because it's too uncomfortable, and you can't ignore a situation that's already being discussed because people will just look for the information elsewhere. Talk openly and acknowledge issues upfront to lead the narrative and set a positive future direction.

Be accurate

Accurate, verified information helps people make informed decisions and enables an appropriate crisis management response. It's vital for stopping the spread of misinformation, protecting reputation and building trust, so it's important that you check all facts and use proportionate language.

You won't know the answer to every question, and that's OK. Rather than make assumptions, it's better to say that some information is still unknown, that the organization is seeking clarity and that you will update when you can.

If mis- or disinformation is swirling, consider a symbol or other digital 'stamp' to show people that information was fact-checked, verified and correct on a certain date or time. If understanding evolves, be sure to remove outdated content and explain that understanding of the situation has progressed.

Be clear

Clarity is at a premium when people are overwhelmed, stressed and short on attention, as too much information will make it difficult for people to process what's most important, and it could lead them to abandoning your content altogether.

Your aim is to make all crisis content as easy as possible to understand, and that is as necessary in subject lines, headings and titles as it is in leadership statements, news articles and FAQ. Short, factual information works best in the acute crisis stage, and a labelling or colour-coding system lets people know instantly when a message is urgent, when it is for information and when it is for action.

Surviving and supporting information should borrow from the news-writing style known as the inverted pyramid, and make the key point in the headline or first sentence. Your second and third paragraphs should contain important supporting details, and finally important but less critical information can be included at the end.

Review every sentence and ask:

- Have I said what I am trying to say?
- Have I used clear and simple language?
- Could this be misinterpreted or misunderstood?
- Are there unnecessary links or attachments?
- Are there any words, sentences or paragraphs that don't add value?

If the answer to any of these questions is yes, go back and change the offending item, making sure the focus is on critical pieces of information, that you cut obscure or complex jargon and that you revise anything that will cause confusion.

If you provide statistics, make them easy to digest. Data is great for showing patterns and a sense of scale, but too much can be overwhelming. Highlight key figures or trends, show patterns visually and explain why the numbers are important.

Be effective

Every piece of content should have a clear objective that reflects the agreed crisis position; supports crisis management, business continuity or business recovery strategies; can be tied to one of the seven key needs (7S) of internal crisis communication; and doesn't get in the way of more pressing crisis activity or understanding. If it doesn't, hold on to it and schedule it for another time.

At the same time, don't omit anything important. Sometimes the people drafting a message are so familiar with the content that they assume others are too. They leave unintended gaps which makes information harder to interpret or understand. If in doubt, let a colleague with less direct involvement check that messages convey the meaning intended.

Be human

Showing care and kindness is not the same as admitting liability, and it is a vital first step towards healing, yet some people speak very formally in distressing times because they want to show they are taking the situation seriously – or because they want to sidestep blame. In doing so, they come across as wooden, evasive and without empathy. Being too formal is damaging when you need to get people on side, and history shows us that organizations who fail to show compassion or understanding for the people affected by a crisis always end up worse off.

As you communicate complex and emotionally difficult decisions, you must avoid further hurt by considering the message and position from the perspective of the worst-affected person. Always imagine you are talking to them directly, and if they are no longer here, imagine you are talking directly to their mother, children or friend. Picture the faces of the people who are most badly affected and be aware how a sloppy message may cause further pain.

A tip to test your language is to read it out loud. If it sounds cold or robotic, go back and review. Other tools such as the CARE Formula and the 5 Cs balance humanity with control in both internal and external communication, and they are extremely helpful.

USE THE CARE FORMULA

The CARE (concern, action, reassurance) formula can be used at any crisis stage.

CARE statements begin with authentic messages of concern, care or acknowledgement of everyone affected, focusing on those who have been hurt, injured or killed. They then explain what action is being taken to understand the situation or put it right, and they end with reassurance that the company is taking a situation seriously, is making progress or that lessons have been learnt.

DEMONSTRATE THE 5 CS

The 5 Cs of crisis communication can be used for different purposes, and they can be brought together in the same message or demonstrated separately as needed. Search online, and you'll find slightly different versions; however, my preference for internal crisis communication is:

- Concern
- Commitment
- Confidence
- Competence (or capability)
- Credibility

Concern   Showing concern is vital when people have been harmed, and it's the first step to enable healing. It's not about admitting fault, it's simply about putting the human first and acknowledging everyone affected.

Commitment   Expressing a commitment to finding and following through on a solution reassures people that the situation is being taken seriously and shows that the company is proactive and in control.

Confidence   Showing confidence is an important internal motivator which energizes people and reinforces a belief in the team's ability to pull through…

Competence (or capability)   … but confidence without competence is transparent, so confidence must be followed with evidence or examples to show the team has the skill, attitude or track record to succeed.

Credibility   Finally, leaders who are considered inadequate or out of touch find it harder to influence and persuade their teams, so messages (and actions) must show they get what's going on and have the qualities and credentials to deal with it.

PUT PEOPLE FIRST

Too often, companies deflate the power of the CARE formula or the 5 Cs by starting a message with an unnecessary, untrue or self-indulgent statement. For example: *'At ABC company, safety is our first priority, and we have an excellent track record'* or *'At ABC company, we work tirelessly to delight our customers.'* Worse, the well-intentioned but self-indulgent: *'As your leader, today has been my own worst nightmare.'*

All these things may be true, and it may be appropriate to say them further down the line, but don't lead with them when harm has been caused. Lead with the human or the team you are speaking to: 'Today, we experienced xxx, and I want to begin by recognizing xxx/thanking you for xxx/ acknowledging xxx/apologizing for xxx.'

Never make the harm an afterthought and recognize that people respond better to a call to protect colleagues, customers or community than they do to protect brand or balance sheet. Make it personal, rather than abstract, and remember that short, factual, empathetic statements that explain 'What's in it for me?' and 'Why should I care?' are more likely to generate trust, advocacy and support than long and rambling ones that feel self-centred, distant or out of touch, especially if the crisis is seen to be caused by poor management and leadership. If your message is neither intellectually or emotionally meaningful in that moment, rip it up and start again.

SAY THANK YOU

Studies show that acts of giving, kindness and gratitude bring physical and psychological benefits in tough times and that sincerely recognizing and saying thank you to employees can lower stress, boost resilience, increase motivation and support healing.

Some people are better at saying thank you than others, and a tip to doing it well is to be consistent and regular, and to include everyone. This means showing the company recognizes all efforts and celebrates the unsung heroes as well as those who stand out for the contributions they have made; and it means saying thank you in different ways – from personal notes and emails, to talking about achievements in team meetings, roadshows and in print and digital channels.

Be memorable

Throughout a crisis, people need clear, helpful and memorable direction. If you send out countless links and attachments, they may find it difficult to identify and remember what matters most, so a tip is to focus on only one or two points per message. From there you can include a footnote explaining where additional but less urgent information has been made available.

When crafting your content, consider how you might use tools such as the rule of three or the rule of repetition to make your content useful and memorable.

THE RULE OF THREE

The rule of three is used in many forms of communication, and it can be helpful when making important points in a memorable way. If examples like *Stop, look, listen* or *Reduce, reuse, recycle* are not familiar, I'm sure you can think of others that are.

Thinking in threes is helpful as you cut through otherwise complex information. Many countries used three-part slogans during Covid for example, and if you lived in the UK during that time, you may remember the slogan: *Stay Home, Protect the NHS, Save Lives,* which underlined the need for lockdown to reduce the spread of the virus and protect others.

The original message was hailed by Lee and Spanier in Campaign magazine (2020) as one of the most effective in the history of UK government communication – but as the situation evolved and lockdown eased, so too did the messaging. The new message: *Stay Alert, Control the Virus, Save Lives* was widely criticized for its ambiguity at a time when many felt the situation was still critical (Massey, 2020).

Of course, not being present as it was developed, we don't know what this second message was designed to achieve, and as with all crisis communication we can't judge it fully if we weren't party to the decision-making process. But what we can see from this example is that while the rule of three can help you develop a mantra to focus or motivate people around a particular outcome, it's not enough on its own. It needs to be clear, precise and actionable if it is to deliver results.

REPEAT, REPEAT, REPEAT

See what I did there? Repetition is important because it draws our attention to key points, emphasizes important messages and creates a rhythmic flow that keeps us engaged. It also builds emotional impact and establishes a clear structure which makes the overall message more memorable. We need only look to Dr Martin Luther King's '*I have a dream*' or President Barak Obama's '*Yes we can*' to know how powerful, memorable and inspiring repetition can be.

Dr King, President Obama and many other persuasive speakers use a powerful literary device called anaphora to make their points in a memorable way. In very simple terms, anaphora involves repeating the same word or phrase at the beginning of successive sentences or clauses. The technique helps create rhythm, emphasizes a point and makes the message more memorable.

Repeating positive phrases like *We will, We know, We can* works well in internal crisis communication because it can give people a shared stake in the crisis, it can inspire hope and it can motivate response efforts, while repeating negative phrases such as Greta Thunberg's '*How dare you!*' surprises the audience and forces their attention towards a critical problem or challenge.

Consider the wider conversation

We've already established that all your employees will have a view and experience of the crisis and company that they will share with others. Without responding to what is said and experienced by your employees, your messages will be confusing, and they may also feel out of touch, tone deaf or downright disingenuous – especially if they sanitize a harmful situation or feel at odds with clearly understood facts and evidence.

So rather than ignoring information that's being discussed or reported elsewhere, think of your internal crisis communication as a conversation. Listen, respond to and acknowledge different crisis experiences so that your messages fit well, feel authentic and generate trust. Crisis communication consultant, trainer and author Amanda Coleman tells me:

> There is a trust deficit in organizations right now. People feel they are being fed a version of the truth, and we need to be careful about that. You simply can't expect people to embrace a version of the truth that conflicts with their own, because in doing so, you are essentially gaslighting their lived experience.
>
> A better approach is to involve people in telling the story, and to let different people share their own versions so that you can build trust and confidence in the bigger picture.

Recognize the power of giving people something to share and advocate for. Get to know what messages will be sticky, shareable and easy for your teams to pass on. If there is a good story to tell, put people in the centre of it so they feel excited and empowered to advocate.

Manage misinformation

At the same time, know that misinformation and disinformation spreads like wildfire in uncertain times. If you don't clarify and offer a factual alternative, people will make sense of the situation using whatever information is available.

Dr Jacqueline Conway is a Founder and Managing Director of Waldencroft, a consulting practice based in Edinburgh, Scotland and working internationally. She tells me a critical internal crisis communication responsibility is to tackle misinformation and disinformation head on:

> What we see time and again is that when things become turbulent, there will be people outside and inside the organization ready to fill the void with nonsense.

That means your employees can jump from a world of strange ideas and conspiracies on social media directly into an official company meeting. If there are no proper updates in the meeting, and questions being asked, of course they will share what they have heard elsewhere.

People want answers, and once the information is out there, it starts moving. Yet leaders panic and stall a correction or an important message because it's not yet perfect. People are arguing about the dot of an 'i' or the cross of a 't' instead of focusing on the message itself. Of course, your content must be factual, clear and well-written, but there is a difference between imperfect and wrong.

You simply cannot delay correcting false narratives because there's a disagreement about grammar or because the people who want to sign something off are doing other things. No one is criticizing the folks spreading fake news on social media because their grammar is not on point. It's what they say that sticks, and any organization that refuses to act quickly to correct misinformation or disinformation is putting people at risk.

Know when not to speak

As you prepare your messages, it's also important to know when not to speak – when you have a duty of care or a legal obligation to protect privacy for example.

Julian Pike is a Partner specializing in reputation management at London law firm Farrer and Co. He tells me that a typical example is an internal, external or regulatory investigation into an allegation of misconduct – such as a #MeToo situation or financial wrongdoing. In these cases, the need and desire among staff to know what's happening must be balanced with the company's obligation to protect the confidentiality and the privacy of the people involved in the process.

Julian explains this means confidentiality and privacy will take precedence, but a business should consider how and what it can communicate as the process proceeds. At certain times, this will be on a need-to-know basis, but it should be recognized that a company must take its staff with it and demonstrate that the matter is being properly dealt with and not brushed under the table.

He says this can involve giving appropriate updates, especially to those more closely involved, which probably will not address the substance, but rather the progress of the process, as the investigation moves forward.

Similarly, he says if a case goes to court, you must not share information that will obstruct justice, or your litigation strategy, before a judgement is released, and that includes not upsetting the judge.

Every situation is different, so it's important for the organization to seek legal advice, in part to avoid spiralling into a second crisis because it failed to meet its legal obligations. Work together with your legal team to discuss what strategies will best meet your obligations while taking staff with you, and make sure that when you do need to pause, you are ready to communicate the moment you are legally able to do so.

Remember too, that any internal content can be leaked to the media or other parties, so you need to be comfortable with your messages becoming public. If you are approaching internal communication in a considered way that meets your obligations and aligns with your overall crisis management strategy, crisis position and company values, that's not necessarily a bad thing. You may even decide it's part of your strategy.

The secret, as always, is to carefully craft every message, to recognize it may be shared, and to consider how it will be interpreted and received by others before you press send.

Control the first messages

In earlier chapters we discussed how first messages must be direct and tightly controlled to deliver the all-important surviving and supporting content needed to keep people physically and psychologically safe, and we also established the importance of stealing thunder to support sensemaking needs and to build trust by ensuring employees hear about the crisis directly from the company before they hear from anyone else.

Both points tell us that timely and well-judged first messages are critically important. They are necessary to deflect harm, reduce anxiety, enhance reputation, and establish the organization and its leaders as the key source of truth. They set the position, the pace, the approach and the tone for everything that will come so it's important to get them right.

As you prepare and agree them, it's important to remember that your role is not to cover anything up, but to prevent harm as you explain what is happening and how it will be resolved. One of the best ways to frame your early internal messages is to clearly and simply offer a statement of concern, care or acknowledgement and then answer the following questions in the most human possible way each time information becomes available, or as an update to confirm nothing has changed:

- What is known (verified facts only)
- What is not known
- What action the company is already taking to manage the crisis
- What action the company will take next
- What employees must/must not do right now
- How employees can get help and support if needed
- Where all official internal and external statements can be viewed
- When, how and from whom the next update will come

If you can't answer one of the questions, you need to say that. Explain the organization is working to get answers then move on to address the next question. Review your message and check it meets all the key principles discussed earlier before you press send.

A tip is to have a pre-agreed adaptable template that uses human language to acknowledge the crisis, confirm how staff can access different resources and get help and support where needed, explain where all internal and external statements will be viewed, and explain when and how the next update will come.

That approach means you will always have something to say immediately, even if there is very little detail about the crisis itself. It also gives you a head start by removing the burden of agreeing language and structure and by giving you cues to add to or fill in as you can. Importantly, it reassures people you're on top of things, and it also buys time to get your facts right in a situation that's unclear.

While it's very important that internal and external communication work hand in hand to ensure a consistent crisis position, it's also important for your internal messages to put the employee first, as internal communication consultant and business owner Katie Marlow explains:

Don't rehash a press release and dress the external news up as the internal news. It's not the same thing – and if nothing else, it's incredibly disrespectful because it tells your people that you care less about them than you do about the shareholders or the media.

Instead, show that the employees and any victims are at the centre of your thoughts. Talk from the employee point of view about how the crisis affects them and the people or things they care about then explain what the organization is doing, what support is available and what – if anything – they need to do.

Keep your messages short and simple until the situation is stable. From there, you can start moving forward, sharing learning, sharing insight and discussing together how you will stimulate, sustain and strengthen activity as you move towards an acceptable future or new normal.

Tell the stories of crisis

Your first messages are crucial, but they are not enough to sustain a full crisis response so your content must evolve from the first moment when the focus is on providing essential information and/or instruction for survival, support, sensemaking, stability and stimulation, then it must inform, engage, enable and sustain people all the way through your crisis journey to healing, recovery, strengthening and a new normal.

Research conducted by David MacLeod and Nita Clarke for the UK Government in 2009 found that a strong, strategic narrative is one of the four enablers of employee engagement, and that companies who can tell an authentic and compelling story about the past, present and future of the organization are more likely to achieve high levels of performance and engagement – something that's critical to success through the crisis and particularly as you sustain people through the chronic stage and begin to strengthen the organization.

Whether it's done through a simple set of vox pops, a presentation, a short film, a poem, a photograph or a long-read article, storytelling is a powerful way to share evolving narratives. It's one of the most impactful ways to set out a vision or call to action, show people where they fit into a bigger picture and evidence progress.

Stories create characters and context that employees can identify with, they show the company is doing what it said it would and they support each of the 7S of internal crisis communication in different ways because they translate the complexity of crisis into a language that everyone understands, and importantly, feels.

Through stories, you can build knowledge, understanding and empathy that helps people make sense of the situation and begin to stabilize. You can stimulate, sustain and strengthen the crisis response by zooming in and out from personal experience to big picture strategy and showing how every person has an important role to play; and you can let people feel the impact of different choices before they make them themselves. Tell them well, and you can engage, empower and enable employees by simplifying complex issues, recognizing effort and giving them a stake in the crisis. But miss the mark, and your efforts will go to waste.

The challenge we face is that stories are often unintentionally told from the top down, and from a management or project perspective. They focus heavily on what business leaders want people to know about the company or its goals, and less about what people share among themselves. In other words, they really do come from 'a land far, far away'. The result is that stories crafted with the best of intentions miss the reality of the situation and feel cold and corporate on one hand, or patronizing and out of touch on the other. Neither is a good outcome when you are demanding that people go above and beyond their normal duties.

So how do we do it well? The answer is in strategy, structure and soul.

Strategy

Like everything else in internal crisis communication, your stories must not include information that's not known or confirmed, and they must be designed with a clear purpose in mind. As the crisis evolves and changes, the employees' physical, intellectual and emotional needs will also change and that means the narrative must change too. Ask yourself which surviving, supporting, sensemaking, stabilizing, stimulating, sustaining or strengthening needs you want your story to deliver on at any given point, and from there consider what people, purpose, policies, activities or values you want to highlight, and what you want people to know, feel and, importantly, do as a result.

Get out and about in the organization, seek out lots of different points of view and record what is happening through audio, video and images. Think about how authentic stories will help you build a deeper, more emotional relationship and connection with the audience, and how they can inspire them to stop, start or continue thinking or behaving in helpful ways, and bring in the views of credible third parties where that is comforting or persuasive. Be creative as you tell unexpected or surprising anecdotes that acknowledge challenges, celebrate success and spark ideas, action and ownership. Put the human being rather than the company in the hero role and tailor content to reflect the things people care about and that they will find interesting.

Structure

Just like all crises, all stories have a beginning, a middle and an end. And just like all crises, they follow a pattern in which tension rises and is relieved. This pattern is widely known as a narrative arc, and there are various frameworks, such as Freytag's Pyramid, which describe how it plays out:

1 Exposition

2 Rising action

3 Climax

4 Falling action

5 Resolution

In other words, our story starts on a normal day. We meet the hero and see the setting. Then the action ramps up – something happens, and our hero faces a problem, a chance or a discovery. As we move towards the climax, we see a defining moment in the form of a turning point, a showdown or a heroic act. Something has changed, and as the action once again begins to slow, our hero starts to solve the problem or grasp the opportunity as we move towards resolution where the problem is solved, and everyone lives happily ever after.

It sounds simple, but reflect on your favourite childhood story, or think about the TV shows or ad campaigns you've recently watched. Can you see the pattern? Whether it's told in a few words or a few hundred pages, this is a structure that works and it's one that works particularly well in internal crisis communication. That's because it allows us to recognize and acknowledge difficult truths in a positive way. It lets us see for ourselves the ramifications of not taking an action, it shows us the gaps that must be filled, it helps us to learn and sometimes it helps us to heal.

Christopher Booker's book *The Seven Basic Plots: Why We Tell Stories* (2004) deepens our understanding of narrative arcs with the proposition that there are seven universal story types: rags to riches; overcoming the monster; the quest; voyage and return; comedy; tragedy, and rebirth. Like every other framework, there are people who argue for two, three, six or more. That's not really the point. The point is that you can use this insight to put your crisis into a context that you know will resonate with your people. You can use this insight to help people make sense of what is happening, and you can use it to motivate them to come out stronger.

In 'overcoming the monster', for example, there's an evil force threatening stability. It's not easy, but our hero fights against it and comes out stronger. In 'the quest', our hero sets out on a long, dangerous journey, and overcomes different obstacles until they are triumphant. And in 'rebirth', the hero falls under a dark spell before breaking free and achieving redemption. You don't have to use them, but it's interesting to understand the different patterns that narrative can follow, and how they might help us engage and inspire people in difficult times.

Carmine Gallo (2016) explains why facing challenge in our stories is powerful:

> Stories of overcoming obstacles provide a dramatic arc to the narrative we tell the world. Inspiring storytellers don't avoid the difficult parts of their arc but rather embrace every step as an opportunity to transform, grow, and to make a deeply meaningful emotional connection with their audience.

By highlighting the difficult parts of our stories, we acknowledge and surface them without blame. We create a culture where it's safe to tackle problems, and we create a culture where every individual knows they can make a difference and be celebrated for that.

Soul

If strategy and structure are the foundations of effective organizational storytelling, it is soul that gives them power, especially in times of crisis. Soul is what grabs our attention and makes us think, feel and do things differently. Soul is what motivates and inspires. It is what gives us goosebumps or moves us to tears. And it cannot be faked.

To be successful, internal crisis communication should not instruct people to 'embrace the challenge', 'move forward with purpose' or 'deliver with confidence' – it should inspire them to decide that they want to do so.

Mike Stevenson is Founder of Thinktastic, and a leading motivational speaker and coach who experienced homelessness, drug addiction and the brink of suicide before turning his life around and founding a multi-million-pound business. Mike has inspired teams at some of the biggest brands in the UK, and he tells me that every well-told story leads with emotion:

> If you want to inspire, move and motivate an audience you need to make a strong emotional connection and you need to speak emotionally. You do that by understanding that people want to see themselves in the world you construct through your stories.

Well-told stories give people a sense of agency, they build connections, find solutions and fix broken things. They reinforce shared values and purpose, they set a path to the future and they encourage people to step forward.

It's important in all internal crisis communication to talk emotionally as well as just informatically if you want people to process and remember your point. So, when you're communicating about your crisis, use a blend of personal and observed stories that show how it's possible to overcome similar things.

Don't just tell – show. And get people talking about the things that have challenged them, the things that have inspired them, where they are having impact. The more people see their name and their department associated with success, the more motivating it can be. It is the ultimate inclusion. Let people see and feel that despite the challenge, they are part of a community that is driving something forward for good.

I call it connecting your tongue to your heart.

Stories with soul are raw, real and sometimes vulnerable. They come from lived experience, and that means to have greatest impact, you must let your people take the stage, become the hero and share their own stories in their own words.

Let them share a vision and a purpose that others can connect to and make sense of. Let them paint a vivid picture of what success looks like through the crisis journey and let them be honest about the barriers they face. Let them speak in their own authentic voice so that other people might see themselves in the struggle, empathize with the challenge and wish for a successful resolution.

Consider your responsibilities

Because the most powerful crisis stories are laden with emotion and personal detail, you must always put the needs of the storyteller before your need for a story. Some powerful stories are never told, and that's OK.

- Be clear with people where and how their story will be told.
- Explain what might happen as a result.
- Let people speak in their own voice.
- Respect their wishes if they prefer to speak with caveats attached.
- Respect their wishes if they change their mind.
- Always give people approval of their crisis stories.

KEY TAKEAWAYS

- Content must flow from the first moment when the focus is on surviving, supporting and sensemaking, all the way through the stabilizing, stimulating, sustaining and strengthening content that will help the organization come back stronger.

- The first message is vital, as it's the one everybody will seek out and remember – but there is much more to say and do beyond that and you must continue to tailor content as the crisis evolves through each stage.

- The key principles of effective internal crisis communication are to be open, accurate, clear, effective, human and memorable.

- Consider how you can use the CARE Formula and the 5 Cs to ensure your communication is hitting the mark, and always put the human first.

- Think about how tools such as repetition and the rule of three can make your content more engaging and memorable.

- Involve staff as advocates and role models as you tell the stories of crisis with purpose, and think intentionally about strategy, structure and soul.

- Consider how you may use narrative arcs and common plots to engage and motivate your people in the crisis response.

- Finally, consider all your obligations and responsibilities and be aware of any legal restrictions on what you can and can't say at different times.

References

Booker, C (2004) *The Seven Basic Plots: Why we tell stories*, Bloomsbury, London

Gallo, C (2016) *The Storyteller's Secret: How TED speakers and inspirational leaders turn their passion into performance*, Pan Books, London

Lee, J and Spanier, G (2020) Single-minded and unavoidable: How the government honed 'Stay home' message, 11 May, www.campaignlive.co.uk/article/single-minded-unavoidable-government-honed-stay-home-message/1682448 (archived at https://perma.cc/WNK4-LDQB)

MacLeod, D and Clarke, N (2009) Engaging for success: Enhancing performance through employee engagement: A report to government, https://dera.ioe.ac.uk/id/eprint/1810/1/file52215.pdf (archived at https://perma.cc/27ST-RCCK)

Massey, M (2020) Government's 'stay alert' slogan not clear enough, says expert, 12 May, https://uk.news.yahoo.com/government-stay-alert-slogan-not-143402987.html (archived at https://perma.cc/5B2W-4BAV)

7

Select the right channels

A considered plan, actionable messages and compelling stories sit at the heart of your success. But if you don't have the means to share them with the right people at the right time, then you can't put your strategy into action, and everything else will be in vain.

Throughout this book, we've established that crises call for a different approach than everyday internal communication. There are several reasons for this, not least the fact that when crisis strikes, the demand for high quality, fast and accurate information is so extraordinarily high.

This means that channel selection is a critical strategic internal crisis-communication activity. More than at any other time, people need clear, consistent and accessible content that is delivered to them in the way that suits them best and when they need it most. If they don't get that from you, they will scrabble among other sources to fill the void themselves, leading to myth, rumour, misinformation, mistrust, inefficiency and mistakes.

Yet internal channel selection is sometimes taken for granted, and organizations send out their most critical information via email lists that go straight to spam, on digital screens that don't work, or on posters, leaflets or stickers that feel frivolous in the moment and sit in unopened boxes on restroom floors.

Sending the information and hoping for the best is not enough. It's also your job to ensure it is received, understood and, where appropriate, further shared. To do this, you first need to know how information flows around your organization in stable times.

Get rid of all assumptions and test what works, what doesn't, why and how. What will encourage your people to seek out your content as an accessible source of truth, and what will push them elsewhere?

This chapter helps you understand what formal and informal channels you have available to you, and it explains how and when best to use them and why. Focusing on different ways to inform, to involve, to engage and to heal, it suggests how you might meet different needs, and choose the best channel mix for your unique crisis. Finally, it offers advice to support tracking and evaluation so you can tweak your strategy in real time if needed.

Understand your channels

Communication channels are the various print, digital and face-to-face methods and platforms you use to keep communication flowing smoothly in all directions around your organization. They are the vehicles for sharing information, bringing content to life, and collecting feedback or responses. They are essential for making and maintaining a connection with large and dispersed groups of people, and if you want to use them effectively, you must first understand how they work.

Getting to grips with the channels that are available in your company is a critical first step to using them well, and many organizations have an internal communication channels matrix that identifies and sets out what print, digital and face-to-face channels should be employed for what purpose, when, how often and by whom.

From there, you need to understand whether they do what you expect them to, and that means flipping your thinking from what's sent out, to understand what's received and consumed by different people and when. You need to know what's delivered, read, watched, listened to, attended, commented on and shared by whom, how often and with what effect so you can be sure that your podcast gets more than three listeners, your information screens are switched on and your emails don't go straight to spam.

Beyond that, it's important to remember that everyone is connected in many ways, and information is also shared through channels that sit outside your established infrastructure. People interact with informal and unofficial communication channels in your organization all the time, but especially when the demand for information is high, and they send and receive information to and from the outside world as well, so if you are to be truly effective, you must understand these too.

Consultant, author and business owner Rachel Miller is a global authority on internal communication, based in England. Her book *Internal Communication Strategy: Design, develop and transform your organizational communication* (2024) explains that when a gap is not filled by official communication channels, people will find their own way to locate and share the information they need. She tells me that this means internal communicators shouldn't just think about how they use the company's 'official' internal communication channels, but that we must have a full sense of how information is traded and shared informally through the organization and the wider industry sector too:

I look for sources of truth inside organizations. Sometimes that's the immediate line managers or shift supervisor or perhaps local leadership. I define a source of truth as a credible, accurate and reliable source of information that employees trust. This could be a conversation with their manager or a leader's statement on the intranet. It will vary in every business and it's crucial you test your assumptions to check who or what you think employees rely on is accurate.

An official way of testing this is my 'snow test'. If I was working inside an organization such as a factory or retail store that required employees to be on site when extreme weather was forecast, who or what would they rely on to know whether it's safe to travel and if their site will be open? Knowing that answer helps you plan effectively. If employees would ask their line managers first, then line managers must be considered a priority channel for crisis communication.

She continues:

Internal communicators need to know how communication really happens inside their company if they want to get the right message to the right people at the right time. You also need to determine where conversation or two-way communication happens as those are the places where employees will seek clarity on your crisis communication and ask questions.

When completing a channels matrix, ensure you capture the shadow comms too. These are the unofficial methods of communication that employees rely on. Sometimes these are closed forums, WhatsApp groups or local email distribution lists. It's rare for an internal communication team to own these channels, but if they are seen as the go-to source of truth for certain employees or parts of your organization, you need to know this. Why? Because during a crisis employees rely on their preferred and trusted source of communication. If you can't tap into this, there may be pockets of the company who will be without the information they need.

By way of example, an internal communication team working in a large multinational corporation may think of their internal crisis communication channels as:

- A global intranet

- Local, regional and global emails
- A global weekly e-newsletter
- Internal social networks
- Noticeboards
- Digital screens
- Team meetings
- local, regional and global digital conferences and presentations

In fact, they should also consider understanding and tapping into:

- Employee networks
- Messaging groups
- Individual or team e-zines and blogs
- Official (and unofficial) company social media pages
- Official (and unofficial) internal and external WhatsApp groups
- Other social media channels
- Other communities of interest

Additionally, they must look at how they give employees messages they feel proud and able to share when talking with colleagues, friends and family so they can answer questions and confidently quash myths, echo truths and advocate for the organization when they are asked.

Rachel says a tip is to identify owners for the shadow comms inside your organization and develop strong working relationships with them before a crisis occurs. Put them on your 'must update' list during a crisis, and make sure they are included on your stakeholder map, so they can pass things on.

Identify channel purpose

Once you are confident you understand all your channels, how they work and how they are used, you need to consider what will best fit each of the 7S of internal crisis communication needs (surviving, supporting, sensemaking, stabilizing, stimulating, sustaining and strengthening) identified in Chapter 2, and if you will develop new channels to meet new or emerging needs.

Bill Quirke (2008) stated that wrong channel choices create overload and confusion, so you need to have a clear sense of which channel is appropriate for a given need. From a crisis perspective, that means knowing which channels will most effectively inform, involve and engage people through each stage of the crisis response, and what will additionally support individual or collective healing, recovery and remembrance if this is needed.

Ways to inform

In Chapters 2 and 6, we established the critical importance of that early surviving, supporting, sensemaking and stabilizing information, and in Chapter 5 we established the benefits of stealing thunder, to make sure your people hear about any crisis from the organization before they hear it anywhere else.

We also established that people are more likely to believe the first message they hear, and they are likely to quickly look elsewhere if their needs are not met and so a strategic internal crisis communication priority is to get clear, factual information and instruction to all the internal community first and fast.

To do this effectively, it is vital that informing channels:

- reach employees immediately
- are reliable and dependable
- are easy for all employees to access
- are free from obstacles or distractions such as passwords, pop ups and codes
- enable targeted or segmented communication with specific groups
- offer a central feedback or contact point should people need to reply

This means it often makes sense to push out informing content through the physical workspace and through personal devices. Every organization and every crisis have different requirements, but you may want to consider a mix of internally and externally hosted systems such as:

- Mass notification systems (MNS)
- Employee communication apps
- Text messages
- Audio messages

- Employee helplines
- QR codes
- Digital screens
- Posters
- Pull-ups
- Desk drops
- Bite-sized videos or podcasts
- Face-to-face updates
- Team briefings
- Online meetings
- Email
- Newsletters
- Webinars
- Intranet or internet sites

Remember that seemingly simple tools like text, email and apps need to be properly maintained and fully tested in stable times if they are to do the job when crisis strikes. Distribution lists, phone numbers and email addresses must be fully up-to-date, and employees must have downloaded and tested all apps in advance.

A simplified intranet or web page can also be preprepared, and some organizations use a dark page to ensure a fast response. Not to be confused with the dark web, this is a private or unpublished page or microsite that's created and populated in stable times then updated and activated if a crisis occurs. It should have minimal navigation and should put critical instruction or statement front and centre, but can include helpful information such as safety protocols, helpline numbers or assistance resources. As the crisis evolves you can add FAQ or myth busters, and you may simplify complicated information with flow charts, listicles, infographics, animation, film or audio if appropriate. But don't add things just because you can – think about the user experience and the unintended consequences of using artificial or mechanical rather than human intelligence.

And don't forget about the importance of printed words or graphics when providing instruction or information. Printed materials can be kept for reference and revisited, so help build both trust and understanding. They can also be 'dropped' or posted to people who have no digital connection;

however, they have a longer preparation and distribution time so are less effective for information that dates quickly.

Ways to involve

Soon after the necessary surviving information and instruction has done the required job, and as you continue to deliver your supporting, sensemaking and stabilizing communication, you'll also need to start stimulating the recovery. Sometimes, that will be needed quickly – within an hour or so. Other times it will be appropriate to wait longer. Either way, the role of your channels at this point will be to build more detailed understanding, and to involve people in conversation, questions and debate as you work together to find and share crisis opportunity and solutions. Involving channels must:

- consider different platforms for different needs
- recognize different time zones and shift patterns
- introduce a level of self-service and content choice
- support longer form content
- bring in different voices
- enable feedback and conversation
- enable people to share ideas
- facilitate collaboration and problems solving
- include different forms of support for those who need it

Involving people means listening to them, and it means implementing their good ideas. We'll talk more about this in Chapter 10; however, key channels for involving people may include:

- site visits
- team meetings
- huddles
- show-and-tells
- social media
- blogs
- project management platforms
- collaboration platforms
- consultation forums

- employee networks
- employee resource groups
- workshops
- knowledge-sharing events
- think-tanks
- hackathons

In person or virtual face-to-face meetings, site visits and consultation forums are all effective ways to deliver sensitive information and receive authentic feedback. They are highly valued by employees as they can help build or rebuild a sense of belonging. They can be as formal or informal as you require; however, they do rely on the skills of the person delivering the message and can be less impactful or even damaging when ill-prepared, unsupported or poorly delivered.

The secret is to make sure your key people are properly trained to communicate face-to-face and to make sure that meetings are properly managed and designed to create a safe space where everyone can ask questions, make suggestions and raise concerns.

Internal and external social media channels are also helpful as they enable employees to form or join communities, share knowledge and get ideas flowing, while knowledge-sharing systems, think-tanks and hackathons give people more agency in meeting the crisis as it evolves. They break down silos, help people 'join the dots' and they can create new ideas, efficiencies, innovation and solutions that they can be proud to own and advocate for.

Ways to engage

As you involve people intellectually, you'll need to make an emotional connection too, especially if you expect them to keep on giving their all through the difficult, chronic stage of the crisis, and if you want them to participate in their role as crisis advocates and ambassadors as the company builds back stronger.

Your engaging channels must:

- establish a shared purpose
- evidence safety
- recognize success
- enable effective storytelling

- introduce multisensory visual and interactive content
- include multiple voices and perspectives
- offer higher levels of personalization
- enable high levels of feedback, conversation and idea sharing
- offer continued opportunities to be involved and collaborate with others
- offer opportunities to recognize and celebrate success
- consult on the future
- show how every individual is important in the bigger picture

Engaging channels can use sight, sound and interaction as they enable lots of opportunity for collaboration, consultation and storytelling, and they should introduce different opportunities to capture imagination and inspire action and hope. They may include:

- video
- podcast
- photography
- music
- art
- site visits
- storytelling sessions
- team-building activities
- recognition events
- milestone celebrations
- celebratory events

Engagement is a two-way process, and organizations must work to earn employee engagement, including through hearing their voice and offering them opportunities to be involved, heard and invited to contribute (MacLeod and Clarke, 2009). That's an undeniable fact, and it's particularly important in times of crisis, but I think it sometimes leads to a belief that all engaging internal communication must be two-way. You may have guessed from the above list that it's not a view I subscribe to. That's not because I don't think two-way communication is engaging – listening is one of the most important themes in this book – but it's because I know one-way communication can be engaging too.

The thing is that engagement is a term often used to describe communication, but it is in fact a separate concept – a dynamic and fluctuating outcome rather than an output, and it is shaped by lots of elements including, but not limited to, communication.

Experts such as Khan (1990) explain that the 'state' of engagement is achieved when employees feel personally valued within the wider team, when they are intellectually and emotionally connected to their role and organization, and when they are enthusiastic about going the extra mile to help the organization succeed. Of course, two-way communication can help achieve all of that, but haven't we all been in situations where it has done quite the opposite?

I once saw a meme in which an internal communication professional was asked to bring people back into the office after the Covid lockdowns through the power of dance. It got a lot of likes. People commented with sympathy, and they shared other weird, wonderful and downright unrealistic things that internal communicators are asked to do. And of course, the joke is silly. But dance is powerful. So is music, so is art, so is comedy. They tell us stories that make us think and feel differently, they foster connection and they evoke emotion. They are deeply engaging.

Broadcast can be a useful channel to create a sense of togetherness among a dispersed workforce, and film is powerful because it combines visual image, spoken word, music and sound effects. It can be edited for clarity, and because we see and hear the characters involved, we form a deeper connection with them.

Blogs, short stories or podcasts that explore the employee journey, interviewing staff about different projects, or offer different perspectives on an issue or opportunity all have a similar effect, while powerful photographs grab our attention and help us experience a place and time that we would otherwise find it difficult to understand.

Supporting all these things with the two-way conversations that enable people to interpret and make sense of them is where the true magic lies, and so a tip is to blend and back up your engaging channels in lots of different ways.

Of course, it goes without saying that actions speak louder than words. If a company is known to lack integrity and its words and actions are out of sync with what it says, highly overproduced and emotional content will seem ridiculous, and it will have an antagonizing and disengaging effect.

Ways to heal

Finally, in the most awful human tragedies, employees need to hear directly from company leaders that their pain is recognized, their sorrow is shared and lessons have been learnt, and they need to believe and trust that this is true.

Damaged people need a way to express their feelings, and they need a place for homage, solace and healing, so grief and anger must not be side-stepped, hidden away or ignored. It is part of the journey towards healing, and the organization has a duty to hear and support all human expression without resistance or defence.

Special consideration should be given to memorials that honour victims and survivors of tragic events, and these must fully include any victims, survivors and bereaved people who wish to be involved.

Working with harmed people can be difficult because everyone grieves differently, and everyone has their own views about the recovery process. Good non-judgemental leadership is essential, and it's important to carefully recognize and accommodate diverse needs while establishing a sympathetic understanding of what happens next.

Memorials can take many different forms. As well as gatherings, the company can offer a book of condolence, participate in a symbolic act, hold an exhibition, create a garden, build a digital archive, illuminate a building, or commission a piece of poetry, music or art. All employees should be supported in deciding what is most appropriate, and in all situations, memorials must:

- put the needs of victims, survivors and bereaved people first
- encompass the whole internal community, including employees, contrac-tors, sub-contractors, freelancers, partners and volunteers
- cater carefully and respectfully to the needs of damaged human beings
- be developed with input from many different voices
- enable a mix of conversation, sharing, solace and reflection
- offer a safe space to grieve
- offer the opportunity to remember, and where appropriate celebrate recovery
- offer legacy or learning
- meet a high standard of quality or artistic excellence
- be fully funded in their creation and maintained for an agreed period

Some companies shy away from creating memorials or marking milestones because they believe keeping the crisis in the public eye will slow financial, operational or reputational recovery. That may or may not be true, but it is not the critical consideration. The critical consideration is human recovery. It is to behave well, to offer dignity to victims and, as far as possible, to do right by those who have been wronged – not just in line with policy, but in line with the deeper values that most people hold.

Beyond this, the reality is that when grief is unsupported, outrage ensues – and an organization or leader that fails to support victims, survivors and bereaved people in their healing needs creates a pain that lasts for generations. That means that what an organization does or doesn't do to help people heal is not a call that should be made exclusively by those with little understanding of the humans harmed, especially in global organizations where the hurt may be felt far from the privilege of head office.

Sue Jane Taylor is an artist known for her visual documentation and interpretation of the technology, engineering and people of the offshore energy sector. In 1987, she spent time as a young graduate artist on the Piper Alpha platform in the North Sea a year before a devastating explosion killed 167 innocent men, and she was asked by the bereaved and survivors to create their memorial. She tells me:

> Piper Alpha haunted me, and it has never left me.
>
> I had been allowed by the company that owned and operated Piper Alpha to stay and document life on the platform in the summer of 1987, almost exactly a year before the disaster, and I was due to exhibit some of this work in a touring exhibition opening at the City Arts Centre, Edinburgh shortly after the disaster occurred. Some of the men I knew and met died that night, and so out of respect to the survivors and families I wanted to see if this was OK.
>
> The survivors and families were strongly in favour that the exhibition must go ahead, but Occidental, the company that had owned and operated the platform, were not keen. They called me to a meeting and asked to see my work, which I showed them, and they then offered a deal to take it all from me so that I would not need to exhibit any of the Piper Alpha related artworks.
>
> It was probably a good deal, but I didn't ask, I just thought of the men and their families. I was a bit green back then – young, naive and not experienced in dealing with big companies, so I was very unsure what to do. I sought legal advice, and that advice confirmed to me I must go ahead with the exhibition.

So, we went ahead and had a special exhibition with a private opening for the families.

It was the right thing to do, and from there I established a good relationship with many of the survivors and families who were already trying to establish a physical memorial for their loved ones, again against the will of the company whose stance was that a book of memorial and their financial compensation was enough.

Still raw in their grief and outrage, the families and survivors pushed ahead. Artists were approached to create the memorial, and in the end, they offered it to me.

The families and survivors wanted the memorial to be a place of homage and solace in Aberdeen, three figures captured in the style of the Spean Bridge war memorial, away from the busy city centre. We agreed we would work together to develop the sculpture from that brief.

I felt it was very important to involve life models. I draw and sculpt from life and felt it essential I involve a survivor as one of my models. It took me time to work out what shape the memorial would take, how I would represent a platform and how I would represent the figures because the men killed were of all different ages, from their teens through to their 60s. But I knew the central figure had to be a survivor, and I asked the memorial committee to choose a survivor to model for me. Bill Barron volunteered as he felt that he needed to help in some way, and it was wonderful to work with Bill because we built up such a strong relationship as the memorial took shape.

It's important to remember I was young. I was chosen not only because of my skills as an artist and my relationship with the men of Piper Alpha but also because the families and survivors trusted me and knew they could work with me. I was working with broken damaged people who were recovering from this terrible, terrible happening and with survivors who were facing such awful guilt, and I felt that trauma deeply too. As he stood for me, Bill would tell me things he has never told anyone else and which I will never disclose. But it was important for him, and it was important for me, and I hope in some ways these things worked into the figures and were reflected in the sculpture.

There is so much sensitivity in working with damaged people, and a need to do them justice. It was very tricky because the disaster was so immense in its consequences. It was the world's worst disaster ever faced in the oil and gas industry, but it was even more painful because the company did not support the memorial being created.

Creating a memorial of this scale is expensive, and without any financial contribution from Occidental, anger built up in the people who were raising the funds. It made them ever more determined, and they took strength to keep going. But they will never forget how appallingly they were treated. In the end, less than £14,000 of the £100,000 required for the memorial was contributed by the oil industry within the North Sea, and the UK government had to step in with the shortfall.

I shut all that out of my mind and focused on my skills and expertise, and I focused on the art and the men. It was more than representing workers, it was about representing people: husbands, fathers, sons.

I wanted the memorial to relate to the North Sea and to its men, youthfulness to the survival suit figure, physicality to the roustabout figure, and survival and maturity to the central figure. We looked at the clothes, the drapes they wore, and Bill advised on that. It was important to research it properly and get it right.

On the figures themselves, some symbolic motifs feature, such as a Sea Eagle and the Tree of Life. The central figure has one hand pointing down to the source of oil; on the other, a spiral of oil coming out from its palm.

We found a place that met the need for solitude as Aberdeen City Council gave a beautiful space in Hazelhead Park. The sculpture was placed in a Rose Garden designed by the council's head gardener. The roses were carefully chosen by the families – the names, the perfume, the colour – and that was part of the healing too.

The memorial to the 167 innocent victims of Piper Alpha was finally unveiled by the Queen Mother of the UK on 6 July 1991 – the third anniversary of the tragedy. It was 32 years later, in 2023, when it was recognized for its national importance as a site of public commemoration and memory and given designated listed status by Historic Environment Scotland (Historic Scotland, 2023).

Like art, music also has a profound ability to transcend language barriers, evoke emotion and create powerful feelings that support the process of healing after trauma. Many studies show the positive effects of music on physical and mental health and there are many examples of music dedicated to victims of tragedy. Sue Jane Taylor shared the example of Tuireadh (Gaelic for 'lament'). Tuireadh is a powerful work created by Scottish composer Sir James MacMillan, who was inspired by a letter from Molly Pearson, the mother of a son just 19 years old when he was killed on Piper Alpha.

Choose a suitable channel combination

Different organizations have mixed needs for everyday internal communication, let alone for crisis, which means channel selection can only be confirmed once the crisis is understood. Start with what you already know about needs and preferences in your organization and then overlay any necessary tweaks your crisis may require. Try to use a mix of timely and accessible one-way and two-way print, digital and face-to-face channels to meet a range of different needs.

Use one-and two-way channels

A mix of one- and two-way communication channels will be most effective to inform, involve, engage and enable your people, and to meet each of the 7S of internal crisis communication identified in Chapter 2.

One-way communication channels enable clear, consistent and unambiguous content that meets surviving and supporting needs, and they are helpful because they get the same information out to everyone in the same way. The transparency offered by published content is key to building trust, but it also increases understanding as people can read and process it in their own time.

Two-way communication channels, meanwhile, help the process of sensemaking, and they help meet the organization's stabilizing, stimulating, sustaining and strengthening needs. They also enable issues, questions and suggestions to be quickly surfaced and dealt with so they are also important to the overall operational response.

Echo and repeat

Research tells us that when we hear information face-to-face, we only take in a small percentage of what is said, so it is important to build in a level of message repetition.

This means that if a senior leader delivers an update on a digital platform, you need to make sure it's recorded and made available to view again, and you also need to follow it up with a strong written statement, an FAQ document, and a properly prepared and supported line manager's briefing to reinforce and translate key points.

Be consistent

Delivering information how and when people expect it is critical to your success.

Missing an update or delaying it without explanation can break trust, so if you can't commit to updating key channels on a specific day or a time, you must communicate that clearly, explain why and share an alternative plan.

Be mindful

It's also necessary to be aware that some of the channels, designs or language you used before the crisis might feel frivolous or in poor taste in the light of the situation as it evolves, and the wrong spokesperson or approach could inflame a situation too, especially when people are angry, grieving or in pain.

Judge the mood carefully and listen to the views of your employees as you decide whether it is necessary to simplify colour schemes, modify logos and avatars, use different voices or fully reschedule planned activity.

Offer choice (but not too much)

In the acute phase of your crisis, you'll have people's undivided attention. This means that clear and explicit content directly delivered through one simple source of truth, backed up and echoed by one or two others will suffice.

But as time moves on, and particularly as you move into the chronic stage of the crisis, you will need to work harder because central updates will not be enough to meet different needs. Concentrate on what's right for your staff, structure, culture and resources, and importantly on what will help you meet your crisis objectives.

Be aware what information is going out, when and to whom. And remember that offering choice means offering different options or alternatives and not just different versions of the same thing. People may value the choice of an article or a podcast, but they won't want to check 20 different microsites to find them.

Put contingencies in place

If you were employed before 2020, you'll remember the profound impact that the Covid-19 lockdown had on internal communication, when, for the first time, companies who had depended heavily on face-to-face communication had to pivot to virtual meetings and chat platforms. The transition was tricky for some, but most made it work, and we all now have a wider range of tools available to us as a result.

But what happens if your people can't come to the office, and your digital channels are unavailable too? It's an increasingly common problem, and one that must be considered. Alison Lochhead was leading the communication team at the University of the Highlands and Islands in Scotland when a cyber incident disrupted systems across its network of 13 colleges and research institutions – including those they'd normally use to communicate with students and staff. She tells me:

> When you are crisis planning, you don't always plan for a situation that will force you to take down all your internal communication channels, but that's where we found ourselves at UHI because in the initial stages of managing a cyber incident, everything – from security entry systems to critical services must be taken offline and tested to ensure against and mitigate further damage.
>
> With buildings unable to open, key systems out of use and the risk of swirling misinformation, we needed to quickly inform and reassure our staff and students, and we needed to point everyone to one single source of truth.
>
> But of course, the incident meant that our go-to channels were not available to us. We couldn't use our intranet, and we couldn't guarantee everyone would get their emails. What do you do? Well, we had to change our approach and use what else we had. That meant the unaffected communication systems outside the university network – our website and multiple social media accounts, which were hosted externally on the cloud.
>
> In essence, our external channels became our internal channels for the first few days of the crisis. We put a single 'cyber incident' link on the website homepage which took visitors directly to all the latest information. This single page contained information for staff, information for students and information for the media, but it was also a rich source of detail for other stakeholders too.
>
> All social media updates linked to it, and, once it was available, all emails linked to it too. Everything was date stamped, and we kept a clear and up-to-

date timeline which answered key questions and let people know what we were doing and what we had planned.

UHI's system worked well and some of the learning has been rolled out as part of a UK-wide cyber incident communication toolkit for the university sector. Alison Lochhead's tip is that when preparing for this type of incident, make sure you build in a backup plan that works for your organization when your go-to channels are down.

Enable tracking and evaluation

If your channels are not working for your people, they will move on and look elsewhere, so you must be sure they are delivering what's needed. As you communicate, keep checking that information is getting through and having impact. We will talk more about measurement and evaluation in Chapter 12, but at a basic level you must make sure that you have systems in place to understand what's going out and how it's received.

This can include:

- measuring reach through online click or open rates
- measuring attendance at physical and virtual events
- measuring log-in frequency to microsites
- analysing likes and shares of different content
- analysing the sentiment expressed in comments and on social media
- checking how well people have remembered important updates
- using focus groups to understand how people have interpreted your messages
- assessing whether tasks are being completed as required

KEY TAKEAWAYS

- Channel selection is a critical strategic activity, yet it's often untested and taken for granted, which means critical information is not effectively shared when it's needed most.

- Your job is to ensure all messages are received, understood and passed on where this is needed, and that all additional needs are supported. This means you must know how information really flows around your organization in stable times as well as through the lens of the crisis.

- Internal communication channels should be planned from the perspective of the audience. What works for them, what doesn't, why and how? What will encourage them to seek out your content as an accessible source of truth, and what will push them elsewhere?

- Channels have different purposes, and so different methods are required to inform, involve, engage and help heal.

- Directive one-way channels are necessary for sending out clear surviving and supporting information first and fast, but these must be supported with more engaging channels to support people, help them make sense of the crisis and strengthen at different stages.

- Some of the channels, designs or language you used before the crisis might feel frivolous or in poor taste as the situation evolves. Judge the mood carefully and listen to employees as you decide whether tweaks are required.

- And finally, crisis is not business as usual so normal channels may not be appropriate or accessible. Put contingencies in place to deal with unexpected situations and unavailable tools.

References

Historic Scotland (2023) Piper Alpha Memorial and Memorial Garden recognised with designated status, 9 October, www.historicenvironment.scot/about-us/news/piper-alpha-memorial-and-memorial-garden-recognised-with-designated-status/ (archived at https://perma.cc/2THF-FVJZ)

Historic Scotland (no date) Piper Alpha Memorial, Hazlehead Park, Aberdeen LB52621, https://portal.historicenvironment.scot/apex/f?p=1505:300::::: VIEWTYPE,VIEWREF:designation,LB52621 (archived at https://perma.cc/D5E6-Q7DC)

Kahn, W (1990) Conditions of personal engagement and disengagement at work, *Academy of Management Journal*, 33 (4) December, 692–724

MacLeod, D and Clarke, N (2009) Engaging for success: Enhancing performance through employee engagement: A report to government, https://dera.ioe.ac.uk/id/eprint/1810/1/file52215.pdf (archived at https://perma.cc/P2HW-JKVF)

Miller, R (2024) *Internal Communication Strategy: Design, develop and transform your organizational communication*, Kogan Page, London

Quirke, B (2008) *Making the Connections: Using internal communication to turn strategy into action*, Routledge, Abingdon

8

Work with your leaders

When crisis hits, every moment of leadership time becomes extra precious. Every one of the senior team will have to juggle multiple urgent and important demands, and they will have to prioritize a wide range of different tasks. As this happens, they might be tempted to push back on their internal communication responsibility and suggest to you that the internal communication team do what's required to keep people updated while they get their head down and concentrate on fixing the problem.

But the reality is that getting their heads down and retreating into a locked room is not a good option for crisis leaders, and neither is relying on others to take on their communication responsibilities. That's because crisis leadership is by its very nature a public thing, and it's because crisis leaders are constantly sending messages to their people whether they intend to or not.

Crises command attention, they spark interest, they attract questions and they provoke concern. And so, as your internal community look to their leaders for information, guidance and support, and for a sense of confidence, control or calm, everything those leaders say (or don't say) will be observed, analysed and interpreted for the conclusions that can be drawn.

This means that your organization can deliver beautifully crafted messages through state-of-the-art channels and tools, but if your leaders are not present and actively participating in the communication process, they'll be unable to secure the trust and confidence of their own people. And that means they'll be unable to secure the employee advocacy and support required to enact the best possible crisis response and strengthen for the future.

This chapter focuses on the vital communication roles and responsibilities of your most senior leaders and managers in times of crisis, and it explains how you can support them in their crisis leadership activity. The chapter begins by explaining what crisis leadership is and describes why communication is a key part of the crisis leadership role. It goes on to outline some key leadership communication responsibilities and it offers advice on how you can best work with your crisis leadership teams to help them succeed.

The central role of the crisis leader

In the simplest terms, crisis leadership sets the standards for the rest of the organization to follow under extreme pressure and in the most difficult of times. It is a responsibility that starts at the very top of the organizational hierarchy, but it can and should also be shared between all the people who are responsible for regions, functions and teams across the whole organization.

Experts such as James and Wooten (2005) argue that while there are overlaps, crisis leadership carries different demands both to daily leadership, and to crisis management, and that it requires different behaviours and a different mindset.

Across a sea of literature on the subject, common crisis leadership responsibilities include:

- crisis anticipation and scanning
- assessing and handling complex, harmful or ambiguous situations
- supporting the sensemaking process
- sharing critical crisis truths
- explaining and advocating for the crisis position
- charting a path out of crisis
- leveraging circumstances to help everyone learn, innovate and create positive change

Most experts agree that visible, decisive, adaptable, empathetic and optimistic leadership is important, and that poor leadership – which is essentially the opposite of all of this – almost always makes a bad situation worse. Many also agree that it must balance the need to be very directive and instructive to contain a potentially harmful crisis with the need to motivate, enable and empower different personalities through the challenge ahead.

All of this means that crisis leaders must take a tight central grip of management and communication at the point of crisis impact, and they must be very straightforward and directive as they set to stabilize the organization. From there, they must set a clear vision and direction, and they must begin to loosen their tight grip on management and communication and share control as they involve different experts and specialists to reimagine and recreate a stronger future.

Having spent three decades with the Federal Emergency Management Agency (FEMA) in the US, Ed Conley has led teams around the globe in response to some of recent history's most significant disasters – including 9/11, Hurricane Katrina, the 2010 Haiti Earthquake and the Deepwater Horizon oil spill. His book, *Promote the Dog Sitter: And other principles for leading during disaster* (2022), is about his personal experiences of crisis leadership, and when I ask him what makes a great crisis leader, he begins by saying something which deeply resonates: 'You want people who are not afraid of the moment. You want people who show up, step up, and take responsibility. You want people who are visible, who let you see instantly that they are there because they want to be there, and you want people who are ready and able to lead.'

It's a wonderful point which shows the clearest difference between brilliant crisis leaders and the ones that are found lacking – a desire to be there.

Lots of people have the intelligence to manage a crisis response, but the best leaders have something more. The best crisis leaders also confront the challenge and its opportunities with a will and an optimism to succeed that can be clearly seen and appreciated by everyone around them. Their commitment and enthusiasm to get things right is catching, and they leave their teams in no doubt that they are the best person for the job as they help others make sense of what has happened and set out to overcome the challenge they face.

Inspiring leaders ignite passion, action, trust and loyalty by acting with integrity and showing trust to others. They speak human to human and recognize that all their workforce has an important and valuable role to play as they pull the organization back into a stronger position.

- They take on a critical role as their organization's most prominent advocate and central source of crisis truth.
- They deliver meaning not just from what they say, but from what they do, and how they do it.
- They role model transparency, credibility, fairness, accountability, reliability, hope and optimism.
- They enable a network of specialists and experts from all parts of the organization to overcome complex problems and seize crisis opportunity.

Communication responsibilities

While different crises bring different demands, clear and trustworthy communication is a critical leadership responsibility. Internal crisis leadership communication generally involves regular, direct and transparent two-way communication that supports each of the 7S of internal crisis communication, first outlined in Chapter 2.

Flexible and adaptable approaches and styles resonate better with different employees in different situations, but difficult subjects must always be discussed, and internal crisis leadership communication usually involves:

- disclosing or promoting the crisis position and response
- creating a sense of security
- helping people make sense of the ongoing situation
- directing and instructing people towards key tasks and objectives
- setting out a vision for the future
- listening, demonstrating learning and implementing change
- recognizing everyone in the role that they play
- demonstrating integrity and inspiring employee trust, advocacy and support

Because crises bring disruption and a sense of shock and uncertainty which can potentially stop people from functioning at their best, the ability to help employees make sense of the situation and instil a level of stability is key. That means that crisis leaders must be aware of all the facts and all the emotions involved in a situation as they help everyone think more rationally, participate more effectively and contribute more meaningfully.

Derek Provan OBE is a non-executive director and business adviser who has led his colleagues through extreme weather, technological breakdowns, aircraft incidents and terror attacks during a 25-year career in the aviation industry. In recent years, he was Chief Operating Officer at London's Heathrow Airport and Chief Executive Officer at AGS Airports in Scotland. He has been a board member at NATS, and he has advised on security in UK aviation at the highest levels. He tells me that crisis leaders must balance the need to deliver directive instruction with the need to carefully listen, involve and recognize people as part of a collective effort:

> Crisis leadership demands that you set a vision and lead from the front, but it also demands that you do this without ego, and you do it without defence.

Dealing with crisis is a collective effort, so while there are times when the leader must be very specific and directive, the ultimate goal is to create an environment where everyone feels ownership for solving the crisis, and where everyone can bring forward solutions, regardless of who they are or where they are in the organization.

This means the leader must foster and role model an environment where everyone can share their views quickly and without fear, especially if they have different perspectives on the task ahead. The leader must hear different views, and they must be encompassing, inclusive and responsive as they make decisions.

As they start to see success, the leader must recognize everyone for the contribution they have made. It doesn't matter whether colleagues are doing a media interview, helping a customer or fixing a machine – everyone feels the same pressure during a crisis. Each person walks away feeling they went above and beyond, so the leader must acknowledge that effort. You don't have to name individuals, but recognizing roles helps people heal, builds goodwill and creates a sense of unity in the organization.

If things are handled and communicated well, the goodwill can last for months, and in environments where crises occur regularly, like airports, each well-handled situation builds trust in the process. Team members come to recognize they're part of the solution, not the problem, and by doing this again and again, the leader helps the organization become stronger.

Role modelling responsibilities

As people across the organization look to their leaders for information, guidance and support, they will observe, analyse and interpret everything those leaders say and do while they make sense of the crisis and form an opinion about what is happening, why, and with what effects. Every formal and informal interaction they have with the top team will shape how your people think and feel about what's going on and why, and every thought and feeling will shape what they say and do next.

This means that if they want to secure the support necessary to effectively confront the crisis, your senior leaders must set the standard. They must be consistently visible throughout the organization, they must walk the talk, and they must consider the intended and unintended impacts of their words and behaviour. In everything they say and do, they should consider how they can evidence integrity; how they can demonstrate the 5 Cs of concern, commitment, confidence, competence and credibility; and how they must speak with empathy and compassion as they hear and play back the things that matter to their teams at each different crisis stage.

Actions speak far louder than words, so if they ask for honesty, they must be honest themselves; if they ask for trust they must show trust; and if they ask people to go the extra mile to support the organization, they must be seen to do this too. They must lead by example and show a crisis understanding and values system that resonates with the wider team, shows their own personal will to succeed and encourages others to follow them. At all times, they must understand, live up to and evidence the standards they ask of others, and they must lead from the front as they role model the values and behaviours they wish to see reflected back at them.

Great crisis role models are competent, visible and active. They are aware of their responsibility, and they are intentional in their efforts to create a culture that will help and enable their people from the earliest crisis warning and all the way back to business recovery and business as usual. They are unafraid to roll up their sleeves and offer clear instruction or direction, yet they are also interested in, and responsive to, everyone around them. They are quick to praise the team and can confidently defer to the expertise of others as they hear different crisis views. They lead with empathy, know what their people want and need from them and they play this back with action as well as with words to leave people in no doubt that they are ready, willing and able to help the whole organization meet the challenge ahead.

Support your leaders

Some people have an instinct for crisis leadership and communication. They thrive in the moment and may even tell you that overcoming a challenge energizes them and makes them feel happy. They have a passion for their organization, a love for their people and a charisma that's evident to all.

Other people can be well-intentioned but need more help because they haven't had the necessary training, because their instincts are not quite as well-developed, because they find it harder to step out of their bubble and relate to other experiences, or because their priorities and values simply are not aligned with those of their people.

Anyone who has worked with them knows that a crisis leader who is not physically, psychologically, emotionally or ethically present will always struggle. But with the right attitude, a lot of planning, preparation and training, many crisis obstacles can be overcome. The internal communication professional is not ultimately responsible for the success or failure of the company's leadership team. But when your leadership teams are willing to work with you, they make your job 100 times easier, and you in turn can offer them extremely helpful support and advice.

Advising leadership is a task that requires tact and objectivity as well as a high level of mutual trust, and your role is to hold a mirror to the organization, to reflect on leadership strengths and to bring concerns to the table as you help to co-create a way forward.

You need to help your leaders see how their words and actions will be interpreted by their employees and explain how experience and attitude affect how people will respond, then from there you need to help your leaders decide what to do and say to achieve their established goals at each stage of the crisis, and you need to put in place the strategy, support and resources they need to do this well.

Help them self-manage

When crisis strikes, the most senior leader must stand at the front of the organization, establish themselves in the role and confirm their legitimacy and authority to lead. Their ability to do this will of course depend a lot on what they say, how quickly they say it and the location they say it from, but it will also depend on how they present themselves in that moment.

That means if your leaders seem hesitant or afraid to get out into the real world, you need to tell them what people will think. If they lash out, languish in their own emotion or let anger get the better of them, you need to tell them how people will feel. If they joke under pressure, you need to tell them how that will be remembered. And if they demand accountability from colleagues while failing to admit their own mistakes, you need to tell them what people will do.

Dr Jacqueline Conway is a Founder and Managing Director of Waldencroft, a consulting practice based in Edinburgh, Scotland. She's also a consultant, adviser and coach who works internationally with developmentally progressive CEOs and their teams to cultivate their leadership. She says:

> We've all been in the situation where you walk into a meeting with a particular leader, and you see they just suck all energy and enthusiasm out of the room. Their negativity spreads, the mood drops and they create a contagion.

And if we've all seen it, then we all know it is possible for one individual's emotion or behaviour to have a significant impact on a group of people. So one of the things that we need leaders to do in a crisis then, is to do the opposite and create contagion in a positive way. To push energy and enthusiasm into the room.

It's not just about what they say, it's what they embody, it's what they represent. It's what they role model as they carry out the leadership duties. And that matters not just in crisis, but all the time. So leaders must prepare in advance to understand their role during a crisis, recognizing that people will rely on them to take action and communicate in ways that create community and a sense of being in it together.

As well as that, they need to be able to manage themselves well, and they need to be able to manage their own fight, flight or freeze mode so from the first moments, they are not contributing to the chaos, they are contributing to the clarity.

The internal communication professional can help them with this by establishing a trusted relationship early on and by preparing for crisis with them so that they are ready and able to quickly make sense of the difficult situation and lead from the moment it hits.

If they are having a wobble, which as human beings they very well might do, the role of the internal communicator is to create the safe space where they can talk everything out before they go out there. And that's not to say they need to remove all the vulnerability. To be vulnerable in a crisis is OK. But there's a sweet spot in the middle because they also need to get it together and show confidence, competence and control.

If you can tactfully and objectively help your leaders reflect on how what they say and do is perceived by others, they will be better able to self-manage. They will find it easier to align their words and actions with their intentions and avoid mixed or confusing messages, and they will also be able to build the support around them that will complement their strengths and support them in their weakness for the benefit of the whole organization.

Help them develop their leadership style

While we have established that the best leaders are visible, decisive, adaptable, compassionate and optimistic, each crisis leader's management style is unique, and that is a good thing because it brings diversity to the highest levels of different organizations.

As long as they are not using the guise of a quirky character or backstory to cause harm or shirk responsibility, a leader's ability and confidence to know and show their own truth can make them more authentic and more compelling. Being honest about their own failures and struggles as well as their successes and strengths can create a greater sense of psychological safety. It can signal to others what behaviours are acceptable in the organization, and it can also help them connect with their own values system and make good decisions when everything feels overwhelming and unclear.

Global crisis communication consultant and trainer Piyali Mandal is the Founder and CEO of The Media Coach and a specialist in reputational, operational and cybersecurity crisis based in Mumbai, India, and she has trained hundreds of senior leaders from a wide mix of international companies and brands. She tells me:

> Great leaders are authentic; they have their own playbook. They have their own unique approach to decision-making, and they know how to use the vocabulary that really connects to their own value compass, and helps them connect with their own values system.
>
> That's very important for a leader to have, because when a crisis feels overwhelming, it's your inner value system and that compass that will direct you to what you can do, what is right for you, what is right for your organization.
>
> So as a leader, some of the key things that you need to do is ask if you know the value system of your organization and if it aligns with your own value system, and you need to be able to play that back to your staff in everything that you say and do.

You can help your leader articulate their value system by discussing how different words and actions fit with the leaders' personal expectations, with the expectations of their employees, and with the more formal rules and guidance that are in place to help them.

When there is a need to share difficult news or communicate tough decisions you can coach them in the use of the CARE (concern, action, reassurance) formula and the five Cs (concern, commitment, confidence, competence and credibility) of crisis communication as discussed in Chapter 6, and you can encourage them to take a more compassionate approach to communication by expressing their awareness of the challenge, setting inspirational but achievable and realistic goals, and expressing hope and optimism for the challenge ahead.

Help them be situationally aware

Some leaders are really creative. They see horizons and boundaries differently to other people. They get excited about quick wins, possibility and the many new ideas that come their way. They may pop into situations, grab an idea, make a suggestion and pop back out again. That's helpful when there is a need to test, create and innovate at pace, but it can also complicate an already volatile and ambiguous situation, or it can come across as ill-judged and opportunistic when it's not anchored in practical or emotional reality.

Big asks and grand visions need to be grounded in the reality of the crisis, the resources available, and in an understanding of what already overstretched people can further tolerate, and this means leaders need to know when an innocent comment or a well-intentioned ask could push their teams past their emotional, psychological or physical limit and backfire.

Great leaders understand their organizations, they get out and work alongside their teams and they seek to hear different views because they recognize that not everyone sees the world as they do, and they realize they need to base decisions on proper insight so they can change tactics if people aren't warming to or joining in with their plans.

You can help your leaders become more situationally aware through the crisis planning, anticipation and understanding of processes discussed in Chapters 3, 4 and 5, by establishing relevant channels for leaders to listen, monitor sentiment, hear different perspectives and collect good ideas as discussed in Chapter 10, and through the measurement and evaluation techniques discussed in Chapter 12.

You can also share your own honest and open observations with them and discuss what you learn as you help them further shape internal messages, activity and plans.

Help them be visible

In earlier chapters we established the importance of stealing thunder, and the need for people to hear crisis news from the company before they hear it elsewhere. In fact, the ideal scenario if you want to quickly build trust and stabilize is that people don't just hear about the crisis from the company – but they hear it from the person in charge, and that applies to all forms of big news.

Beyond that, people want to respond and feed back their own views on this information, so knowing that the top team are out and about, observing and responding to the reality of the situation and listening to different views can not only help them feel more calm and secure but it can also boost engagement and morale.

Lucy Easthope is a global disaster responder and author who has advised on everything from the 2004 Boxing Day tsunami and the 7/7 bombings to the Grenfell fire in London and war in Ukraine. She says:

> Sometimes the senior team think they are getting out and about, but people don't register that because they don't know who they are, or they miss them because it is not their day on shift or because they don't see them and the moment is lost.

> That means you need to let people know they are there. You need to jazz it up a bit. Have them wearing the lanyard, have them in the gilet. People need to know that they're there and they need to know what they've done and what they've seen and heard. It's not about the photo shoot, it's about the support they are there to offer to their teams.

You can help your leaders to become more accessible to the internal community, coach them to play to their strengths and offer them relevant and regular point-to-point, face-to-face and digital communication channels that they will want to use in a range of different situations.

Walk around the organization with them and put an official programme of drop-in sessions in place. Make sure they visit colleagues in the worst-affected departments and locations first, and make sure they interact with real people. Help them offer sensemaking and support to those on the frontline, and if this can't be done physically then ensure there are online opportunities to connect instead.

Talk about leadership roadshows or visits in other communication channels before and afterwards, and encourage leaders to mention what they have done, seen or heard in their regular messages to the company so that if people missed them, they would still know they were there, and they will know what was done and discussed.

Help them be inclusive

Build in lots of opportunities for company leaders to engage with people inside the organization as well as to get out and about more generally. As they get out and about, help them leave their comfort zone and speak to lots of different individuals.

Sometimes a leader will know one or two people in the operation and will refer to them constantly as they seek to understand the voice of the troops. That's better than nothing, but it doesn't really give them an insight into the full diversity of views within the organization, and sometimes it may even confirm bias and assumptions that are already in place.

Crisis leadership is all about seeing different perspectives, recognizing different skills and expertise, and encouraging collaboration among diverse groups and internal crisis communication can play a role in many ways.

As you get out and about with your leadership team, tell them how much people are enjoying seeing them, and play back to them what you found interesting or valuable about the experience. Ask simple reflective questions such as: *Did you manage to hear different voices today? What did you hear today that surprised you? What did you think of that meeting? How do you think we can build all these ideas or feedback into our decision-making? And what do you think we should do to increase our visibility further?*

If the experience has been challenging, and people are angry, encourage all your top team to consider why other views might be legitimate, coach them to understand other emotions while managing their own and agree how the organization might show greater compassion.

Help them inspire

Remind your leaders of the need to create a collective sense of hope and possibility, and explain to them to do this best, their internal communication must be specifically tailored to the wants and needs of the internal audience, as well as to the demands of the crisis as it evolves through different stages and that key behaviours must be role modelled from the top.

Talk to them about the need to be explicit and direct when this is required, give them the tools to ask questions and create conversation at other points. Work with them to present a clear and inspiring vision of the future and help them evidence and demonstrate strength and adaptability when setbacks occur.

Encourage leaders to take responsibility for their own actions, to communicate with compassion, and to show how they are adhering to their own personal values as well as the rules and policies in place to guide them, and look at different ways in which they can encourage and enable others to contribute and grow.

Help them learn

As well as challenge, crises bring opportunity for growth, innovation and strengthened relationships, so help your leaders explore the crisis without judgement or defence and encourage them to play back what went well and what went badly so that the whole organization can learn and implement lessons for the future. We will talk more about this in Chapter 12.

Help yourself

To have a full impact on the organization, experts such as Quirke (2008) advise that internal communication and its strategy must have full support of the board. To support them best, this means that you need to know your leaders well and importantly, they need to know, like you, trust you, and sponsor and commit to your plans. Achieving this means building a close and positive relationship with them in stable times, discussing your strategies and agreeing clear internal crisis communication expectations and objectives with them from the outset.

Get to know all the different personalities, so you can influence, persuade or satisfy them appropriately, and make sure that anyone who is asking you for advice or allocating you tasks knows who you are, what you do and the value you bring. Ask organizational administrators to make sure your name is on the right distribution lists, and that you are included in important face-to-face or digital meetings, so that you are front of mind from the outset.

Leadership coach and consultant Dr Jacqueline Conway says:

> One of the most important things you can do to prepare for success is to build your own personal credibility as a strategic adviser and helpful support to the senior leaders and crisis managers in the organization. That means when the crisis hits and you walk into the room, all the key people think 'Thank goodness you're here' rather than 'Who are you?' or 'Why are you here?' If you can do that, you are already on the front foot.

> Establish your value early by building positive relationships with everyone you'll be expected to support. Evidence your track record, ability, trustworthiness, judgement and reliability in the organization, and be explicit in your understanding of what your company leaders want to achieve and how you can provide support.

> Make sure that internal crisis communication plans and policies are explicit about the role and necessity of crisis leadership communication and make sure that once you have their support, you also do the necessary early preparation with the senior team in a safe space so that they are ready and able to lead from the moment a crisis hits.

Discuss how different messages and behaviours will be received and encourage senior leaders to practice speaking to the internal audience as they do for external stakeholders.

As you advise, remember that you are there because you have value to add. Show that you understand the company and that you understand the crisis. Listen to the conversation, ask relevant questions and share your observations and expertise. Be clear how your advice will help the organization to achieve crisis goals.

Sharing your thoughts and observations, especially when the situation is volatile or when the feedback is negative can be challenging so be clear about what you're there to do, and how you can help. Be honest and open, use the language and communication style that resonate with the leaders you are talking to, bearing in mind that their organizational reality is different to yours, and so you might need to explain background or experiences they have not previously encountered.

Listen to what they say, focus your advice on the strategic priorities they care about most in that moment, and back up your arguments with real-time data and actionable insights. Don't just tell your leaders what they want to hear, but at the same time, avoid presenting problems without observations or potential solutions if you can. Instead, offer ideas and suggestions that are appropriate in context of the crisis and that align with wider crisis management and organizational goals.

As you advise, take comfort in the fact that if your leaders are asking questions, it's because they are interested and invested in what you have to say. By listening to them and incorporating their ideas, you'll demonstrate that you're working towards shared objectives, and you'll be more likely to secure their commitment to your plans.

KEY TAKEAWAYS

- Great leadership is vital in times of crisis and many people believe it's the single most important element in whether an organization will fail, or whether it will come out stronger.

- Internal communication professionals have a vital role in supporting organizational leaders to communicate regularly and consistently to engage, empower and enable their colleagues and to help build the necessary trust, advocacy and support across the whole organization.

- Crisis leadership is different to normal leadership and internal crisis leadership communication is different too.

- Leaders are critical role models and influencers who need to know that saying nothing sends a powerful negative message. That means they must be visible, they must lead from the front, and they must create the time to prioritize regular and direct two-way communication with the whole of their internal community throughout the whole of the crisis.

- Internal communications professionals have a vital role in supporting internal crisis leadership communication, but work needs to begin early, and trusted relationships need to be in place before the crisis hits.

- Internal communications professionals can help their leadership teams by advising on strategy, advising on messaging, holding up a mirror to behaviour, and supplying the tools and communications infrastructure they need to do the job.

- You can also help them self-manage, develop their leadership style, be situationally aware, visible, inclusive and inspirational, and you can help them continue to learn.

- The secret to success is to build a long-term relationship with leaders in stable times, to evidence your value, and to set clear internal crisis communication objectives with them from the outset

References

Conley, E (2022) *Promote the Dog Sitter: And other principles for leading during disaster*, Lioncrest, Nevada, US

James, E and Wooten, L (2005) Leadership as (un)usual: How to display competence in times of crisis, *Organizational Dynamics*, 34 (2), 141–52, https://jamesandwooten.com/wp-content/uploads/2020/04/Leadership-as-unusual-Org-Dyn.pdf (archived at https://perma.cc/F3N5-SMD6)

Quirke, B (2008) *Making the Connections: Using internal communication to turn strategy into action*, Routledge, London

9

Support your line managers

While leaders map the route out of crisis, it's line managers who keep everyone on track. They are daily leaders, influencers and role models, and their impact at every stage, from pre-crisis to crisis management, business continuity and business recovery cannot be underestimated.

That's not just because their direct understanding of daily workflow and operations gives them a detailed understanding of crisis opportunity and challenges, it's also because they sit right at the heart of all human connection in the organization and whether they engage face-to-face, on the phone or through a digital platform, they can foster the genuine connection, understanding and real-time responses that other methods simply can't replicate.

As the main bond between employees and organization, managers know the human beings in the company better than anyone else. They know their strengths and weaknesses, they know their aspirations and frustrations, and they understand the real-world possibilities and setbacks their teams face every single day.

In many ways, they define the reality of the organization. They have the power to make or break every single day, and their active support is essential if the organization is to build meaningful, trusted relationships in stable times, and if it is to provide the emotional, psychological and practical support necessary to help people survive, thrive and deliver what the company needs through every crisis stage.

Yet despite their importance, we know that across all industries and around the globe, managers are squeezed, stressed and poorly supported, with heavy pressure exerted on them from both above and below. To meet their crisis potential, they need help and support from company leaders. And they need help and support from internal communication professionals too.

This chapter highlights the critical role of line managers in internal crisis communication. It explains how the line management community is uniquely placed to deliver the close, personal and credible communication that's required when crisis hits; it explains how managers meet a range of different emotional, psychological and practical crisis needs; and it describes how they are the vital link that enables information to flow up, down and around all parts of the organization in a meaningful way. To best support them, the chapter suggests you must think intentionally about where they will and won't add value to the organization's internal crisis communication activity, and you must give them the time, tools, training and trust needed to properly do the job.

The critical role of line managers

Line managers are all the people with a direct managerial responsibility for others in the organization. They exist in all departments, regions and levels of the hierarchy, from the C-suite through to supervisors and team leaders. Their role involves planning, leading and enabling day-to-day activities and it also involves supporting their team's personal needs and development, so they play a vital role in meeting each of the 7S of internal crisis communication (surviving, supporting, sensemaking, stabilizing, stimulating, sustaining and strengthening needs) identified in Chapter 2. They can make or break a colleague's day, they can make or break a colleague's career, and they can also make or break the organization's crisis response.

Anyone who has done the job knows it's not always easy – there's a delicate balance to be achieved in keeping employees motivated, engaged and productive. Lots of people get it wrong, and that's an issue that needs to be tackled. But the ones who get it right can deliver extraordinary and occasionally life-changing impacts for their people, for their teams and for their organizations.

Wigert and Maese (2019) perfectly capture their value when they describe managers as:

> The bridge between leadership's vision and the hard realities of the front line. They are often your most committed employees, and they can also be your best critics – providing valuable feedback that moves the organization forward while avoiding roadblocks and blind alleys. Great managers help their leaders make better decisions while helping employees understand organizational dynamics and making them feel like valuable contributors to an important mission.

When a crisis strikes, a company's line managers may be physically, intellectually and emotionally closer to the action than the senior leadership team, and this means they fully understand the challenge, they fully understand the opportunity and they fully understand the impact. They are best placed to feed analysis, advice and information in different directions around the organization, and they are best placed to personalize and translate complex messages for very diverse and decentralized groups of people.

Communication is in their DNA, yet many organizations fail to empower and support their management community in their crisis communication role and focus on the mass distribution of company-wide messages and statements instead.

That's a mistake when you consider that engaging managers are one of MacLeod and Clarke's four enablers of employee engagement (2009), and when you reflect upon research by academics such as Mazzei and Ravazzani (2011) who observed that employees can find hierarchical and formal crisis communication to be distant and cold, and they can see the central distribution of written content to be a tactic to avoid discussion about the more ambiguous and difficult aspects of the situation.

Simple, consistent and centrally led content is of course necessary for all the reasons previously discussed in this book, and it's particularly important in the earliest moments of crisis when the key points need to be communicated to everyone, at the same time and in the same way. But the research tells us that the central message is not enough on its own, and it must be supported by something more personal and contextual if it is to fully satisfy and meet different needs – particularly in large, diverse and dispersed organizations where a level of explanation and interpretation is needed, and where mutual trust and understanding is strongest at a local level.

More than almost any other organizational content, internal crisis communication must be human-focused and user-centred. It must address the fundamental questions *What does it mean to me?*, *Am I safe here?* and *What can/must I do now?*, and it must offer instant opportunity for clarification if that is needed.

Internal communication consultant and business owner Katie Marlow explains how a well-intentioned central message can cause stress rather than soothe when it is not backed up and reinforced by something more tailored and personal:

> Employees get really frustrated when they consistently receive messages that don't feel tailored to their unique needs. Across the company, you have different people, with a different perspective on what's happening, and different needs from crisis communication.

When crisis news feels impersonal, it doesn't build trust or the will to address the challenge. In fact, what it does is quite the opposite – it distances people, it makes them care less, and it makes them less inclined to say and do what's required.

If you want it to connect, you need to be more personal, more contextual, and you need to recognize that your managers play a crucial role in passing on or interpreting the message, clarifying and reinforcing the key points, and bringing it to life for wider discussion.

Bill Quirke (2008) is a leading global authority on internal communication. His writing emphasizes that communication is not just about sharing information, but also about encouraging collaboration, co-creation and shared meaning across all levels of an organization. Quirke says managers have a critical role to play in this, not just because they create understanding, but because they create value by putting big-picture information in context. The manager's role, he says, is 'less about instructions and directing, and more about making interconnections clear, engaging colleagues to identify issues and working together to solve them.'

In a time where digital communication and remote working and the use of AI is common, organizations still depend on human interaction to properly function. Every social connection has an impact, and properly tailored one-to-one communication is valued. High-quality human relationships and a sense of formal and informal togetherness are critical to building trusting relationships, and they are necessary to avoid workplace isolation, cynicism and even paranoia, especially when people are shocked, traumatized or afraid.

Good line managers are uniquely positioned to identify, understand and resolve brewing misunderstanding in their teams. They can foster warm and meaningful relationships that help regulate emotions and move people out of their fight, flight or freeze crisis response; and they can interpret and explain crisis impacts and recovery in a trustworthy and credible way which makes direct personal sense and resonates more deeply with their people.

Their power is real, and their role is essential as HR strategist Marion Anderson explains. Marion is Founder and Chief Executive of The Fearless PX. Now based in Arkansas, US, she has led people functions for corporations including Apple and IKEA across three continents, and speaking from her own crisis experience, she tells me:

In any workplace crisis, line managers or shift leaders are usually first on the scene. They arrive well before senior leaders arrive, and they stay long after the leaders leave. They are a vital link in the organizations, and they are so important in challenging times.

When managers build strong, trusting relationships and create a sense of psychological safety in their teams, they are better placed to offer people the personal support that they need, they are better placed to share useful information smoothly in both directions, and they are better placed to ensure big picture vision is informed by frontline demands and vice versa.

Ultimately, a manager's role in a crisis depends on trust and psychological safety. When a manager knows their team members well, and vice versa, everyone feels like they're in safe hands. This 'credit in the bank' of trust makes navigating a crisis smoother, more confident and more compassionate for everyone involved.

Meeting emotional needs

In any type of crisis, people will feel many different emotions, and they will have many different experiences. Even if they are not directly exposed to trauma, they will feel uncertain and insecure and will require one-on-one support and care to increase their crisis wellbeing, especially if they have other difficulties in their lives and at work.

To survive and thrive, the internal community will rely on high-quality, meaningful human relationships and human connections. They will need the ability to offload and be heard in a safe space, and they will need the ability to talk or simply be with people who they know, who care about them, and who have shared the same experience.

You can't expect any human being to deal with the shock and confusion that a crisis brings and then pack up and go home as normal, because regardless of crisis type, people need help from trusted and influential managers to process and make sense of what has happened so they can continue to function well in the organization and can turn up and deal with the crisis again the next day.

A personal conversation needs to take place to help people engage on a deeper level, and from the manager's perspective, it might be as much about watching, listening and picking up on behaviour, body language and tone of voice as it is about passing content on. It is also about letting the team know it's OK to not be OK. It's about using words and actions to show them that they are safe, they are supported and that everyone will work together to help each other – and it's about pointing them towards other important sources of crisis truth, support and assistance inside the team, and inside the organization.

Managers play a key role in building close human connection and responding to emotion in their teams before, during and after crisis. They have a critical role in listening, understanding capability, demonstrating empathy and compassion, supporting physical, mental and emotional wellbeing and referring people for additional assistance and support if this is needed.

Crisis communication consultant, trainer and author Amanda Coleman explains:

> Before you can do anything else, you need to understand how people are feeling. You need to step out of the corporate cape, recognize what's actually there and connect as humans. You can't fight emotion with facts. And if you think you can go into an emotional, distressing situation and give people a bank of facts thinking they'll accept it and perform at their peak, then you are mistaken.

By accepting, understanding, acknowledging and responding to a wide range of emotion, managers can help people feel valued and cared for. Through words and actions, they can help soothe distress after trauma. They can be alert to those who need extra help, and they can be subtle and informal as they build the trust and confidence needed for different personalities to move forward, go back into the world and participate in the crisis response or business recovery.

Because of their closeness to the individuals in the organization, managers are also uniquely placed to recognize that their team's feelings are not linear, and that different people will have different needs at different times.

They may recognize that feelings go up and down as new information becomes available and new milestones are reached. They may recognize passions, fears, frustrations, disengagement, burnout and emotional triggers that central functions don't see. They may know what information is easier to process and what creates overwhelm when it's not broken down into messages that are easier to understand and to act on.

Importantly, they can take this insight and feed it back through the organization to make sure that central messages and activities are acceptable and resonate effectively, and they can use it to give people the individual support they need, as HR strategist Marion Anderson explains:

> Effective managers understand emotion. They understand how each team member prefers to be communicated with, and they tailor their approach

accordingly. For example, if they know one team member feels anxious, a manager might adjust their approach, tone and task allocation to be extra reassuring while at the same time recognizing a different team member needs only the go-ahead and support to get on with the job at hand. Senior leaders often don't have these close, personal insights into how each of the different teams work, and that makes it even more important for managers to act as this bridge when sensitivity and compassion is required.

Meeting psychological needs

Psychological needs can relate to our ability to process and make sense of the situation, and they can relate to our ability to stabilize and become re-engaged in a sense of purpose as we begin to tackle the task at hand; so again, line managers play a critical role in not just echoing the central message, but in offering clarity and meeting different internal crisis communication needs in a meaningful and actionable way.

Carolyn Bowick led the marketing and communication team responsible for communicating with 3,600 'behind-the-scenes' employees at NHS National Services Scotland (NSS) as Covid-19 hit in 2020. Carolyn's colleagues were responsible for everything from sourcing and supplying PPE, to managing the technology that would enable the vaccine roll-out and taking care of the logistics, planning and set up of a temporary Covid-19 hospital. She tells me that the line manager community held a vital role in interpreting and making sense of the central message:

> In an organization like NSS where you have a diverse mix of teams, line managers are crucial for giving a local context to central information. This was even more important in the early days of Covid-19 because our people had such a critical role in supporting the wider health service through a situation that was still very unclear. It was not a time to miss the mark, and while the general public was out on the doorsteps clapping the frontline heroes of the NHS, our teams needed relatable, actionable information together with a clear understanding of how their work was also recognized and valued.
>
> Those of us crafting content from the safety of a bedroom or a dining room were aware of the need to talk meaningfully to our operational colleagues. Take somebody who's working overtime picking things off the shelf in the procurement warehouse, for example. How can we reach those people and how do we talk to them about the things that they want and need? It's not just normal comms, there's also an emotional and psychological need to think

about when people are so exhausted and overwhelmed. They need simple tailored guidance around where they fit in and what they must do; and they need answers, or at least the chance to chat through questions like: What's happening? Am I going to be OK? Is my family going to be OK? Am I safe here? Am I valued? And so on.

Line managers were crucial in taking key central messages, tailoring them to meet their own local context and turning them into conversations that would give them relevance. We encouraged and supported them to be open, we let them know it was OK not to have all the answers and we asked them to tell us if they felt our central messages were not hitting the mark. We encouraged them to gather and return feedback, and we empowered them to deliver the key message in a way that would work for them, and their people so we could cater to a full range of needs.

Meeting practical needs

Managers are also best placed to help people complete the work necessary to stimulate, sustain and strengthen the business continuity and recovery processes at the local level. In this sense, their role is to make sure people are aware of all the latest information and resources, to offer clear guidance and instruction, to help people to explore and fix problems, and to enable and empower them to get on with the job while quickly passing all necessary insight and ideas from the frontline back up the hierarchy and elsewhere.

As they carry out this critical role, they can meet very specific team needs in a way that central communication cannot, and so they must be helped to add this value. Rather than forwarding information, they should be supported and enabled to become the curators and translators of information, and the co-creators and facilitators of the conversation. They must be allowed to gather and pinpoint what is most interesting and important about the key message for their team, to offer their own insight, and to create an environment where people can chat openly about crisis experiences and learning as they come to better understand how their daily work contributes and adds value to the wider crisis response.

Importantly, line managers can also role model and enable expected behaviours by making sure people continue with skills development and professional growth, helping people to monitor and manage their workloads, offering flexible working or paid time off to those who need it, and facilitate team-building activities and a collaborative work environment.

All of this enables people to play to their strengths and support one another, and it also helps them understand what actions and behaviours are expected as the crisis moves from stage to stage, as HR strategist Marion Anderson explains:

> Employees often look to their managers for cues on how to react in uncertain situations, especially if it's their first time facing a crisis. A manager who stays calm, confident and compassionate signals to the team that everything is under control, which not only reassures and enables them but also sets an example for how to handle the situation, while a manager who is visibly distressed or absent will leave the team feeling lost and unsupported with potentially devastating wider effect.

Feeding back

Finally, line managers have a significant role when it comes to listening, understanding and interpreting what's happening in every nook and cranny of the organization and feeding this information back up through the hierarchy.

Listening across the whole company is not just helpful, it's essential for many reasons, as we will learn in Chapter 10. Specifically in this instance it helps gather the intelligence and understanding necessary to check if the centrally crafted messages are resonating and hitting the mark, or if they need to be tweaked or altered for better effect. It's also important to empower the most efficient and effective crisis response, and to get a diverse mixture of people involved in gathering information and discussing what's going right, what's going wrong and what must happen next.

Managers recognize and understand changing questions, emotions, behaviours and trends in the organization, perhaps before anyone else. And they see important strengths, weaknesses, opportunities and threats that can inform crisis communication and crisis response.

This means that great managers don't just collect questions, they collect ideas, suggestions and challenges and then they interpret, translate and feed these back through the hierarchy to those people with the authority and resources to enact them in a meaningful and compelling way.

Help your line manager community

While your managers have a significant role in passing crisis information forwards and receiving it back, they are not a communication channel to be switched on and off at will. If you want them to succeed, you must:

- think intentionally about where they will and won't add value
- give them the content to do the job
- explain why they play a critical role
- help them to communicate to the best of their capability

In the first instance, that means deciding which messages and resources will benefit from manager support and interpretation, and which won't – either because they cannot be modified or distorted in any way, or because the burden created by tailoring and modification outweighs the value gained at such a critical time.

Everyone has different emotional, intellectual and physical limitations – so if a fast, factual and undiluted message is required, then it may be better to deliver it point-to-point – direct from the senior leader via face-to-face gathering, online platform, video, podcast, email or text.

But if there's space or necessity for tailoring and interpretation, then you must make sure the content is useful, easy to understand and easy to share; and you must give all managers the time to absorb what they are being asked to deliver, and let them deliver it at the time (within reason) and on the terms that best suits their team.

If communication experience doesn't work for them, they can't make it work for others. And if a briefing feels like an unnecessary or overly complicated piece of corporate puff at a time when there's critical work to be done, it will go to the bottom of the to-do list and stay there. HR strategist Marion Anderson explains:

> They are not mind readers and they have an awful lot else going on, so you need to make the briefing experience work for them. Think about the content and the process from their perspective. How can they pass on information when they have been given nothing specific, meaningful or useful to interpret or share? How can they engage others if they have not been engaged themselves? How can they offer support when they are feeling alone and unsupported themselves?

> When crisis strikes, your managers will feel a huge amount of pressure from either side, so they need more, not less, leadership and communication support than many of your other internal stakeholders.

If you need them to say or do something, you must explain this to them and you must make sure they feel safe, supported and certain in their communications role. You must be clear what, when and how, and you must check if that is possible and acceptable within the current context. Be clear what you expect from them, when and why – then give them time to process, question and interpret information before passing it on.

Let your managers know what other sources of information are available to them and their teams. Point them to the organization's trusted sources of truth, support and assistance, and allow them to discuss, challenge and co-create or lead the message where they have a greater understanding of what their own people want and need.

Give them time

Time is one of the most valuable resources available to any of us, and in crisis it's in very short supply. This means that all too often, managers are asked to come out in front of their teams and deliver a PowerPoint presentation they've received two minutes earlier, and never seen before. And like a rabbit in the spotlight, they read the presentation in front of their people, and they add nothing.

If they are not adding anything, or if the message is too urgent to be cascaded, they don't need to be doing it. But if they do need to be doing it, you need to build in the time for them to understand the message, to process the content, to prepare to discuss it, and to organize and hold the conversation. You can help them by:

- telling them in advance when a message is expected for onward distribution
- committing to an embargo system that gives them time to process and prepare
- being mindful of time zones, shift patterns and flexible working agreements
- building communication time and space into the working day

Remember that managers will be processing and making sense of the situation too, and they will need time to talk about what's happening and ask questions of their own before they pass any information on. In these circumstances, offer the opportunity for them to get together physically or virtually to receive the briefing themselves and to:

- share experience and ideas for delivery

- co-create content and FAQ
- discuss what further help and support is required

Give them tools

Everyone needs the right tools to do the job, and internal communication consultant and business owner Katie Marlow says this means you must give line managers the context, key messages, updates, facts and figures, milestones, templates and guidelines necessary not just to pass on a message, but to talk about it too.

> Give them the information they need to share the message and to engage their colleagues to discuss it further. Help them identify issues, join up dots and work together to solve problems. Give them the talking points, conversation starters and questions needed to discuss the details that matter most to them. Help them to have grown-up, meaningful conversations that make people feel safe, supported, willing and able to overcome the challenge ahead.

And remember that as well as the central message, you also need to give managers tailored internal information to help them have real-world conversations as well. Internal communication consultant and trainer Dan Holden reflected on his own experience in dealing with crises in the aviation and manufacturing industries as he told me:

> After something has gone wrong, once they have had official notification, your employees will be thinking: What does this mean for me? Will I be based in a different location? Will I need to focus on different tasks? Do I need to make arrangements for my kids because we're now in crisis mode and working late?
>
> It's important to build in what managers need to be able to answer these practical questions, and it's important to help them have an ongoing conversation. So, after 48 hours, when everyone is exhausted, how do we help managers cope with changing needs? What about business continuity? Disruption to schedules? Shifting priorities? To the outside world, the crisis may be over, but inside, people are still dealing with the knock-on effects. As communicators, we need to ensure they have what they need to guide their teams effectively.

Help your line managers by:

- putting technology in place to stay in touch with remote colleagues
- making budget and facilities available for people to gather in person as required

- giving them official messages and practical answers
- giving them guidelines for facilitating respectful conversations
- offering a mix of supporting and engaging one-and two-way channels and resources to lighten the load – such as newsletters, leaflets, videos, webinars, podcasts and apps

Give them training

Research from the CMI and YouGov (2023) tells us – in the UK at least – four in five people with some kind of management responsibility don't have the training needed to do their day job let alone deal with complex and uncertain situations. They are 'accidental managers' who are thrown in at the deep end and struggle to sensitively deal with the issues their team members face. By failing to properly support these people, the research found that organizations are seeing damaged culture, damaged productivity and damaged staff wellbeing as a result.

Properly trained managers are not guaranteed to be perfect, and we all know that. But they are more likely to know how their organization works, more likely to be effective in their managerial duties, and more likely to have had opportunities to develop their communication style and to understand how to create a positive and responsive work environment in good times and bad.

Having worked for large corporations over three continents, HR strategist Marion Anderson says that with a few notable exceptions, a lack of training for managers, and particularly those at the beginning of their career, is a global issue, and she tell me that's not just related to crisis needs. Lots of organizations overlook the importance of providing any strong support for high-performing employees who want to move into management roles:

> Just because someone is a popular colleague, or a great individual contributor, doesn't mean they'll automatically excel as a manager. Engineers, for example, may love their technical work, but when they become managers without proper training, they can struggle day-to-day, let alone when times get tough.

> That's because most organizations don't offer enough training for new managers. While they may provide safety training or technical training, most overlook crucial elements like how to support team members emotionally and

professionally in challenging times. This lack of preparation means managers are forced to 'wing it' when things become difficult, and if they don't wing it well, their team members will become collateral damage.

The answer is to be honest about the skills gaps in your organization and to commit to offering early and continuous training, support and exposure that helps build confidence and competence over a period of time and that helps all managers thrive in a wide range of different situations.

That means offering a strong and long runway for high-performing, high-potential employees who show an interest in management roles, and it means including all the essential elements required to build a strong crisis backbone. This includes having difficult conversations, handling uncertainty and ensuring effective employee communication, as well as driving performance, encouraging innovation, and supporting, motivating and empowering a team.

Marion continues:

> We also need to give our managers the space and the comfort, the psychological safety to know that it's OK to not feel OK. When crises happen, everyone looks to a leader to get them through the moment. And they're looking for someone who's strong. But your line managers are not made of Teflon. Things impact them in the same way that they impact everyone else, and they can find it hard when they have not dealt with something like this before.

> So as well as formal training, there is a critical role for senior leaders to show more junior leaders the way. To support, mentor and coach them. To act as a sounding board and to offer advice, to explain that this is a learning journey that comes through life experience and through exposure, and to reassure them that we're all human, and we will all support each other.

> It's essential to provide all this support early so that new managers can develop their skills and avoid burnout, high turnover and mental health issues. If organizations take care of all their people and create a supportive learning environment for the management community, everyone benefits – especially in difficult times.

Use training workshops, case studies, skills guides and tips to help line managers better deliver a message, understand and respond to comments, exercise judgement and gather feedback, then back this up with informal guidance and coaching on how to work with difficult information, how to prepare it, how to deliver it and how to gather feedback on it. Help managers get comfortable with saying 'I don't know, but I'll answer that when I can', and make sure they understand communication is a continuous, ongoing two-way process. You can also:

- Be clear about the company's responsibilities to candour and also to privacy.
- Set clear and realistic expectations about what can be communicated remotely and what should be done in person.
- Specify preferred channels and response times for different conversations.
- Explain how to use communication tools and channels effectively.
- Establish boundaries for out-of-hours communication.
- Role model from the top through every level of the management hierarchy.
- Make it easy for managers to access personal or tailored advice and support.

Trust them to do the job

Finally, organizations demand trust from their employees in crisis situations but stall goodwill and progress when they are slow to give it back in return. If you ask managers to take on a crisis communication role, then you must trust them to do the job required.

That means respecting their capability, acting on their feedback, and supporting them without controlling their approach. Internal communication consultant and business owner Katie Marlow says:

> If you have decided to enable your managers to lead the conversation, let them lead it. Trust them. Don't then say, 'Oh, that's way too much, we don't want that much. We want them to interpret the information, but we don't want them to go off-script.' Because, of course, that's not possible and you'll end up with a disconnect, and possibly even a bigger challenge than you had before. Give them the tools, give them the backup and empower them to do the job. You'll get stronger engagement, increased accountability and better outcomes as a result.

KEY TAKEAWAYS

- Line managers are some of the most important people in your organization at any time, and in crisis they have a critical role. That's because they have a direct understanding of daily workflow and operations and it's also because they sit right at the heart of all human connection in the organization. They are the vital human link.

- As the main bond between employees and organization, managers know the human beings in the company better than anyone else and so they are better placed to support them and communicate with them in a meaningful way.

- Managers provide the emotional, psychological and practical support needed to bring credibility and meaning to more distant central messages and they help people survive and thrive in every stage of the crisis response.

- They are also crucial to supporting the flow of information around the organization and to passing on feedback that will enhance centrally led crisis communication, and crisis response.

- Not all crisis communication needs to be shared by line managers, so it's important to decide which messages and resources will benefit from manager support and interpretation, and which cannot be modified and should be delivered to everyone from a more central source

- To support managers well, you must recognize their needs. You must make sure the content you are asking them to deliver is useful, easy to understand and easy to share, and you must give them the time, tools, training and trust to do the job.

References

CMI and YouGov (2023) Taking responsibility: Why UK PLC needs better managers, www.managers.org.uk/wp-content/uploads/2023/10/CMI_BMB_GoodManagment_Report.pdf (archived at https://perma.cc/3QYS-P9MW)

MacLeod, D and Clarke, N (2009) Engaging for success, https://Engageforsuccess.org/engaging-for-success/ (archived at https://perma.cc/8ZVQ-RTM4)

Mazzei, A and Ravazzani, S (2011) Manager-employee communication during a crisis: The missing link, *Corporate Communications: An International Journal*, 16, 243–54, www.emerald.com/insight/content/doi/10.1108/13563281111156899/full/html (archived at https://perma.cc/APB7-MHP2)

Quirke, B (2008) *Making the Connections: Using internal communication to turn strategy into action*, Routledge, London

Wigert, B and Maese, E (2019) How your manager experience shapes your employee experience, www.gallup.com/workplace/259469/manager-experience-shapes-employee-experience.aspx (archived at https://perma.cc/6XRJ-BW7V)

10

Listen to your people

Effective listening is a key interpersonal skill in difficult times, but it's also a key strategic internal crisis communication activity that is necessary to build engagement and organizational resilience before, during and after a crisis occurs, and that helps effectively deliver each of the 7S of internal crisis communication identified in Chapter 2.

Listen well, and you'll not only help the organization to avert many of its most dangerous crises before they ever cause harm, but you'll also be more authentic and effective in your bid to support, engage and enable colleagues when they do occur, and you'll be best placed to learn and adapt for whatever comes next. But get it wrong, and you'll miss important warning signs, aggravate an already challenging experience, and risk catapulting the organization into a different problem entirely.

This chapter explains that to be most effective, listening should be embedded and threaded through all internal crisis communication activities, and it should be supported by dedicated policies, systems, structures and resources. It discusses how listening is important in everyday internal communication as well as in times of crisis, it explains how listening can be used to support and strengthen the organization through each different crisis stage, and it offers advice on how to listen and respond well in difficult times.

What is organizational listening?

Listening, in its widest sense is about receiving, understanding and responding to the different ideas, questions, messages and perspectives that come our way, and it's about making sure we have given others a voice. It's not always easy to do well, and in large or complex organizations where many voices can and should be heard, it takes planning, effort and skill to get it right, but it's important to build meaningful relationships, to make good decisions, and to set the company up for best operational and reputational success. Employee voice is also one of the four enablers of employee engagement identified by David MacLeod and Nita Clarke in their 2009 paper, Engaging for success.

Dr Kevin Ruck is an academic internal communication researcher and author with interests in crisis communication and organizational listening. He tells me that effective listening is vital for creating strong and thriving companies, and that for best effect, we must listen consistently and in a considered way:

> Effective organizational listening is not about an annual survey or an occasional 'You said – We did' campaign. It's an ongoing process that's embedded into day-to-day internal communication plans and crisis communication plans using multiple methods and multiple levels of analysis. If you want to do it well, you need to spend as much time listening as you do broadcasting, and you need to understand, analyse and act on the issues that are raised.

> Great listening involves fully understanding people in the organization and encouraging them to share their experiences, ideas and expertise on an ongoing basis. Effective listening ensures that all thoughts are taken into consideration and either acted upon or given good explanations why not.

> When employees feel their input is valued and understood – even if their suggestions aren't implemented, they are more likely to believe the organization is fair and trustworthy, and they are more likely to be engaged. That means that as they listen, leaders and internal communicators must acknowledge and pay attention to what is being said, they must try to hear lots of different viewpoints, and they must carefully consider and respond to what they have heard. They need to be honest about what can and can't change, explain their decisions clearly, and treat every conversation as an opportunity to learn and improve.

Like all other strategic internal communication activities, effective organizational listening involves considering a range of different needs. Experts such as Macnamara (2017) argue that it must be purposefully planned, supported and backed up by policies, systems, structures and resources.

To make it 'stick', and to make people feel safe to use the infrastructure available to them in the most effective way, it should also be actively encouraged and role modelled by leaders and line managers across the organization, through conversations that are inspired by curiosity and by a desire to enable all employees to participate fully in the organization.

It should be built around a genuine interest in who the internal community are, how they feel, what they can offer and what they need to thrive in any given situation. Listening involves asking questions, hearing stories, practising compassion and digging beyond superficial feedback to build meaningful connections, and mutually beneficial relationships in good times and bad.

Listen through crisis

Listening both formally and informally is fundamental to proactive and forward-looking crisis management and internal crisis communication success. Experts such as Coombs (2015) talk in detail about its importance in the crisis prevention scanning process and others such as Mazzei and Ravazzani (2022) observe that discussion and disclosure is also a critical antecedent to internal crisis advocacy. It's the only way to:

- be fully alert to the danger and opportunities ahead
- ensure the people with information and experience about the day-to-day reality of the crisis are understood by those with the power to make strategic change
- recognize misunderstanding or misalignment and test if the proposed crisis position, messages and activities are supported by the internal community
- fully involve and engage people in the crisis recovery and strengthening process
- check that crisis activity is having the desired effect

When their organization is in crisis, people want and expect to have their say. Listen well, and you'll enhance trust, engagement, decision-making, performance and innovation. But get it wrong – particularly in the hardest of times – and you'll aggravate an already challenging experience, fracturing goodwill, advocacy and support.

Having spent three decades with the Federal Emergency Management Agency (FEMA) in the US, Ed Conley has led teams around the globe in response to some of recent history's most significant disasters – including 9/11, Hurricane Katrina, the 2010 Haiti Earthquake and the Deepwater

Horizon oil spill. He says that listening is one of the most important parts of the job:

> When you're dealing with crisis, listening is huge. It's where you get the raw data, the situational awareness, the scope of the challenge. It tells you where you are now, what you are missing, and whether you are making progress and achieving success.

> Listening is an important, exciting and interesting part of the job. It's not done well in every crisis, but if you can get it right, it's one big thing that helps you get better. It's the only way to pick up emerging issues, judge how people are feeling, and be ready for whatever might come next. You have got to embrace it.

Like every other aspect of internal crisis communication, listening can be applied strategically to maximize impact in different situations, and it can bring forward different benefits at each crisis stage. Academic internal communication researcher and author Dr Kevin Ruck explains:

> Listening has distinct benefits at each crisis stage. First, it can surface operational and reputational issues at an early stage, so help the organization avoid the crisis all together. Second, it can diagnose problems and facilitate solutions. Third, it can help bring forward future learning; and fourth, it is associated with positive relationships, trust, engagement and wellbeing – all of which are essential for fostering general resilience, solving problems and driving innovation.

Listen before crisis

We have already established that the best way to manage a crisis is to prevent it from happening, and listening is a critical driver of this kind of crisis success. That's because employees can provide insight that doesn't just help organizations seek and optimize opportunity, it also helps identify and mitigate threat, and it helps build psychologically safe cultures where people feel confident to have open conversations, and to share their questions, ideas and concerns.

Experts agree that employees can help a company get ahead of a problem and prevent a crisis by detecting and alerting others to growing problems before they cause harm, but they also recognize far too many missed opportunities. Perlow and Williams (2013) say that's because many organizations send verbal or nonverbal messages that falling into line is the safest way for people to hold on to their jobs and further their careers, while Edmondson (2019) argues that a culture of silence infuses the whole organization when psychological safety is low. As academic internal communication researcher and author Dr Kevin Ruck explains, that comes at a huge cost:

> Surfacing operational and reputational problems is a critical part of crisis mitigation, and it's something that we talk about in the book *Leading the Listening Organisation: Creating organizations that flourish* (2024) when we share crisis stories that reveal that people in the business knew things were amiss but either felt that they couldn't speak or tried to do so, but didn't have their voices heard. Wells Fargo, Boeing, Volkswagen and the UK National Health Service are all examples of organizations that have suffered serious crises which might have been avoided with more effective listening.

> What this tells us is that failing to listen in the pre-crisis stage can be extremely costly, and that organizations who wish to be more resistant to crises of their own making need to create a climate of psychological safety in which people feel able to talk about the things they feel are important without worrying about ridicule, humiliation or criticism.

Ignorance can have devastating consequences, yet organizations consistently fail to understand, acknowledge or address visible red flags and warning signs, or they fail to recognize real or perceived systemic barriers and existential risks for those speaking out, and it's a problem that former BBC journalist and crisis communication consultant Kate Betts knows well. Kate has advised on many of the highest profile and most complex crises in the UK, and says:

> I've worked with too many organizations who went on to experience a crisis because leaders and managers failed to listen, or because they glossed over known problems and tried to create an illusion of success or normality by pushing issues away instead of dealing with them.

> Meanwhile, the idea that it's better not to speak up spreads and takes hold elsewhere in the organization, and soon people with legitimate fears or frustrations stop raising concerns. More people then stay silent because they think that if they do speak up, they will be seen as ignorant, incompetent or disruptive – and because they think they will be seen as someone who is trying to rock the boat rather than as someone who is trying to help the organization to do right.

> The problem with not listening and not encouraging people to speak is that it leads to a lack of awareness, and the problem with a lack of awareness is that you don't know about the train until it's about to hit you in the face.

Listening to prevent crisis involves all the risk anticipation and tracking activities we discussed in Chapter 3, but it also involves actively seeking different perspectives as the organization seeks to surface and tackle the issues that sit beneath potential difficulties.

Derek Provan OBE is a non-executive director and business adviser who has led his colleagues through extreme weather, technological breakdowns, aircraft incidents and terror attacks during a 25-year career in the aviation industry. In recent years, he has been Chief Operating Officer at Heathrow Airport and Chief Executive Officer at AGS Airports. He has been a board member at NATS, and he has advised on security in UK aviation at the highest levels. He tells me that every organization facing a crisis must learn to listen without defence:

> Listening is a skill all on its own. It's something you must learn how to do, and one of the most important things you can learn when facing crisis is to listen without defence.

> If you've worked hard to create an environment where people feel that they can speak up, then the last thing they need when they do speak up is for the organization to become defensive. Because immediately that signals to them that there is a say-do gap. It tells them that the company is saying that it wants to hear about the full range of issues, but it doesn't really mean it.

> There are so many organizations who say 'We have an open, honest, transparent culture. We want to hear what you think. We want to take your views on board', but it's not what happens and unfortunately people stop speaking up.

> That means you must invite challenge, criticism and concerns as well as ideas and innovation, and you must listen to a wide range of voices, not just those that say what you want to hear. And if you invite all feedback, you need to receive all feedback and respond to all feedback. As hard as it is, and as personal as it might be, you can only make good decisions if you understand and respond to every experience. Don't worry who said what, or even if you disagree, just accept that this is what your team are telling you.

> Take it all, put it all on the table, and play it back, so people can see that you have considered it. Sometimes that can be painful, but ultimately people will have more respect for a leader or an organization that listens to all feedback and either better explains a situation or sets out to deal with it.

Good organizational listening in the pre-crisis stage involves creating a culture where everyone understands they have legitimate rights to speak and be treated with respect. It recognizes that different people see the organization in different ways, and it seeks to better understand organizational strengths, weaknesses, opportunities and threats for the benefit of everyone concerned.

Yet getting the whole truth can be challenging in organizations where people are afraid or mistrustful of management, or where it feels that feedback is not valued, and researchers such as Professor Rosabeth Moss Kanter have observed that when problems mount inside organizations, the likelihood of secrecy, and isolation grows too. People tend to either blame or avoid one another, and even if they don't consciously hide information, they find reasons to avoid discussing it, causing a spiral of decline. In Moss Kanter's 2003 article for the *Harvard Business Review*, she says:

> Finally, the ultimate pathology of troubled companies takes hold: collective denial. As in the fabled village where the emperor showed off his new clothes, people unwittingly collude. Rather than volunteer an opinion that no one else seems to share, people engage in collective pretence to ignore what they individually know. It's a phenomenon known to psychologists as pluralistic ignorance.

Pluralistic ignorance and similar recognized organizational phenomena, such the MUM effect (Rosen and Tesser, 1970), which refers to the tendency of people to withhold information that could make them look bad or to alter it to seem less damaging, highlight how organizational dynamics can lead to the problems that Dr Kevin Ruck and Kate Betts both identified earlier.

The good news is that decline can be reversed when a culture of secrecy, blame and denial is confronted and changed. That's easier in some companies than others, but if there's a history of organizational trauma or blame, you can:

- Role model non-defensive listening and accountability.
- Create and promote a policy which states the organization is open for listening and advises how people can get involved.
- Use internal communication content and channels to encourage dialogue, and make sure all comments receive a response.
- Tell stories that celebrate mistakes as learning opportunities.
- Celebrate signal detection and crisis aversion.
- Evidence how every voice is valued as the company scans for and identifies warning signs.

Don't assume silence necessarily means agreement, and beyond that, recognize that sometimes anonymity is important. Sometimes people with very important information feel more comfortable to share it anonymously, and so you must allow them to do that. Beyond that, named and/or anonymous whistle-blowing is essential to stop unethical or illegal practice because, ultimately, it protects everyone, so inform people about whistle-blowing opportunities in a non-defensive way and position it as an opportunity to improve the organization for everyone.

Listen in the acute stage

Like other internal crisis communication activities, the purpose of listening changes at different crisis points, and in the earliest moments it must take multiple quick, direct and regular forms to enable critical surviving, supporting and sensemaking needs.

Soon after the initial crisis statement – or within it, if appropriate – the organization must make an early internal statement to confirm an environment where anyone can speak out quickly and directly about crisis, and to tell them how to do this. Simultaneously, it must use general observation and channels such as face-to-face or virtual meetings, site visits and employee helplines to:

- understand the crisis
- understand urgent employee needs and expectations
- assess whether employees are getting timely and factual information
- check that employees understand and can deliver the task ahead
- assess how employees will respond to different positions and asks

If you need to gather insight, quantitative methods such as surveys, questionnaires and polls will give you information at scale, while qualitative methods such as interviews, and focus groups or general observation will help you dig deeper into what people are thinking, feeling and doing, why, what that might mean and how that might change.

And as you focus on practical things, recognize how listening can be used to support people through shock, complexity, ambiguity and grief. Regardless of the level of harm felt, employees will need to be heard as they process and make sense of the situation, and they will want to take back a snatch of control through the use of their own voice.

Suzanne Goldberg has led internal crisis communication at Channel 4 television, the Royal National Lifeboat Institution (RNLI), BBC News and Burberry. She has specialist experience supporting welfare and trauma response for employees working through human crises and she told me that as well as listening for specific reasons, it's vital that we also allow people who have experienced or seen trauma simply to be heard:

> Listening in traumatic situations is vital. Consider welfare drop-ins that anyone can join. Let people go along and talk about the support they need, and just to vent and be heard. That kind of internal communication support is vital, and it must be done right.

Regardless of what they have to say, whether or not you give people the opportunity to be heard will affect how they feel and what they do as the crisis evolves. Academic internal communication researcher and author Dr Kevin Ruck tells me:

> The reason passion turns into anger in times of crisis is because people feel ignored. So, it's important that leaders listen to their employees on an ongoing basis. Rather than seeing angry people as problematic, it's better to recognize their passion and ensure they are given scope to express their views in a safe environment. This is far more effective than doing nothing and eventually have the same problem played out externally.

The crisis itself will determine whether you need to create a new channel for listening, or use existing channels that already work well. Either way, check that you can meet a range of different employee needs, that multiple opportunities are built into the plan, and that you have a robust process in place to ensure formally submitted questions, feedback and concerns are anticipated, welcomed, captured, understood and answered at regular intervals.

Jane Leaker has worked in the internal communication and engagement function at Transport for London (TfL) for 20 years. In that time, her teams have experienced everything from terrorism to cyber-attacks to other complex incidents on the network. She tells me that if you want to hear lots of different voices, you must give people choice in how they speak:

> It's important to foster the kind of supportive environment where staff feel confident to voice concerns or quickly put their hands up if they have a question. In an organization like TfL, you need to give people different ways to do this. We are big users of social and digital channels to understand real-time sentiment and to enable open dialogue across the organization, but we also

hold regular virtual and face-to-face meetings with leaders, we have a robust and healthy cascade that allows for conversation and questions, and we use feedback forms and surveys to collect specific insights.

Listen in the chronic stage

As the organization makes the profound step from acute crisis stage to the chronic stage, the listening changes once again, and while it's still very important to support people and help them make sense of what's now happening, the focus moves to involving people and giving them back a sense of agency and control as the company sets out to stimulate and sustain business continuity and recovery efforts, rebuild relationships and find and implement crisis solutions.

Keep the conversation going as leadership teams get out to thank and encourage everyone in stimulating, sustaining and strengthening the organization. As people get tired, leadership visibility and role modelling are key to keep morale high, reinforcing positive behaviours, and checking in on changing need and emotion, so look for lots of ways for leaders to interact, connect and converse with as many people as possible. Crisis communication consultant and trainer Ben Verinder tells me:

> You can't be in two places at one time, but often the organization has multiple offices or facilities in multiple locations. That means you need multiple leaders in the organization who can cover all bases.
>
> A tip to help them is to generate a central script, talking points or suggested questions which they can use to begin conversations in their own parts of the company and collect ongoing intelligence that can be brought back to the centre. Rehearse common questions and coach them to be honest if a situation is not clear. This approach builds understanding that a situation is evolving but that nothing is being deliberately withheld.

Site visits are a great way to get to know what is happening in different parts of the organization. If possible, they should offer the opportunity for a general walkabout and show and tell as well as group gatherings and private conversations.

Internal communication consultant, author and business owner Advita Patel tells me that active listening is necessary to keep people feeling involved and included as the crisis moves forward, and that means that as leaders and internal communicators visit people on their own patch, they should observe how people are behaving as they listen to what is being said:

> As the crisis continues, you can help leaders establish channels like roadshows, walk-the-floors, drop-in sessions and virtual meetings first so they can listen and directly respond, but also so they can see things for themselves and pick up stress signals.

> Go along with them and observe. Look at body language and interactions. Observe who is dominating meetings and who hasn't spoken for a while, who continuously keep their cameras switched off, and who gets interrupted more than others. Those observations can offer a real sense of changing needs and what you need to support.

> Be aware of your biases and make sure that you are listening to people who have diverse views and experience of the situation so that you can pick up different cues, spot the gaps, and get a better understanding of what is really being said. If people are hesitant to speak, reframe the questions and ask what they need from the organization or how you can help them succeed. Encourage the conversation by using phrases like 'It's OK to disagree' or 'Thank you for your honesty' and 'Let's give everyone a chance to speak'.

If the crisis means it's not possible to get physically out and about in the organization, you can build in virtual opportunities to listen instead. Online forums offer a genuine opportunity to engage staff in key issues and take part in an ongoing conversation. In Chapter 9, Carolyn Bowick explained that line managers played a crucial role in enabling successful conversations with 3,600 'behind-the-scenes' employees at NHS National Services Scotland (NSS) as they supported the country's healthcare services through the Covid-19 pandemic. But she tells me that the line manager conversations were just one part of a wider listening strategy, and organizational-wide listening led by the chief executive was also critical to uncover and respond to what employees wanted and needed in such a challenging and unprecedented time:

> We created large live online forums to support listening on a bigger scale. The format was like the town hall meetings we ran before Covid, but we moved them online, made them bigger, and held them more often so we could touch base and capture all feedback from people on different shifts, in different roles and in different locations on a more regular basis.

> We had capacity for everyone in the organization to join the live sessions, and we were specific that everyone was welcome, and we would try and accommodate different needs. Because we had high levels of shift working and overtime, questions could be submitted in advance, and recordings were also

made available for those who could not attend, as well for as those who wanted to watch again. At times we had 1,400 people attend each live session, so we knew they were needed, and they were popular.

The format was simple. They'd start with a short introduction and perhaps a short presentation from people in different parts of NSS – just three or four minutes to introduce different colleagues, to recognize efforts and to touch on the challenges and opportunities that they were facing in that strange time. From there, the chief executive would offer a few observations and then invite questions or feedback.

Questions and comments that had not been pre-submitted were welcomed live through the chat function and the event moderators would speak on behalf of the audience. We prescreened for swearing or inappropriate language, but no topic was off the table, every question and comment was answered, and every question and comment was treated respectfully. Sometimes, it was so busy that we couldn't get through everything, but we always responded to everything, and we made sure everyone got an honest and meaningful answer, even if the answer was that we don't yet know.

It was important that people knew this new opportunity was available for them, and that we used it effectively, so we really promoted the events and the recordings. We needed to understand what employees wanted and needed, because nothing was the same as it had been six months before. We could not afford to make assumptions, and we could not afford to be slow to respond.

As well as collecting all those important questions and feedback, I hope the fact that we were so open to listening gave a sense that all colleagues are valued and looked after. You know in every organization there's a cohort of people who are deeply cynical about everything, but I think we were successful in easing some of that by letting people see the commitment to listening and the positive intention.

I also found it interesting that in the early days the first questions were all about safety. I guess for want of a better word, survival. Those real 'What does it mean for me?' type things. But then as those questions were answered and people began to feel safe, they slowly started asking about strategy. By five or six in, we started to see a shift from. 'Am I safe?' to 'What does this mean for the future? What will life look like after Covid? What impact will the cost of Covid have on NHS strategy?

I think the reason for that was that it reflected a growing psychological safety. Everyone had seen other people ask questions. And they had seen all those questions had been treated respectfully and they had been given a respectful answer. They had seen that nobody got fired because they'd asked a difficult question, you know?

So over time, that snowballs in a positive way. People see they can ask difficult questions; they can talk about the things that need to be spoken about, and they take another step forward. Their immediate needs are satisfied, and they open up to a bigger picture. They are interested to start talking about what's next. I thought it was really interesting to see that difference and hear that interest from people as they felt more supported, because psychologically, I don't think they would do that if they didn't feel safe and respected.

When people have had their surviving and supporting needs met and they once again feel safe in the organization, you can offer back a sense of control and re-energize and reinvigorate them in problem-solving groups, in co-creating solutions generally, or in sharing ideas related to their specific areas of personal interest and expertise.

Remember too that as the crisis evolves, misinformation and disinformation may continue to be shared. This is dangerous not only for the impact that it can have on the organization and its reputation but also for the psychological damage it can cause to employees as fatigue sets in. If they see and hear inaccurate messages time after time, they may begin to wonder if there is something in it. That means it must continue to be tackled, and you can use employee listening to support this. Global crisis communication consultant and trainer Piyali Mandal is the Founder and CEO of The Media Coach and a specialist in reputational, operational and cybersecurity crisis, based in Mumbai, India. She tells me:

We live in a world of virtual reality. Videos can be morphed. Voices can be morphed. People can create misleading information, so you need to tell employees what is happening, and you also need to hear what they are seeing and hearing themselves.

In situations where there is a lot of misleading information flowing out, we tell employees that if you see some information or a post that you feel is misleading, you must share it back with the team. That way we can very quickly let people know that this is fake. Here is the real video. Here is the real information. The power in that is making sure that people not only get the correct information, but that they also feel valued and involved as part of the solution. They know what team they are on, and they feel more encouraged to help and to protect the reputation of the organization.

Listen post-crisis

As the crisis comes to an end, the conversation must continue. At this point it is about revisiting the sensemaking process, understanding and acting upon opportunity to rebuild and renew, and it's about re-establishing a strong positive culture where everyone continues to feel seen and valued for the significant role they have played.

Where grief has been felt, people must voice whatever they want to say, and everyone must be able to talk about their struggles and triumphs as they recover. As well as giving people a safe space simply to speak and make sense of what happened, you must also create opportunity for them to come together and reflect on what went well and what went badly so that the whole organization can learn, implement lessons and evidence action.

Remember that crises bring opportunity for growth, innovation and strengthened relationships, so look at where the organization can adapt and learn even when the insights are hard to face. Create safe and supportive environments for people to come together and reflect on what went well and what went badly so that the whole organization can learn, implement lessons and strengthen for the future. We will talk more about this in Chapter 12.

Respond to feedback

Earlier in this chapter, academic internal communication researcher and author Dr Kevin Ruck explained that considering and responding to feedback is part of the listening process, and employees are more likely to believe the organization is fair and trustworthy when they feel their input is valued and understood.

That doesn't mean that your organization needs to implement or agree with every employee suggestion, but it does mean that key people within the leadership, crisis and business continuity teams need to carefully consider and respond to what has been said at every crisis stage, and it does mean the company must clearly explain why decisions are made.

When vulnerable people share feedback and do not receive a response, the silence is both deafening and disconcerting. Every hour without a response adds to the stress, it adds to the pain, it adds to the confusion, and it erodes trust – so when a question or comment cannot receive an instant answer, a simple and heartfelt holding statement thanking people for their idea and letting them know when they will receive a considered reply is vital, and an update is required if and when the agreed response time is not going to be met.

As you help craft organizational responses, begin with a word of thanks and replay the question, comment or idea back in simple words, including the full original text as an attachment or link for reference. Evidence fairness in the process, and where possible include examples to show purpose or consistency in decision-making. Be clear about expectations and be open and honest about risks, weaknesses and threats, but also talk about opportunities for success. Answer questions with facts and evidence, build in key crisis messages if this is appropriate, and clearly show people a way forward.

Put systems, processes and service level agreements in place to make sure all formally submitted feedback is quickly, correctly and honestly responded to, and if possible, take inspiration from your company's CSR (Customer Service and Relationship) logging systems to keep track of key questions, interactions, feedback and themes so that you can understand an employee's history with a specific question or issue and offer better help.

Some companies make all employee feedback openly available across the organization and they even let others comment upon colleagues' questions or suggestions or vote them up and down. That's great practice in some situations, but it's more challenging when issues are complex and fraught, so again consider the organization's approach to publishing feedback in the light of the needs of the crisis, the company and the community before deciding whether it's right for the situation.

There are times when some feedback can't be shared with a wider audience, and that's OK, but it's still helpful to openly acknowledge key themes and it's always useful to have a published policy in place to manage expectations around the publication of feedback and to ensure consistency of approach.

Where internal feedback is being actioned and is having positive impacts, you can build a sense of employee trust and involvement by recognizing and celebrating this. Use internal communication channels to publicize what changes have been made and to explore key questions or themes in internal articles, interviews, case studies or face-to-face events, and it's helpful to develop a staff FAQ or knowledge repository of data, policy, procedures, guidelines and action taken on key issues.

KEY TAKEAWAYS

- When employees feel their input is genuinely acknowledged and appreciated, they are more inclined to view the organization as fair and trustworthy, and they are more able to participate effectively in every stage of the crisis response.

- To be most effective, listening should be embedded and threaded through all internal crisis communication activities, and it should be supported by dedicated policies, systems, structures and resources at each crisis stage.

- Listening should be built around a genuine interest in who your people are, how they feel, what they can offer and what they need to thrive in any given situation.

- Surfacing operational or reputational problems is a key part of crisis mitigation, and it's important to create a psychologically safe environment where all feedback is welcome and everyone can be involved.

- In the acute stage of the crisis, listening can be used to meet key survival, supporting and sensemaking needs. It can be used to stabilize, stimulate and sustain everyone in the recovery as the crisis enters the chronic stage, and it can be used to generate good ideas and innovate through the strengthening process.

- For best success you must carefully consider and reply to what has been said at every crisis stage. Put systems and processes in place to make sure all feedback is logged, understood and quickly, correctly and honestly responded to.

References

Coombs, W T (2015) *Ongoing Crisis Communication: Planning, managing, and responding*, Sage, Los Angeles

Edmondson, A C (2019) *The Fearless Organisation: Creating psychological safety in the workplace for learning, innovation and growth*, Wiley, New Jersey

MacLeod, D and Clarke, N (2009) Engaging for success, https://Engageforsuccess.org/engaging-for-success/ (archived at https://perma.cc/7SPX-H3UG)

Macnamara, Jim (2017) Toward a theory and practice of organizational listening, *International Journal of Listening*, 32 (1), 1–23, www.researchgate.net/publication/319922463_Toward_a_Theory_and_Practice_of_Organizational_Listening (archived at https://perma.cc/U87D-6JUP)

Mazzei, A and Ravazzani, S (2022) Chapter 19, The strategic role of internal crisis communication, *Research Handbook on Strategic Communication*, Edward Elgar, Cheltenham

Moss Kanter, R (2003) Leadership and the psychology of turnarounds, *Harvard Business Review*, https://hbr.org/2003/06/leadership-and-the-psychology-of-turnarounds (archived at https://perma.cc/9XWR-SRXC)

Perlow, L and Williams, S (2013) Is silence killing your company? HBR's 10 must reads on communication, *Harvard Business School*, Boston, US

Pounsford, M, Ruck, K and Krais, H (2024) *Leading the Listening Organisation: Creating organisations that flourish*, Routledge, New York

Rosen, S and Tesser, A (1970) On reluctance to communicate undesirable information: The MUM effect, *Sociometry*, 33 (3), 253–633, https://doi.org/10.2307/2786156 (archived at https://perma.cc/X4BH-KLB6)

11

Take care of yourself

Communicating during a crisis is an intensive, high-paced and high-pressure activity which takes hard work and bravery. It involves juggling urgent and important demands, and it involves acting quickly and decisively, sometimes in the centre of very traumatic or emotionally charged situations, often outside of your comfort zone, and often at the expense of your own personal time, personal activity and personal relationships.

Most of us want to make a positive difference at work and to learn, grow and contribute to our organizations in good times and bad – but when a crisis hits, the pressure to be immediately available, to make quick decisions in an unclear and potentially harmful situation, and to deliver important information at speed can be exhausting. It can be easy to forget about your own emotional, psychological or physical needs as you attend to the needs of others, but it's important to pause and take care of your personal and professional wellbeing so you can stay well and thrive through the challenge you face.

This chapter explains that all crises affect us in different ways. It explains some of the natural feelings, conditions and challenges you might experience as you communicate through a workplace crisis, and it explains how they reveal themselves. It suggests that the first step to staying well is to recognize and accept when your personal and professional needs are not met, and it offers advice to cope if your mental health is suffering. It also shares advice on wellbeing, self-care and on setting yourself up for professional success. The chapter ends with tips that will help you set professional boundaries, manage your workload, and manage your professional wellbeing while staying positive and looking for ways to learn and grow from your crisis experience.

Acknowledge your feelings

The demanding nature of crises means that they all leave a mark on the people involved, particularly when they involve harmful, tragic or traumatic events. It's natural to experience a wide range of emotions, thoughts and memories as you navigate such an intense situation, and it's natural to feel 'up' one day and 'down' the next.

Everyone reacts in their own way, and your feelings will be shaped by the nature of the crisis and by your own unique personal and professional history and experiences. Even very resilient people are affected when they witness trauma or when they face intense professional pressure and an unrelenting workload, and no one should be forced to take on more than they are equipped to deal with.

As you negotiate the personal and professional challenges a crisis brings, it can be tempting to push back your own feelings and focus on other people's needs. But it's important to accept that you also need time to make sense of challenging situations, and that you also need to stay well, rest and recover in your own way.

Whatever your circumstances, it's helpful to pause from time to time and acknowledge the emotional, psychological and practical pressures that you are under, to reflect on how you are feeling and why, and to ask for whatever you need to help you thrive as well as you possibly can.

Look after your mental health

Stewart Kerr is Head of Mental Health and Wellbeing for the School of Nursing at the University of the West of Scotland, and he is also responsible for supporting staff wellbeing in times of crisis. He offers some helpful insight and advice:

> Everyone feels a little stressed or anxious at times, and it's normal when we face challenges at work. Sometimes, short-term stress can be helpful, as it can sharpen your focus and motivate you to prepare for important events or tasks. However, it's important to recognize when stress or anxiety becomes excessive or persistent, as this can negatively impact your wellbeing and performance.

> We all have different thresholds, but if stress or anxiety is interfering with your daily life, work or wellbeing, then you should reach out for support. Keeping a good work-life balance and seeking help early can keep you thriving as you face

workplace challenges, and it can prevent more serious mental health issues from developing.

You can look after your mental health in lots of ways. One step is to look for self-help books, apps, websites and other resources that might help. But you can also ask for materials from your healthcare provider, you can talk to supportive individuals or groups and you can seek advice as to whether medication might be beneficial. There are no right and wrong answers, and sometimes you may take a combination of different measures. You will know what feels right and comfortable for you.

As well as stress and anxiety, it's also possible to experience conditions such as depression or post-traumatic stress disorder (PTSD) after you've witnessed or been involved in a workplace crisis. Information from the Royal College of Psychiatrists (2020) explains that depression has a range of causes, and while it may be triggered by a stressful or distressing event, it may equally have triggers that are harder to identify. PTSD on the other hand is more likely to be directly linked to a traumatic event (2021) and so people who experience a crisis are at greater risk.

If you think you are dealing with either depression or with PTSD, there is help available to you, so you should reach out for help and support. Some more information is included in the references at the end of this chapter.

Turning specifically to PTSD, Stewart Kerr says:

Not everyone who experiences a crisis will get PTSD; however, there is evidence to suggest that the risk of developing PTSD is higher for people in jobs with greater exposure to traumatic events. Symptoms can start immediately after you experience the event, or they can start weeks or months afterwards, and they can be triggered by seemingly unrelated things such as a smell or sound.

If you have PTSD, you may re-experience the crisis event, you may have nightmares, or you may experience intense, disturbing or debilitating thoughts or feelings related to the trauma. You may feel emotionally numb or detached from your surroundings, you may feel the need to avoid situations or people that remind you of the event, and you may choose not to return to work.

PTSD can have a significant impact, but it's important to know that help is available, and recovery is possible. If you think you might be experiencing symptoms of PTSD there are various treatment options and support pathways to consider, and many people find it helpful to connect with support groups or individuals who have had similar experiences. If you're unsure where to start, reach out and speak to a trusted friend, colleague or health professional.

If your organization, industry or professional networks offer support through mental health and wellbeing apps, portals or other resources, support groups, telephone helplines, employee assistance programmes, counselling, therapy, or psychiatric support, take whatever you think might be helpful to you. And if you prefer to speak to a healthcare professional or someone who can offer religious or spiritual pastoral support separately to the company, you can do that too.

If someone offers you help, consider their advice and how it might be beneficial. Be open to their suggestions and remember that different things work for different people.

If you have a pre-existing mental health condition, you should continue with your treatment plans, and you should monitor and report any new or changing symptoms so that you can get help to deal with these.

If you need help right now, there are several free and reputable helplines or internet chat services that are staffed by people who are properly trained to help you and ready to listen. Some are available 24 hours a day, 365 days a year and most are available globally so can offer support in your preferred language. They won't judge you, and they could help you feel better.

The Samaritans in the UK can be reached by calling 116 123. This number is free to call from any phone, at any time of day or night.

Look after your personal wellbeing

Taking time to rest, recharge and look after yourself is important when you are pushing yourself physically, mentally and emotionally at work. It's vital if you are to avoid professional exhaustion, and it's also necessary if you want to stay clear-headed, confident and thriving in challenging times.

Again, mental health and wellbeing specialist Stewart Kerr emphasizes that we should focus on what is comfortable, and he tells me that research published by the UK National Health Service (2022) shows that there are five key things everyone can do to improve their wellbeing. These are:

- connect with other people
- be physically active

- learn new skills
- give to others
- pay attention to the present moment (be mindful)

Connect with other people

Spending time with family, friends and colleagues is a necessary part of self-care, and we must not let connections slip in difficult times, as mental health and wellbeing specialist Stewart Kerr explains:

> There's lots of evidence to show that strong social ties enhance our health and resilience, and this applies as much to our professional relationships as it does to our personal ones.

> Peace, quiet and calm is sometimes necessary, but try to avoid the instinct to isolate yourself in difficult times. Instead try to keep up with family, friends and colleagues. Conversations are cathartic and so we must always give ourselves permission to talk about our thoughts and fears. Build supportive relationships inside and outside of work and speak as openly as you can about how you are feeling.

The importance of conversation and connection came up time and time again as I spoke to different individuals about how they stayed well and thriving during their crisis experiences, and for many people their memories of friendship or shared experience were as vivid as their memories of the incident itself. Many people spoke of doing good work, receiving help and enjoying positive relationships as they made sense of what was happening or had happened around them.

Crisis expert Gillies Crichton reflected on the power of a simple cup of tea and a gentle check-in conversation after a particularly traumatic accident early in his career. Visual artist Sue Jane Taylor remembered watching TV and sharing food with fellow artists as she decompressed from the intense and important work of creating the Piper Alpha Memorial. FEMA disaster responder and NATO adviser Ed Conley spoke of co-workers making the effort to find each other and say thank you face-to-face after a job well done. Others spoke of bowling, hill walking and getting together in restaurants and bars to support each other or to celebrate a job well done.

Gathering and being sociable in challenging situations is easier for some people than it is for others. But maintaining positive connections takes many different forms and guises. Having, or being, a friend can make a difference, so don't retreat from the people who care for you. Reach out to others, respond to those who reach out to you and spend time in special places or with beloved animals. Start where it feels comfortable and go from there.

Be physically active and learn new skills

Having spent three decades with the Federal Emergency Management Agency (FEMA) in the US, disaster responder and NATO adviser Ed Conley tells me that staying physically and mentally balanced is helpful to everyone. He says:

> Often, at the time, you don't realize how much of yourself you give. You don't realize how much of yourself you pour into it. But working these kinds of events takes a physical and mental toll, and it's important to recognize that and to think about how you will balance your job with your life. Are you going to take long walks? Are you going to take naps? Do you have a spiritual outlet? Do you play an instrument? Do you paint? Do you read? Do you swim? Everyone needs balance to get through.

We all have different preferences, and what matters most is that you focus on healthy and enjoyable forms of activity and release. When you finish your shift, pause to recognize that your workday is over, and be intentional about how you will rest and enjoy your time off so that you can come back strong and well tomorrow.

It's OK to check in with a major update, but don't become consumed by 24-hour news channels or by your social media feed if a high-profile situation stays in the public eye during your rest time, and don't let unhealthy or harming habits such as drug or alcohol misuse become the way that you cope with the additional physical, mental or emotional burden. Instead, consider activities such as dancing, cooking, painting or meditation to help you stay well.

Visual artist Sue Jane Taylor saw first-hand the trauma that an immense and catastrophic crisis such as the Piper Alpha oil disaster had on everyone in the organization, and she witnessed the overwhelming impact that it had on the survivors and on the victim's family, friends, colleagues and communities for decades to come. She told me how safe spaces, solace and therapy are vital in healing from such devastation, but she also spoke of the value of creativity and the arts when practising self-care and processing what has happened:

> I believe in the power of art and the humanities. We saw how the families and survivors took comfort in art, music and poetry after Piper Alpha, and we saw the comforting power of these things again in a different way during the Covid

lockdowns. How many people took up painting, writing, knitting or dancing? How many learned instruments or joined virtual choirs or other groups? For lots of people, creativity is part of the help or the healing, and we should recognize its value and importance.

Give to others

Research also suggests that acts of giving, and kindness can improve your happiness and wellbeing. Seeing colleagues pull together or helping in the local community can alleviate feelings of hopelessness and it can boost our resilience.

Generosity doesn't always have to be material. A smile, a nod or a simple thank you is an act of giving, as is offering someone your full attention or stepping in when they need help. Recognizing a job well done, sharing resources, or bringing someone food or a drink when they are busy can make a big difference to them – and to you.

If you are a team leader, mentor or manager, remember that those people who look to you for guidance and support will also be feeling the pressure. Give them your time, allow them to offload in a safe space, and look for ways to recognize, thank and help them in their efforts. If you're worried about someone, regardless of the professional relationship, let them know they matter to you. Consider some conversation starters:

- How are you feeling about everything that has happened?
- I've noticed you seem quieter than usual, how are you today?
- You are working hard just now, how can I help?
- You are juggling a lot, what can I do?

Approach the conversation with empathy by listening carefully without judgement and taking action to help or offering flexibility where you can. Let colleagues know they're not alone and that you'd like to help. Not everyone welcomes physical closeness at work, so carefully read the cues you are given, but when words are hard to find, a caring hand on someone's arm or a hug can also make a big difference to some.

Be mindful

Finally, being mindful or in the present moment can improve your mental wellbeing. This means being attentive to your thoughts and feelings, your body and the world around you.

Mental health and wellbeing specialist Stewart Kerr tells me that mindfulness can be as simple as taking a walk outdoors and noticing the changing seasons or appreciating the taste and texture of your food as you eat. Being mindful can help you enjoy life more and understand yourself better. It can positively affect the way you feel about life and how you approach challenges.

Mindfulness can help reduce your worries and it can provide a sense of perspective in difficult times. Because it encourages you to focus on the here and now, it can also reduce tendencies to catastrophize about past events that you cannot change or about future scenarios that have not yet occurred.

Look after your professional wellbeing

It's reasonable to expect everyone to do a bit more, a bit faster when crisis hits. Most people can accommodate the extra rush of activity and challenge, and some thrive on it for short bursts of time, but there's a difference between helping your organization through a crisis and sacrificing yourself to it. That means that just as you should support your personal wellbeing, you should also support your professional wellbeing and enjoy professional balance, satisfaction and fulfilment in difficult times.

To do this you must:

- take your seat at the table
- set realistic goals and objectives
- review your workload and areas of responsibility
- establish reasonable boundaries
- push back on unacceptable demands
- deal with difficult people
- deal with mistakes
- think positively
- look for opportunity to learn and grow

Take your seat at the table

A crisis can bring closer contact with senior leaders and with the crisis management or business continuity teams. Whether you are working in internal communication at a strategic or tactical level, and regardless of your experience or status in the organizational hierarchy, this means you need to be ready to take your seat at the table.

You can't offer your best advice if you are playing catch-up, so as a first step, make sure that anyone who is asking you for advice or allocating you tasks knows who you are, what you do and the value that you bring. Build your credibility early, so people can see the benefit of keeping you in the loop and be clear what information you need if it doesn't seem to be forth-coming. Make sure your name is on the right distribution lists, that you are included in important face-to-face or digital meetings from the outset.

From there, don't be shy to join the conversation. Listen carefully to what is said and respond in ways that show you understand the strategy and the priorities, and that clearly joins the dots between what the organization needs to achieve and the impact that internal communication will bring. Speak in simple language to make sure people understand what you're saying and what it means to them and their areas of responsibility.

Know before you enter every meeting what you want to achieve from it. Are you there to provide an update, look for direction or ask for resource? If you are clear about what you want and need you will be more likely to get it. Do your homework and make sure that you enter every meeting prepared. Understand concerns and potential objections to your advice so you can influence and persuade as required.

Be as helpful and flexible as you can. Recognize the occasional need to pivot from one thing to another and know there is a need to muck in with others, but don't feel obliged to drop important internal communication priorities because someone misunderstood your role and asked you to pick up an extra task that will distance you from your strategic goals. Clearly explain what you are working on, why that's both urgent and important, and suggest an alternative person or solution to do the secondary task.

Try never to leave a meeting unsure of what has been agreed, or uncertain of what you are expected to do. If it's not clear, replay what you have heard and confirm that's correct, or ask for further explanation, detail or guidance. A simple way to do this is to say: 'Thank you, I'm gathering all my actions to be sure nothing slips – can you please replay to me what you'd like me to do and by when?' Write them down then read them back.

Set realistic goals and objectives

Because you are not working in business as usual, your normal goals and objectives may need to be paused so you can focus on the task at hand. Test this by asking:

- Do my personal objectives align to the crisis objectives?
- Are they achievable with current resources?

- Are they realistic given the current situation?
- Do the objectives complement each other?
- Can I measure or evaluate my impact?

If the answer to one (or all) of these questions is no, go back to the drawing board and agree with your line manager what you need to do and when.

Review your workload and areas of responsibility

If you revise your objectives, you'll need to review your workload to accommodate this. That means some of your regular tasks may have to be paused, stopped or reallocated and some new tasks may be added to help achieve the challenge at hand.

Write a full to-do list then break large tasks into smaller steps, group similar tasks together and consider how each item on the list helps achieve your new objectives. Focus on impact as you consult with your manager and use an Eisenhower Matrix to sort the tasks by importance and urgency:

- If a task is both urgent and important, you must prioritize it.
- If it's urgent but not important, you should delegate it to someone who has the time and capacity to take it on.
- If it's important but not urgent, you should schedule it for later.
- If it's not important or urgent, you can remove it.

Make the necessary changes then let colleagues know what you expect to deliver, when you expect to deliver it and what help you need from them to succeed. Use tools like checklists, whiteboards and shared calendars to stay on top of everything.

Establish reasonable boundaries

Crises demand that you set, and reach, stretched targets, but that doesn't mean you lose your right to switch off or to set reasonable boundaries. Keep perspective not just on how much you can deliver, but also what you can realistically emotionally, psychologically and practically tolerate before you hit a wall.

The World Health Organization (2019) describes burnout as an *occupational phenomenon* caused by persistent stress that has not been successfully managed, and they explain it results in exhaustion, negativity and professional disconnect.

Burnout is a global problem, and it can affect everyone. Indeed, research from Mental Health UK (2024) found that one in five workers in the UK needed to take time off work in the previous year due to poor mental health caused by pressure or stress, with high workloads, unpaid overtime, job insecurity and being bullied or intimidated at work all being cited as problems.

The reality is that in every situation, we all need time to pause and take a break. Even if that's for a few minutes, even if it's for a few hours and even if it's for a few days. Pausing lets us take a breath and come back stronger, so you must rest. If out-of-hours working becomes the norm, or a 24/7 crisis response is required, you should ask to agree an on-call schedule or rota system and stick to it.

Try to manage expectations on what communication can deliver and what needs to be seeded elsewhere, for example by leadership or HR. Politely but firmly decline additional or unreasonable tasks and activities by reminding people of your crisis priorities and explaining that you are already active in the crisis response, and consider putting an automated response on your email and voicemail to explain that you are in the office but temporarily focused on a critical task and may be slower to respond to unrelated issues. Point people to key resources or manage expectations around the response time for less urgent requests.

Tell colleagues what is possible with the time and resources available and be clear about the help you need to deliver additional demands. Don't be embarrassed to claim recognition for the important work that you are already doing as you suggest reallocating or reprioritizing less urgent and important tasks.

Push back on unacceptable demands

Beyond the sheer volume of work, decision-making may be clouded when people are stretched, conflicted or pressurized.

If something doesn't sit well with you, you have the right to say no. Acknowledge the complexity of the situation and use logic rather than emotion to widen the conversation in a rational and diplomatic way. Refer to policy, standards, codes of conduct, general guidance, past examples and public expectation as you pose simple reflective questions that play forward different scenarios, then suggest or invite alternatives that work better for everyone.

If you are shut down, but you remain concerned, pause. Take advice from a trusted mentor or a professional helpline. Many industries, organizations and professional bodies including the Chartered Institute of Public Relations offer decision-making tools and advice lines that you can call in confidence to receive unbiased advice.

In extreme situations, the ultimate recourse to protect yourself and others is to walk away, and potentially to whistle-blow. Of course, that's easier to advise than it is to do. But it is always a better option than doing something you know to be wrong. At the end of the day, your professional and personal integrity may be at stake, so don't let a toxic situation or a toxic individual steal your future.

Deal with difficult people

Intense and stressful situations can cause people to act in unexpected ways, and you may find yourself feeling undervalued, undermined, or dealing with colleagues and leaders who are rude, aggressive, demanding, arrogant, slippery or out of touch. In some cases, this can become harder to deal with than the issue itself, as a PR professional who prefers to stay anonymous told me:

> It was really difficult. There was a negative news story about a senior person that everyone was talking about. I was the only comms person in the company, fairly new, and not that high up the hierarchy, so I asked two other managers how we might address a press cutting that had been shared internally. They were furious that I thought it was appropriate to say anything and questioned whether I understood my role.
>
> I was instructed not to escalate anything and focus on getting good PR, but the top team didn't like my ideas, and they didn't have any of their own. Everything just got very uncomfortable. To begin with, I was quite confused about the whole thing, but I increasingly came to feel foolish, and very lonely. I wanted to please, but I began to second-guess everything, and I would overthink every interaction.
>
> I began waking up in the middle of the night thinking about work and unsure if I was dreaming or if I wasn't. I would wake bolt upright then not sleep for hours. I was damaged mentally, and I think physically too. I wouldn't have time to eat properly at work and then at night I would just binge on everything.
>
> My grandfather knew. He told me I was working too hard. He was right, but he said it in the wrong way, at the wrong time, and I reacted badly. I was angry and I regret that, because I know now that he was trying to help.

Anyway, we are talking about history. I look back now and more than anything I feel sorry for the wasted time. I should have left sooner, but that's easier said than done. How do you do your best in a job hunt when your confidence is broken? How do you ask for time off to go to a second or third interview when you are already in the bad books? What do you say when they ask why you are leaving?

If you are deep in that kind of situation, you worry about everything, and you begin to expect that more will go wrong. But you need to take a step back and ask, 'What's the worst that can happen?' In the end making the decision to tell them it wasn't working for me was very liberating. In a strange way, I think they were shocked, and in that moment, I recognized that it wasn't me, it was them.

Every situation is different, and I know that people deal with bigger crises and trauma than I did, but I also know now my experience is not uncommon. My advice to anyone feeling as I did is to be kind to yourself and look for ways to stay positive and productive. Don't benchmark how good or bad things are, just trust your gut when it tells you that something's wrong and try to be optimistic as you consider how you can fix it – because you can fix it, and you will be happier when you do.

Also, don't get mad with the wrong people, and don't isolate yourself from the people who truly care. Ask for help and accept help. The problem I had was that I was kept in the dark. I didn't know the details of the situation, only the rumours, so I couldn't make an informed decision about what was actually going on and from there I got pushed further and further out. As I felt cut off at work, I was embarrassed, so I also cut off a bit from life and that was a mistake.

It took me a while to rebuild, but I'm more confident now. I'm more likely to call out bad behaviour, and I'm more likely to celebrate success. I enjoy my work, I think I'm good at what I do, and I think I'm a good manager. I'd always rather make someone's day than break it, and I think that makes for a better team, and a better company.

Dealing with any type of crisis is difficult enough when you have not been kept in the loop, but it's much worse when one or more colleagues refuse to engage or support.

We see time and time again that when people are scared or angry, they say and do things that they don't really mean. Often their behaviour is a reflection on how they are feeling in the moment, and there may be multiple things going on with them that you can't even guess at. Keep your head high and don't take it personally.

Handle conflicts, disagreements and rude behaviour with diplomacy, focusing on finding solutions and common ground. Remember that you were given the job because you were deemed capable and worthy of inclusion, and that means you must be properly treated in the role.

Stay calm so that you can have helpful conversations and make well-judged decisions, and also for your own comfort and resilience. Don't enter high-profile battles, simply treat others as you wish to be treated and do not take it personally when you are not afforded the same courtesy.

If the situation continues, be clear that it is not acceptable. State your case firmly and politely, explain how the behaviour is affecting you personally and professionally, and be clear about what you would like to see change. If it's helpful, use your job description, objectives or an industry code of conduct to guide the conversation. Often this is enough to encourage someone to back off, but if it's not, the next step is to involve a neutral third party and look to move out of a damaging situation.

Deal with mistakes

It's impossible to be perfect in a situation you've never experienced before, and the intensity and uncertainty of crisis may cause the most capable professional to make mistakes. If that happens, and even if it feels difficult, you must always deal with it as quickly and honestly as you can.

This means taking accountability for the error, understanding why it happened, taking steps to fix it and asking for help to make sure it doesn't happen again. Tell someone you trust what has happened – then agree who else needs to know, and what you must do next. The saying 'a problem shared is a problem halved' is as true in a crisis as it is at any other time. It is always easier to find a solution to a shared problem, and it is never too late to put things right.

As you set out to resolve the issue, show people that you're listening, that you're flexible and that you're working to fix the problem. Listen to feedback, take it on board and explain how you are applying it.

At the same time, if you acted with the best intentions in a situation that did not go well, don't let it eat you up, and don't be unfairly judged by those who have different agendas, different perspectives or who were not in the room at the time. They don't know what really happened, and they don't know what they would have done in your situation.

Think positively

As hard as things get, try to approach even the most difficult situation with an optimistic mindset. Shift your thinking from *Why did this happen?* to *What can I do? What can I learn?* or *How can I help?* and approach your important task with the belief that you will succeed.

Hold true to your values, praise others and accept praise as you celebrate kindness, celebrate courtesy and celebrate the fact that, when they are treated well, more people will always want to help rather than hurt each other. Recognize your own growth, learning and successes and note different personal milestones as you reflect on the vital work that you do and the value that you bring.

Look for opportunity to learn and grow

Finally, remember the more you face challenges, the more you learn from them. We will discuss organizational learning in the next chapter, but personal learning is important and should be prioritized and celebrated too.

As things get busier and more complicated, look to become more innovative, stronger and more resilient. Try to be curious and keep an open mind as you embrace challenges as opportunities for personal and professional growth and learn from each difficult situation.

As often as you can, make note of a barrier that you faced, how you dealt with it, what worked and what you could do differently next time. Look for new skills or new responsibilities and observe the behaviour of those around you. Who are your role models and mentors? Who do you aspire to be more like and who don't you want to become? Reflect regularly on your crisis experiences and interactions and consider how they're shaping your outlook or understanding, and how they are making you even better at the job that you do.

KEY TAKEAWAYS

- It is natural to experience a wide range of thoughts, experiences and memories when you navigate a crisis and this means that taking care of your mental health and personal and professional wellbeing is important for immediate relief, as well as for long-term recovery and resilience.

- Everyone reacts differently, and even very resilient people can be physically, mentally and emotionally affected by a crisis at work. Pause to acknowledge how you are feeling and what you need, so you can stay well and thrive in the moment and afterwards.

- **If you have a pre-existing mental health condition**, you should continue with your treatment plans, and you should monitor and report any new or changing symptoms so you can get help to deal with these.

- **If you need help right now**, there are several free and reputable helplines or internet chat services that are staffed by people who are properly trained to help you and ready to listen. Some are available 24 hours a day, 365 days a year and many are available globally so can offer support in your preferred language. They won't judge you, and they could help you feel better.

- Remember that self-care is important. Be kind to yourself and try to focus on healthy rather than unhealthy ways to switch off and release.

- Consider how you can connect with other people, be physically active, learn new skills, give to others and be mindful to improve your mental wellbeing.

- Review your objectives and workload to accommodate the ongoing situation and set boundaries so that you are able switch off and relax.

- Know that you have the right to push back on demands that don't sit well with your values, and don't say or do anything that risks your professional reputation.

- Know that anyone can make a mistake. If you get something wrong, then deal with it as quickly and honestly as possible.

- And finally, remember that all crises end eventually. Try to think positively and see the crisis as an opportunity to help others and to learn and grow yourself.

References

Mental Health UK (2024) The Burnout Report, https://mhukcdn.s3.eu-west-2.amazonaws.com/wp-content/uploads/2024/01/19145241/Mental-Health-UK_The-Burnout-Report-2024.pdf (archived at https://perma.cc/5PSZ-VKRS)

NHS (2022) 5 steps to mental wellbeing guide, www.nhs.uk/mental-health/self-help/guides-tools-and-activities/five-steps-to-mental-wellbeing/ (archived at https://perma.cc/H98G-AHSV)

Royal College of Psychiatrists (2020) Depression in adults, www.rcpsych.ac.uk/
    mental-health/mental-illnesses-and-mental-health-problems/depression (archived
    at https://perma.cc/6B3B-KUPG)
Royal College of Psychiatrists (2021) Post-traumatic stress disorder (PTSD), www.
    rcpsych.ac.uk/mental-health/mental-illnesses-and-mental-health-problems/
    post-traumatic-stress-disorder (archived at https://perma.cc/M8WW-5B34)
World Health Organization (2019) Burn-out an 'occupational phenomenon':
    International Classification of Diseases, www.who.int/news/item/28-05-2019-
    burn-out-an-occupational-phenomenon-international-classification-of-diseases
    (archived at https://perma.cc/ND52-VEH3)

12

Evaluate efforts and learn for next time

As it evolves and lingers, your crisis will feel complex and unending. Each stage will bring new challenges, and there will be times when it's hard to reimagine normality. But it will end eventually. At some point, the pressure will lift, and your world will begin to feel balanced again.

When that happens, you could be tempted to seek comfort in old ways and never look back. But if the old ways caused the problem in the first place, going backwards without seeking to reflect or learn from what happened would be a mistake that would hinder your own growth, hinder the organization's growth, and remove the very real opportunity to bring forward positive and meaningful change.

As well as challenge, crises bring opportunities. They bring opportunities for progression, innovation, positive change and new beginnings, and they bring opportunities to do good and be better – if the organization is open to them. Being open to opportunities means being ready to explore the crisis without judgement or defence, and it means being willing to adapt and learn even when the insights are hard to face. It means making time to measure and test success as you go along, and it means creating safe and supportive environments for people to come together afterwards so that the whole organization can implement lessons and strengthen a muscle memory that will help drive crisis outcomes and:

- improve real-time crisis performance
- build resilience
- prevent future crises
- improve crisis outcomes
- repair relationships and build trust
- regenerate and strengthen the organization
- make positive change

All of this means the organization must embrace learning as an opportunity, and it must seek to understand different perspectives as it implements a considered programme of measurement and evaluation to understand how it has performed at each crisis stage. Beyond that, it means using the insight gained to reflect on organizational behaviour and to innovate, adapt and build reliability and resilience for the future.

This chapter is a call to action through reflection and learning. It explores short- and long-term measures in relation to the wider crisis response and to internal crisis communication activities, and it advocates for a considered and joined up approach that recognizes the unique needs brought about by the crisis itself. It suggests the measurement tools you might use in different situations, and it gives some tips for interpreting, sharing and actioning the learning so that the company can re-establish trust and support, and so that it can stabilize, strengthen and secure permission to grow into the future.

The benefits of learning

Internal communication authorities such as Quirke (2008) have long argued that an ongoing commitment to measurement and evaluation is the foundation of any great internal communication strategy, while crisis communication thought leaders such as Mitroff (1994) and Coombs (2015) reflect that remembering and learning from what has happened is a critical crisis responsibility, and propose that ongoing measurement and evaluation is essential to help deliver continual improvements.

This means that while running surveys and collecting data may seem a low priority as volatility and ambiguity abound, meaningful learning is an essential part of each stage of the crisis process and it's critical if your organization is to effectively dismantle future risk, increase crisis resilience and build opportunities for improvement and growth.

From an internal communication perspective, knowing what works, what doesn't and why also ensures that you inform, engage and listen to your people in the most effective way as the crisis evolves, and it helps you ensure your communication is driving the necessary action or behaviour change. Sense-checking what people think, feel and do at key stages throughout the crisis also helps you:

- test that messages are received and understood as expected
- test that questions, suggestions and responses are returned and understood
- understand employee attitudes towards the crisis

- track progress towards objectives
- identify the value of different communication activities
- refine messages, activity and channels
- better allocate resources
- assess and evidence your impact

This means that the need for ongoing measurement must be built in at the crisis planning stage and it must be used to strengthen the organization at many different critical crisis points.

Not all crisis measurement and evaluation are the responsibility of the internal communication team, of course, but it's important that you measure internal crisis communication impact, and it's important that you support broader organizational goals by reflecting crisis learning, and by sharing crisis insights and actions with the wider team.

What to measure

Measurement isn't just about collecting information – it's about using it in a helpful way to improve crisis outcomes in both the immediate and longer term. This means that your normal approach to measurement and evaluation may need to be paused or altered as you focus on the impacts of the crisis and on the performance of internal crisis communication.

As with everything else, measurement in the acute phase of the crisis must be very simple, specific and focused on key crisis needs, and it can then broaden out as the crisis evolves. Crisis communication consultant and trainer Ben Verinder explains:

> The measurement techniques you use don't necessarily differ too much, but the circumstances do. This means you need to think carefully about what insights you need and when, and you may also need to pause 'normal' employee surveys and research so you can focus on building understanding in relation to the difficulty at hand. It also means you need to be sensitive to the ongoing situation and be careful that you're not conducting research that will take up too much time, aggravate the difficult situation, or otherwise make things worse.

> In the very early stages of a crisis, for example, we know the focus is on survival. Any measurement must be attentive to that. It must cut out distraction and focus on whether those first messages have been received and understood by staff and whether they are working to help people and assets survive.

The requirement at that time is for very straightforward measures of outputs and out-takes – but don't confuse straightforward with unsophisticated. Basic measures such as 'How much stuff have we sent out?' won't cut it. In the immediacy of a crisis, you need to know about employee consideration of the message, understanding of the message and retention of the message so you can use that understanding to confirm or change your approach. But we are talking about short, sharp measurements to support rather than interrupt other activity.

Quickly on the back of that, you want to start understanding employee attitudes and views of difficulty and you want to start understanding what they are saying and doing because of those attitudes and views – again with short, sharp measures. It's only as you move out of the acute crisis stage that you should introduce a greater mix of methods in the form of focus groups or in-depth discussions as you begin to explore the impact of the situation on internal relationships and reputation, or to understand how staff feel, how they are behaving, what they need personally and what else you must do to support and motivate them through the crisis response.

Every organization will have different internal crisis communication objectives, so make sure that what you are measuring is strategically meaningful and will either directly support the efficiency and impact of your internal crisis communication activities, facilitate wider crisis understanding, improvement or change, or otherwise support the immediate crisis needs of the people in the organization.

Beyond this, be aware that national or international agencies may also ask the company to share specific insights or learning objectives so that industry-wide safety standards, guidelines or training can be improved after a crisis occurs. Mandated measures and actions must always be reported and published as a priority, and while it's important that the internal communication function is involved in the full process of gathering, reflecting and sharing insights, you must also be clear with colleagues that crisis learning objectives rarely relate to internal communication alone, and you must be specific about who holds responsibility for different forms of learning and action.

Crisis management

Many large or high-risk organizations have detailed systems and processes in place to manage and learn from crises, and they have specialist experience, expertise and insight in the people who have been allocated this responsibility. This means your job as an internal communication professional is not to lead or manage that part of the process but to support it by reflecting the implications of what is being suggested, and to communicate learning, action and opportunity to different internal audiences.

Some of the things that the organization may want to understand include:

- if and how a looming crisis was successfully averted
- how effectively the plan was activated to deal with the crisis
- the impact of the crisis versus best- and worst-case scenarios
- the impact on relationships versus best- and worst-case scenarios
- the success of internal crisis communication against established objectives

A common way to do this is for the crisis steering group, crisis management team, crisis communication team and business continuity team to come together and first answer questions around plan activation such as:

- How quickly did the different groups come together?
- How effective was the interaction between them?
- Did the crisis plan, processes and resources deliver what was expected?
- Did effective group interactions stay in place through each crisis stage?

From there the same team can move on to discuss the impact of the crisis faced, and the harm it caused against some of the scenarios that could have reasonably been anticipated. In such situations, it's common to compare the crisis impact to what could be expected if no action was taken to manage it, and it's also common to compare it to the agreed crisis management, business continuity and business recovery objectives.

For example, let's imagine I am out walking with a friend, and we realize I am in the path of an oncoming vehicle. Anyone can predict the outcome will be different if I take action to move out of the way, or if I take no action and stay in the road:

A   I move in good time, and everyone is fairly relaxed.

B   I am slow to move and have a close encounter but feel no physical harm.

C   I am slow to move, there is contact, and I have a minor injury.

D   I don't move, the vehicle hits me, and I am hurt.

E   I don't move, the vehicle hits me, and I have a life-changing injury, or I am killed.

In this example, not being hit would be a positive outcome, and being hit would be a negative outcome, and so, assuming I survive, I would learn to move more quickly next time. However, reality is more complicated than this, and the outcome might be affected by many other things. These might include the type and size of the vehicle, the speed of the vehicle, the driver's awareness of my friend and I, the driver's ability to control the vehicle and even the driver's intent in causing or preventing harm. Beyond that, what if there is a bigger, faster and heavier vehicle in the other lane? All these factors change the nature of what we consider a positive and negative outcome and importantly, of what we would consider useful learning.

If I see the vehicle in good time, my objective is to step out of the way and avoid all harm. But if it appears fast, close and out of control, I might consider a minor bump to be a lucky escape. My objective changes, and the learning outcomes might differ too if we consider not just my experience, but the experience of the driver, and that of my friend as well.

That example is very simple, but all crises can have different best- and worst-case outcomes and they have complex dependencies so it is important that you are honest in assessing your success and learning through what occurred, and also through what could have occurred.

Dr Timothy Coombs (2015) says that the organization 'must not inflate the potential damage or lowball their objectives if the exercise is to be meaningful', and this is a critical tip if you want to maximize future safety and success.

Internal crisis communication

Beyond the organizational learning that comes from the crisis itself, you also need to understand the performance of your internal crisis communication activities and the impact of the crisis on internal reputation and relationships.

Research conducted by Mazzei and Ravazzani (2011) found there can be a misalignment between management and employee perceptions about the success of internal communication, so it's important that you ask the right questions and listen to a wide range of views if you want to move beyond a tick-box exercise and get the meaningful insight that will help you improve and keep getting better.

Speak with individuals at all levels and from all parts of the organization to dig into how they feel and why, and seek to understand what they want and need not just through the crisis but also through the process of healing, reconciliation and repair. Internal communication consultant, author and business owner Rachel Miller says:

> It's important to consider all evaluation from an employee perspective. What communication went well for them and what was a complete disaster? Involve your employees and listen to them as you assess what went well, what went badly, and how you get better next time.

Think about the clear, simple and unambiguous questions you might ask to capture information and build actionable learning about employee understanding, satisfaction and engagement with internal crisis communication in key areas such as:

- crisis management planning and processes
- crisis understanding
- crisis messaging and position
- communication channels
- organizational listening
- issues reporting
- communication with leadership and management

And beyond that look at how you might measure the achievement of specific crisis management and communication goals, or understand issues and outcomes such as:

- engagement
- motivation
- advocacy
- capability
- discretionary effort
- pride
- trust
- ongoing concerns

Off-the-shelf only takes you so far, and that is especially true in turbulent times. If you want actionable insights, you must clearly link your research to your specific internal communication objectives so you can test when, how and why your crisis communication has been successful, and when, how and why it missed the mark.

Make sure that you are gathering the data that you think you are by making sure all questions follow a very simple structure and use simple words to avoid misinterpretation or conflation – and consider response options too. Are you asking for a simple yes, or no answer? Are you going to use a scale? If so, what kind and why? Are you going to offer the opportunity to add comment? Or are you going to use your questions as discussion points and let others lead the way? Each of these approaches will generate different insights so must be approached intentionally and with an understanding of what constitutes best practice. Similarly, if you want to understand changes in trust, attitude or behaviours, you need to have something meaningful to benchmark against.

Consider connections

Thanks to the work of global experts such as Dr Jim Macnamara (2015) and specialist bodies such as AMEC – the International Association for Measurement and Evaluation of Communication (2020) – it is commonly understood that effective measurement goes far beyond counting what you created, sent, broadcast or delivered. It is instead about looking at the issue within its context or situation and taking a holistic approach to understanding the connections between and impacts of a full series of activities.

- Objectives: your original aim for crisis communication
- Inputs: the learning, insights and circumstances that informed your approach
- Outputs: the content, channels and activity experienced by your audience
- Out-takes: the thoughts and feelings shaped by your outputs
- Outcomes: the subsequent intended and unintended responses or behaviours
- Impact: the overall influence of your communication inputs, outputs, out-takes and outcomes on your original objectives, and of course on crisis recovery

How to measure

When you are clear about what you want to measure and why, it's time to decide how to do it, and to make sure that you can get a wide range of different people involved. The right choice of measurement tools and techniques will depend on the crisis stage and impact, as crisis communication consultant and trainer Ben Verinder mentioned earlier, but it will also depend on the issues you wish to better understand, the degree of sophistication required, the size and geographical spread of your organization, and the resources and budget available to you.

Different organizations will have different expectations of which techniques should be used and why, but either way, once you have moved out of the acute crisis stage, it's helpful to use a mix of both quantitative and qualitative measurement, if they are possible within the confines of the situation at hand. Ben Verinder says:

> Certain types of perennial measurement will not be appropriate in times of crisis, but that's not your only consideration when deciding what techniques to use. It's also important to recognize that some measurement channels might not be available as a result of the crisis. For example, in a cyber breach, some of your normal digital channels could become unavailable and you will need to seek meaningful alternatives.
>
> And even if all your normal channels are available, be aware that the uncertainty, stress and exhaustion people feel may lead to lower response rates, poor-quality answers or employees abandoning the survey altogether, and so other techniques may be more effective.

All of this means that results should be carefully scrutinized, and where possible cross-checked rather than taken at face value.

Use quantitative measures to track patterns

Quantitative measurement (which can be conducted through polls, surveys, questionnaires, content analysis, audits and online analytics) involves collecting and analysing large amounts of data to help you understand scale and trends. It is helpful to test whether the loudest voices really do reflect the most widely held view; it's helpful to recognize shifts, changes and trends; and it's helpful to assess whether the same patterns exist across the whole organization, or if different people in different roles, locations or groups do things differently or hold different views.

Quantitative measures can be designed specifically for your needs, or they can be brought in as standardized surveys that have been used, tested and benchmarked elsewhere. In crisis, as we established earlier, it is usually more helpful to measure directly against your established objectives if you want actionable insight to inform immediate goals and strategic priorities.

Ben Verinder advises that it's always helpful to pilot your research to catch any confusing or misleading questions before launching it widely. His general tips when designing surveys for use in crises include:

- If you are designing a survey that is intended to be anonymous, beware asking questions that, taken together, might identify (or be perceived to identify) colleagues.

- If using questions that employ a Likert scale – commonly used when exploring strength of feeling towards an issue – ensure that a midpoint is included in the scale, to allow respondents to express neutrality on an issue, and that, separately, respondents have an alternative option to say they 'don't know'.

- If including a ranking question in any survey, remember that it will typically provide insight into the order of preference or aversion, but not the strength of feeling.

- Always consider sampling and check to what extent respondents are representative of the population under study. If a survey is anonymous, it can be very difficult to assess this, but you need to be alive to that tension in discussing your results.

Use qualitative measures to gather insights

Qualitative measurement (which can be conducted through focus groups, interviews and analysis of written feedback, letters, comment and reviews) can be used to help you explore different ideas so that you can better understand why the quantitative data is as it is.

It offers a deeper insight into the meaning behind the quantitative figures, and it can give a more nuanced understanding of different experiences, attitudes and perceptions relating to crisis challenges, opportunities and threats as well as towards the organization and its activities at any given time. From an internal communication perspective, it helps you more sincerely understand and connect with your audiences, and it can also be helpful if you are deciding how to influence or persuade people to stop, start or continue with a specific action or behaviour.

The quality of a focus group conversation or interview is shaped by many different factors including the questions, the context, the environment and by the skill of the person leading the conversation. A great moderator helps people speak freely while remaining fully objective. They can probe deeper into superficial statements, they can make sure that conversations focus on reflection and not on blame, and they can ensure that everyone has their say, so that any learning can be built directly into future crisis management and communication plans.

Include everyone

Remember that data is always open to interpretation, and if you want to learn you must not ignore what's right in front of you. Make sure that everyone is aware of the opportunity to take part, knows how to get involved, and feels safe, supported and valued as they share their own crisis truth.

As you invite people to step forward and share their views, make sure that you encourage everyone to participate. In her book *Influential Internal Communication: Streamline your corporate communication to drive efficiency and engagement*, internal communications author and consultant Jenni Field (2021) explores the role of internal communication data and diagnostics in detail, and she offers tips on the messaging that will encourage people to participate in internal communication research during busy and chaotic times. Some of her key tips are to acknowledge the difficult situation while being clear why you're doing the research and why it's important and emphasizing that results and actions will be delivered quickly to prioritize employee support.

Listen to those who have tried to retreat from sight as well as those who are loud in grief or anger. Try to make sure no voice is forgotten, pay attention to what is being said and done in different regions and teams as the organization deals with the crisis and seeks to strengthen.

Interpret your findings

Once you have checked it, you need to process, interpret and make sense of the knowledge you have gathered so you can identify what went well and what could have gone better, and then put your learning into action.

There are different ways to do this, and a good idea is to involve as many employees as possible as you discuss key outcomes, sense-check understanding, and decide which actions will really move the organization forward in future. Some organizations choose to do this through workshops and hackathons, while others prefer to hold more reflective conversations. By way of example, the communication team at Bromford, a housing association responsible for more than 44,000 homes across central and southwest England ran a Rose, Bud, Thorn evaluation after a cyber incident pushed them to disconnect all their online systems.

Bromford's former Digital and Brand Lead Jarrod Williams tells me that Rose, Bud, Thorn is a simple way to reflect upon and evaluate the effectiveness of your crisis communication activity, and it involves identifying what went well (Rose), what new opportunities were created (Bud) and what must be improved (Thorn). Exercises such as these are helpful because they encourage detailed but balanced reflection after the complexity and ambiguity of crisis, and because they allow you to acknowledge effort and celebrate success while putting actions around learning and continuous improvement. Jarrod says:

> No one ever thinks about losing everything, but that's where we were. We had to protect ourselves and our customers, so we flipped the switch, and everything went off. We had access to nothing – no CRM, no HR systems, no office access fobs, no fuel cards and of course no internal communication channels. It was totally unprecedented, so we were taking no risks. We were quick to activate our crisis plans, and as we confirmed that our data had not been breached and we began to switch on again, we knew it was important to review what had happened and to identify and share learning for the future. The Rose, Bud, Thorn exercise helped us do that in a positive way.

> From the word go, it was clear that our Roses stemmed from the positive connections we had already established in the company. My strong relationship with the Chief Information Officer meant I was first to be told when the red flag was raised. This kept me ahead of the curve, meant I was in conversations from the outset, and meant I could be proactive at every new development. Crucially, for example, it gave me time to export all employee phone numbers minutes before the system was shut down, and those numbers were a communication lifeline.

> Having the numbers meant we could set up a formal third-party text messaging service for all employees, wherever they were. We were cut off from our customers and suppliers through all normal means but we had to maintain an emergency service so we used these texts to share critical updates for staff as

well as information that they could pass on. We backed this up with a more involving and engaging manager-led WhatsApp network that enabled a more human connection, and facilitated listening, idea sharing and real-time issues reporting to make sure every voice was heard as we worked to get back to normal service.

WhatsApp turned out to be vital in unexpected ways too, as our cyber-savvy employees interpreted the very first third-party SMS message as a phishing scam and refused to click the link! But having WhatsApp messages from real people in trusted networks meant we were able to reassure people that the new text service was legitimate, it would message them every day going forward, and it would point them to that all important source of truth.

Even when we didn't have all the answers, we made sure employees understood the situation, why decisions were made and when updates would come. This openness helped maintain credibility and foster trust across the organization.

Given the high levels of challenge and uncertainty, Jarrod tells me another Rose was the ability to quickly repurpose the IT helpdesk so colleagues could get directly in touch with teams such as HR and finance for other necessary sources of support, as well as repurpose the external website as an intranet. Taking a totally open, transparent and human approach worked well for them too:

Because our colleague pages had to be hosted on our external channels, our internal communication was accessible to anyone in the outside world who wanted to find it. I think this was a Rose because it evidenced our transparent approach and reassured everyone that nothing was being hidden.

You must remember that Bromford are a housing association. There's a lot of important work to do. Some of our customers are vulnerable and they have urgent needs related to homelessness or domestic abuse. Those vital services can't just stop, and so I think another Rose was the fact that there was real energy among colleagues to smash normal bureaucracy and ensure this vital side of our work continued against the odds. Staff are the keepers of customer relationships, and our approach meant they were empowered with real, clear information to make things happen for the people who needed it most. This meant that throughout the crisis, innovation thrived, creating opportunities to do things differently and rewrite processes from the ground up. This shift had a lasting impact on the organizational culture.

Identifying and acknowledging the things that went well offered a real boost for the team who had pulled out all the stops and changed all normal ways of working to survive and thrive in a fully unforeseen situation, and Jarrod tells me that it enabled them to be more open to learning too.

> We recognized the distribution of work within the comms team as a Thorn. For example, a colleague event that was happening as the crisis hit meant that my team, which is mainly digital and brand, took on the initial internal comms response. When our teammates came back, we probably didn't bring them up to speed as fast as we could have done and that meant the pressure was on too few people. The very nature of crisis means they don't run 9 to 5, and they don't wait until everyone is available. That means team members will potentially always have to take on different or additional roles, especially in the earliest moments, so I would better plan how we make this process work better for everyone, and how we enable that tracking and handover of work.

> Another Thorn was the need for clarity around the approvals process because we wasted time when people disagreed on the focus or wording of the message. Related to this, we also identified a need for people to be realistic about the demands being placed on the communication team. We were sometimes asked to put out a message at 12 pm, for example, but we only got the information at 11.30 am and still had to get sign-off before it went. Everyone was busy, so getting hold of people was difficult and in future I'd try and get that lead time and sign-off process agreed up front, in our crisis comms plan.

> And when it looked to the outside world that normal customer service resumed, our colleagues were using workarounds or brand-new processes to make that happen. These new processes created additional layers of complexity that slowed things down as employees got used to them. There needed to be more recognition of this extra workload by leadership and in our comms, as it meant our day-to-day operations were impacted still.

> As for the Buds, one was our relationship with the chief executive and the senior leadership team, who saw the power of comms first-hand. They got an appreciation for our work, and they got fully involved in internal as well as external communication, recording regular videos and getting fully involved in the WhatsApp groups. They really embraced and enabled our work, demonstrating a commitment to our principles of regular, human-centred and transparent communication. From the outset, their visibility and empathy were crucial, and their hands-on approach not only boosted employee morale and boosted trust but also established a precedent and tone for future engagement, inside and outside of a crisis.

Jarrod tells me that having a clear vision of what all your different people need personally and professionally, while remaining agile, is vital in a crisis.

From the outset, he said, his team's focus was about getting out the message that there had been an attack, followed by the news that data had not been breached. But it was also about enabling and empowering people to continue with their vital work as disruption to the system lingered on. Flexibility and innovation are necessary when you are trying to implement solutions in a situation that can't be fully predicted, and he says a top tip is to build flexibility into your plan, so you are best prepared to find solutions in unpredictable situations.

Share learning and evidence action

Its widely agreed that showing how the organization has listened, learnt and grown is an important part of the crisis recovery strategy because it sends a vital signal that the company is technically, intellectually and emotionally competent to operate in the crisis aftermath. Disclosing and being open about what went wrong, why and how it will be addressed is critical to re-establishing trust and support, and it is also critical to strengthening reputation and securing future permission to grow.

That means a final key step is to bring people back together to discuss all the feedback and analysis the organization has gathered, and to agree and communicate what different parts of the company need to stop, start and continue.

Publish top level organizational actions in a central, accessible place, such as on the company intranet or on posters and pull-up stands in operational areas. Build them into meeting agendas at every level of the organization and encourage teams across the company to create and share their own associated or linked actions with a process, an owner and a timeline to commit to them and address them.

Turn the problem into a target or opportunity that people can be proud to reach for and meet, then (keeping victim and survivor needs in mind) share success quietly or more publicly as these targets and opportunities are met. Remember, as we discussed earlier, progress in the chronic stage of the crisis can be slow, and improvement doesn't happen overnight, so make sure internal crisis communication plans offer milestones and points of reflection on the journey, evidence fairness and consideration in the new ways of doing things, avoid blame and show a clear understanding of what people have been through as you involve everyone in the future, share lessons learnt and pinpoint progress.

As always, include as many stories, as many voices and as many ideas as possible, and let people talk about learning and improvement in their own words and through multiple channels and platforms. Simple ideas might include publishing everyday steps to prevent future crises, and promoting updated tools, techniques, policies and strategies, while more complex actions may involve implementing wider systemic or cultural change that will take many years to fully resource and embed.

Regardless, it is important to publish crisis learning, share this widely and give detailed updates or milestones as change is introduced and embedded for a better future. Concrete rather than abstract descriptions of progress are always more effective, and this is something that can be continued by sharing news, stories and case studies through your normal internal communication channels.

Finally, be aware that some people may be feeling bruised and others traumatized from their crisis experience, so a duty of care is required to show how the whole organization is learning valuable lessons to stay strong and making sure it does not fall back into bad habits.

KEY TAKEAWAYS

- Alongside challenge, crises bring opportunities for progression, innovation and positive change.

- As well as creating opportunities to measure and test success as you go along, it's important that the organization can also create safe and supportive environments for people to come together afterwards to learn and implement lessons.

- Crisis measurement is an ongoing activity that should take place at each crisis stage – but what you can and should measure at different crisis stages can change, so you must be attentive to what is happening in the organization as you decide what measurement is helpful and appropriate.

- Measures in the acute crisis phase should be short, sharp and focused, but they can become more mixed and detailed as the pressure lifts.

- Don't just count what you did – consider objectives, inputs, outputs, out-takes, outcomes and impacts to build a full picture.

- Consider both strengths and weaknesses without judgement or defence.

- And finally, publish your learning, share this widely and give detailed updates or milestones as your actions are implemented and embedded for a better future.

References

AMEC (2020) Barcelona Principles 3.0, https://amecorg.com/barcelona-principles-3-0-translations/ (archived at https://perma.cc/D6SK-3S96)

Coombs, W T (2015) *Ongoing Crisis Communication: Planning, managing and responding*, Sage, Los Angeles

Field, J (2021) *Influential Internal Communication: Streamline your corporate communication to drive efficiency and engagement*, Kogan Page, London

Macnamara, J (2015) *Organizational Listening: The missing element in public communication*, Peter Lang, Lausanne, Switzerland

Mazzei, A and Ravazzani, S (2011) Manager-employee communication during a crisis: The missing link, *Corporate Communications: An International Journal*, 16, 243–54, www.emerald.com/insight/content/doi/10.1108/13563281111156899/full/html (archived at https://perma.cc/MPN8-TC6N)

Miller, R (2024) *Internal Communication Strategy: Design, develop and transform your organizational communication*, Kogan Page, London

Mitroff, I I (1994) Crisis management and environmentalism: A natural fit, *California Management Review*, 36 (2), 101–13, https://journals.sagepub.com/doi/10.2307/41165747 (archived at https://perma.cc/EZ7A-DWQY)

Quirke, B (2008) *Making the Connections: Using internal communication to turn strategy into action*, Routledge, London

INDEX

Abercrombie & Fitch 41
Aberdeen City Council 122
'accidental managers' 156
accountability 77–81, 140
accuracy 93
active listening 169–70
acute crisis stage 8, 21–22, 85–88, 124,
        167–69, 196–97
adaptability 45, 47, 102, 132
advocacy 83–84, 99
ambiguity 98
anaphora 98
Anderson, Marion 147–48, 149–50, 152,
        153–54, 156–57
anger 11, 22, 168
        see also outrage
anonymity 167, 203
anxiety 178
Arnett-Morrice, Lulu 64–65
art, power of 182–83
assessments 72–73
authenticity 23, 104, 107, 116, 137

Bailey, John 41–42, 49
Barron, Bill 121, 122
Betts, Kate 4, 164, 166
biological crises 37–38
blogs 83, 112, 118
Boeing 737 MAX crises 38, 164
bolstering strategies 81–82
        see also celebrating success; recognition
boundary setting 186–87
Bowick, Carolyn 150–51, 170–72
broadcast channels 118
Bromford 205–08
Buds (Rose, Bud, Thorn exercise) 205, 207
burnout 186–87
business continuity teams xi, xii, 9, 28, 35,
        50, 51, 198

call trees 46, 49
capability (competence) 96, 134, 136
care 96
CARE formula 95, 137
celebrating success 30–31
central communication strategies 27,
        146–47, 149, 153, 169

CERC Crisis and Emergency Risk
        Communication 86
champions 78
change 29
channel selection 109–27
Chartered Institute of Public Relations 188
chat platforms 125, 171, 180, 192
checklists 46, 68, 186
chronic crisis stage 8, 85, 88–89, 124,
        169–72
clarity 94, 140, 154
climax (narrative arc) 105
coaching 42, 135–36, 138, 157, 169
'Cobra' crises 5, 80
Coleman, Amanda 68, 149
collective denial 166
colour-coding systems 94
commitment 96
communication teams 49–50, 198
company information 58, 82–83
competence (capability) 96, 134, 136
        practitioner 141–42, 144–59, 197–99
concern 96
confidence 96, 136, 137
confidentiality 100–01
conflict management 188–90
confrontation crises 38–39
Conley, Ed 131, 162–63, 181, 182
connection 181–82
consistency 124
consultation forums 116
content creation 91–108, 153
contingency planning 125–26
Conway, Dr Jacqueline 99–100, 135–36,
        141–42
Coombs, Dr Timothy 86–87
Covid-19 pandemic 64–65, 98, 125,
        150–51, 170–72, 182–83
credibility 96, 104, 141–42, 185
Crichton, Gillies 45, 48–49, 51, 181
crisis, defined 2–3
crisis activation 45–46
crisis anticipation 34–41
crisis assessments 72–73
crisis communication teams 49–50, 198
crisis development 7–9, 66
crisis 'flashover' 49–51

crisis positions 74–82
crisis response activation 51–52
crisis scanning 5, 6
crisis stage 8
crisis steering teams 49–50, 198
culture
    learning 30, 140–41, 182–83, 191,
        194–209
    organizational 31, 57, 106, 164
customer service and relationship logging
        systems 174
cyber crises 39, 125–26, 202

dance 118
dark pages 114
data collection 195–96
    see also evidence gathering
data presentation 94
Deakin, Leona 11, 26
deception crises 40
decision trees 49
demands, responding to 187–88
demographics 58–60
denial 76–77, 166
difficult colleagues 188–90
digital platforms 123–24
diminishment 77
direct instruction 85, 140
disinformation 76, 85, 99–100, 172
    see also fake news
distribution lists 114, 185
diversity 136–37, 140
double crises 9
drop-in sessions 139, 168

Easthope, Lucy 75, 80–81, 84, 139
effective listening 12, 28, 42, 69, 117,
        148–49, 152, 160–76, 183
Eisenhower Matrix 186
Elizabeth, The Queen Mother 122
email addresses 114
embargos 154
emotions 106–07, 136, 148–50
    see also anger; feelings; outrage
empathy 66, 87, 95–97, 102–03,
        134, 149, 183
employee assistance programmes 80
employees
    as advocates 83–84, 99
    as champions 78
    demographics 58–60
    emotional needs 106–07, 136, 148–50
    engagement of 116–18, 146, 161
    information requirements 10–13,
        43–44, 55–70, 73, 140, 199–201

participation (involvement) 28–29, 99,
        115–18, 119, 139–40
practical needs 151–52
psychological needs 150–51
roles (responsibilities) 60–63
sensemaking needs 21, 24–26, 69,
        87–88, 113, 139, 173
stabilizing needs 21, 26–28, 69, 113
stimulating needs 21, 28–29,
        115–18
strengthening needs 21, 30–31
supporting needs 21, 22–24, 87–88, 91,
        94, 113, 139
survival needs 21–22, 67, 85–86, 91,
        94, 113, 171–72, 196–97
sustaining needs 21, 29–30
environmental crises 29–30, 36, 37, 38
evaluation 204–08
    see also reflective practice
evidence gathering 50–51
    see also data collection
evidence sharing 208–09
exhibitions 120–22
expectation setting 187
expert input 131
exposition (narrative arc) 105
external triggers 6

face-to-face communication 26, 60, 116,
        123–24, 167
fact-checked 'stamps' 93
    see also verified information
fairness (parity) 81, 88
fake news 76, 93, 100
    see also disinformation; misinformation
falling action (narrative arc) 105
FAQs 88, 114, 124, 169, 174
fatality crises 80–81
feedback 152, 165, 173–74
feedback logging systems 174
feelings 178
    see also emotions
'fight, flight or freeze' response 9–10, 136
financial crises 29–30
Fink's four stage crisis model 8, 85–89
first (initial) messages 51–52, 86–87,
        91–92, 101–03, 113, 167
5Cs of communication 96
'flashovers' 49–51
flexibility 185, 208
focus groups 126, 204
Freytag's Pyramid 105–06
Fukushima tsunami 37

giving to others 183

Glasgow Airport terror attack xi–iii, 89
goal setting 185–86
Goldberg, Suzanne 22–23, 168
graphics 114–15
Grenfell Tower fire 40
grief 81, 119–20, 124, 173
growth mindset 191

hackathons 116, 205
Haiti earthquake 41
Harrods 41
Hazelhead Park 122
healing strategies 119–23
helplines 47, 180, 187–88, 192
Holden, Dan 61–62, 155
holding statements 47
Horizon scandal 39–40
HR teams 58–59
humanity 95–97
'Humans of Healthcare' campaigns 64–65

impact 201
inclusion 139–40, 204, 208–09
incompetence crises 78–79
    see also mismanagement crises
industry measurements 197
Infant Formula Action Coalition 38
informal communication channels
        62, 110–12
information
    employee requirements 10–13, 43–44,
        55–70, 73, 140, 199–201
    inverted pyramid of 94
information gaps 95
information presentation 94
initial (first) messages 51–52, 86–87,
        91–92, 101–03, 113, 167
inputs 201
instruction, direct 85, 140
integrity 118
internal communications
        practitioners 141–42, 144–59,
        197–99
    see also coaching
internal crisis communication 18–32
internal crisis communication plans
        32, 44–49
internal crisis communication strategy
        44, 45, 71–89
internal triggers 6–7
intranets 114
inverted pyramid of information 94

judgement 124

Kerr, Stewart 178–79, 180, 181, 184
key contacts 48
    see also call trees; distribution lists;
        email addresses
kindness 183
King, Dr Martin Luther 98
knowledge sharing 116

labelling systems 94
language use 94, 185
leadership 30, 63–65, 78, 81, 119,
        129–43, 169
leadership roadshows 139
leadership self-management 135–36
Leaker, Jane 5–6, 27, 168–69
learning culture 30, 140–41, 182–83, 191,
        194–209
life models 121
Likert scale surveys 203
line managers 27, 78, 111, 144–59, 170
listening skills 12, 28, 42, 69, 117, 148–49,
        152, 160–76, 183
litigation 101
Lochhead, Alison 59–60, 125–26
logging forms 46

MacMillan, Sir James 123
malevolent acts 39
management teams 46, 49–50, 198
management values crises 40
Mandal, Piyali 93, 137, 172–73
Marlow, Katie 146–47, 155
measurement (metrics) 126, 167, 196–204
meeting skills 185
memorable content 97–98
memorials 119–22
Mendonsa, Sister Patricia 65
mental health 30, 178–80, 192
Miller, Rachel 44, 110–11, 200
mindfulness 183–84
misconduct crises 41, 100
misinformation 85, 99–100, 172
    see also fake news
mismanagement crises 39–40, 75
    see also incompetence crises
mission statements 45
mistakes 190
moderators 204
monitoring (tracking) systems 41–42, 126
mood judgements 124
moral violation crises 79
Moss Kanter, Professor Rosabeth 166
motivation 29–30, 63–65, 106–07
MUM effect 166

music 122–23
myth busters 88, 114

narrative arc 105–06
National Health Service 150–51, 164,
    170–72, 180–84
National Services Scotland 150–51, 170–72
natural crises 37
Ndone, James 13
Nestlé boycott 38
neurodiversity 44

Obama, President Barak 98
objective setting 74, 94–95,
    185–86, 201
observations 58, 62, 66, 167, 170
Occidental 122
on-call schedules 187
one-way communication channels 117–18,
    123, 127
    see also direct instruction
online forums 170–72
openness (transparency) 82, 92–93, 123,
    142, 166, 206, 208–09
operational crises 29–30
organizational change 29
organizational context 73
organizational crises 2–3, 4–7, 36–41
    impact of 1, 9–13, 17
organizational culture 31, 57, 106, 164
organizational information 58, 82–83
organizational listening 12, 28, 42, 69, 117,
    148–49, 152, 160–76, 183
out-takes 201
outcomes 201
outputs 201
outrage 3, 22, 40, 120, 121
'overcoming the monster' (narrative
    arc) 105–06
Oxfam GB 41

pandemic, Covid-19 64–65, 98, 125,
    150–51, 170–72, 182–83
parity (fairness) 81, 88
Patel, Advita 61, 63, 169–70
pausing (self-care) 177, 178, 182, 187
pausing (work activities) 78, 79
Pearson, Molly 123
photographs 118
physical activity 182–83
Pike, Julian 100–01
pilots 203
Piper Alpha explosion 120, 123
Piper Alpha memorial 120–22
planning 34–52

pluralistic ignorance 166
podcasts 110, 114, 118
positioning statements 47
positive thinking 191
post-crisis stage 8, 173
Post Office scandal 39–40
post-traumatic stress disorder (PTSD) 179
practical needs 151–52
pre-crisis stage 7, 8, 163–67
pre-existing mental health conditions
    180, 192
printed materials 114–15
prioritization 67–69
privacy 100–01
problem avoidance 4–5
problem-solving exercises 26, 29–30
professional body helplines 187–88
professional wellbeing 184–91
Provan, Derek 132–33, 165
psychological needs 150–51
psychological safety 43, 106, 137, 148,
    157, 163–64, 171–72, 173
psychology theory 12–13
purpose 26, 28, 63–65
'Python' crises 5, 79–80

qualitative measurements 167, 203–04
    see also focus groups
quantitative measurements 167, 202–03
    see also surveys
'quest' (narrative arc) 106
questioning techniques 50–51, 140, 170,
    183, 203
    see also FAQs
Quirke, Bill 113, 141, 147, 195

Rana Plaza disaster 40
ranking questions 203
'rebirth' (narrative arc) 106
rebuilding 77–81
reciprocity 12–13, 57
recognition 29, 30, 31, 89, 133, 183
    see also 'thank yous'
reflective practice 26, 31, 36, 65,
    140, 173, 187
    see also evaluation
relationship building 32, 57–58, 59–60,
    141–42, 147–49, 181–82
remote working 147, 155, 158
    see also virtual meetings
repetition 98, 123–24
reputational impact 7, 13, 29–30
research 58
    see also focus groups; surveys
resolution (narrative arc) 105

response activation 51–52
reward systems 82
    see also recognition
rising action (narrative arc) 105
risk registers 35–37
role models 78, 83, 133–34, 136, 151–52,
    161–62, 169
Rose, Bud, Thorn exercise 205–07
Ruck, Dr Kevin 161, 163, 164, 168
rule of three 98

Samaritans, The 180
sampling 203
saying 'no' 187–88
scanning 5, 6
scenario planning 5, 42–44, 45, 46, 198–99
self-care 177–92
self-indulgent statements 96–97
sensemaking needs 21, 24–26, 69, 87–88,
    113, 139, 173
7s of internal crisis communication 20–32
shadow communication channels 111–12
shock crises 4
short stories 118
silence, culture of 164
site visits 116, 169
situational awareness 138
Situational Crisis Communication
    Theory 75–76
skills development 182–83
    meeting skills 185
    see also listening skills
small wins 27
SMART objectives 74
'snow test' 111
social connection 181–82
social identity theory 11
social media 100, 116, 125–26
    see also WhatsApp
social psychology 12–13
societal impact 5–6
soul 106–07
Spean Bridge war memorial 121
specialists 131
spokespeople 83
stabilizing needs 21, 26–28, 69, 113
stakeholder information 47
stakeholder maps 112
statistical information 94
Stay Alert, Control the Virus, Save Lives 98
Stay Home, Protect the NHS, Save Lives
    campaign 98
'stealing thunder' 87, 101, 113
steering teams 49–50, 198

Stevenson, Mike 106–07
stimulating needs 21, 28–29, 115–18
storytelling 103–08, 118
strategy 44, 45, 71–89, 104
strengthening needs 21, 30–31
stress 178
    see also burnout
supporting needs 21, 22–24, 87–88, 91, 94,
    113, 139
surveys 195–96, 203
survival needs 21–22, 67, 85–87, 91, 94,
    113, 171–72, 196–97
sustaining needs 21, 29–30

taking seat at the table 184–85
Taylor, Sue Jane 120–23, 181, 182–83
team reflections 26
technological crises 38
    see also cyber crises
templates 102
testing 48–49
'thank yous' 97
Thorns (Rose, Bud, Thorn exercise)
    205, 207
Thunberg, Greta 98
time management 154–55
Tokyo Electric Power Company
    (TEPCO) 37
Tomlinson, Victoria 43
tracking (monitoring) systems 41–42, 126
training 135, 156–58
transparency (openness) 82, 92–93, 123,
    142, 166, 206, 208–09
Transport for London (TfL) 5–6, 27,
    168–69
trauma crises 80–81
triggers 6–7
trust 13, 59–60, 99, 138, 158
Tuireadh 122–23
two-way communication channels
    117, 123, 132
Tyagi, Dr Vedang 65

unacceptable demands 187–88
uncertainty 24–25
Union Carbide accident 86
University of the Highlands and Islands in
    Scotland 125–26
updates 88, 100

values 63–65, 137, 140
values crises 40
verified information 93, 102
Verinder, Ben 2–3, 169, 196–97, 202, 203

virtual meetings 125, 167
visibility 134, 138–39, 169
vision 78, 88–89, 107, 138,
        140, 207–08
Volkswagen 164
vulnerability 136

walk-abouts 62–63, 66, 68–69, 139,
        140, 169, 170
web pages 114, 125
welfare drop-ins 168

wellbeing 177–91
Wells Fargo 164
WhatsApp 206, 207
whistleblowing 40, 41, 167, 188
Williams, Jarrod 205–08
working groups 29–30
workload reviews 186
workshops 205
worst-case scenario planning 43

X/Y axis tracking system 41–42

Looking for another book?

Explore our award-winning
books from global business
experts in Marketing and Sales

Scan the code to browse

www.koganpage.com/marketing

More from Kogan Page

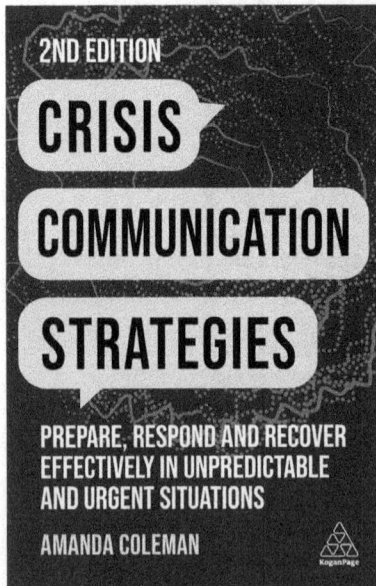

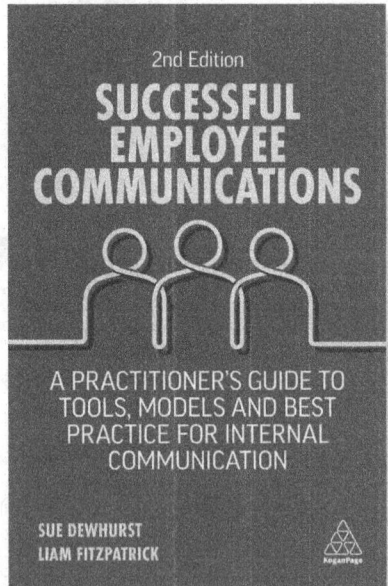

www.ingramcontent.com/pod-product-compliance
Lightning Source LLC
Chambersburg PA
CBHW071554210326
41597CB00019B/3243

* 9 7 8 1 3 9 8 6 2 0 5 9 9 *